Andrés Iniesta is widely considered one of the greatest footballers of his generation.

After graduating from La Masia, the fabled Barcelona youth academy, Iniesta made his first-team debut in 2002, aged 18. He became a regular in the 2004–05 season and has remained in the side ever since, helping Barca to an amazing string of trophies, including eight La Liga and four Champions League titles.

At international level he has well over a century of caps, and has twice won the European Championships. In 2010, he scored the winning goal to hand Spain their first World Cup.

# ANDRÉS INIESTA
# The ARTIST

With Marcos López and Ramón Besa

Translated by Peter Jenson and Sid Lowe

headline

First published in 2016
by HEADLINE PUBLISHING GROUP

7

Cataloguing in Publication Data is available from the British Library

ISBN 978 1 4722 3233 5

Typeset in Bliss Light by Palimpsest Book Production Limited, Falkirk, Stirlingshire

Printed and bound in Great Britain by CPI Group (UK) Ltd, Croydon CR0 4YY

Headline's policy is to use papers that are natural, renewable and recyclable
products and made from wood grown in sustainable forests. The logging and
manufacturing processes are expected to conform to the environmental
regulations of the country of origin.

HEADLINE PUBLISHING GROUP
An Hachette UK Company
Carmelite House
50 Victoria Embankment
London EC4Y 0DZ

www.headline.co.uk
www.hachette.co.uk

## ANNA

For just being you, for loving me the way you do, and for being the person that you are. You gave me back the joy of living and gave meaning to my life. Meeting you was the most magical thing that could have happened to me; destiny brought us together so that we could share our lives. You have given me the opportunity to become a father, form an incredible family and feel what complete happiness is alongside you and our children. We have already shared so many unforgettable and unique experiences, but I know that by your side the best is always yet to come.

My life would make no sense without you, '*Mami*'.

## MAMÁ

We only get one mother and I could not have had a better example in life than you. You have made me the person I am today. And the things that you have taught me, I would like to teach my children. You are my role model. I cannot imagine what you went through after I left home to live in La Masia when I was only 12 years old. Without you, all of the things that I enjoy now would not have been possible. You were always happy to be in the background, away from the limelight, but no one is more indispensable than you. We have cried and suffered a lot together, but now every moment that I spend with you I enjoy and appreciate for the precious thing that it is. I am eternally gratefully to you for everything you have done for me, Mamá.

## PAPÁ

You have always been my guide, my coach. You are the father every kid would love to have protecting him as he grows. It would be very difficult for me to appreciate where I am today and how far I have come without you being by my side. You never dreamed of Champions Leagues, European Championships or World Cups; you just dreamed that your son would become a professional footballer and we made it. We cried and suffered along the way, but now we can both enjoy it together. I am forever grateful to you for all that you have given me. And above all, for all the countless things you taught me along the way, Papá.

## MARIBEL

You will always be my girl. Because being without you for five years was not easy; and because, although we fought when we were young and I would love to tease you from time to time, I could not have a better sister than you. You have such a big heart.

We have the same blood and that makes us closer than ever. I love you so much, more than you realize.

I know that you are always there for me. Thanks for being by my side, 'My girl'.

## Valeria and Paolo Andrea

My treasures. My princess and my little terror. What wonderful things life has given us! What complete happiness. The princess of the house and the champion of the house. What a pair you are!

One day you will read this wonderful book and realize so many things. You are my inspiration.

## Andrés Jnr

How could I forget you? People don't know you, but I do. I know you and I know that you are beautiful. Even though you are not here with us in the flesh, you will always be with us in spirit; our angel who we fought so hard for, and who we will never forget.

# CONTENTS

## SECOND HALF
### From the Touchline

## AUTHORS' NOTE

This is not an orthodox biography. Nor is it a traditional one. More than Iniesta's book, it's the book of Andrés; nothing more, nothing less. Perhaps it seems that in this long story, he rarely appears at the forefront – accustomed as we are to authors of autobiographies being the all-action heroes of their own life stories; spicing up the epic and playing down the doubts and fears.

Here Andrés takes a different approach. But even when you don't see him, he is there. He is in every one of the lines that we started writing together in 2012. He is present far more than it first appears, and if you asked him he would probably say that he appears in the book too much. What he most definitely wanted to appear was every last detail of his long and patient climb to a summit he never thought he would reach.

Not in his wildest dreams would he have imagined the career that he has had. And nor did anybody tell him, when he was a 12-year-old boy left in La Masia, separated from his parents, just how tough it would be sometimes. Football, it turns out, would not always free him from life's problems. He first began to run with the ball at his feet in Fuentealbilla, in Albacete, and he remains intrinsically connected to the small Spanish village that he ended up putting on the map. Having reached this point in his career, captain of Barcelona and a symbol of the style of football that conquered Europe and the world – be it with Rijkaard, Guardiola or Luis Enrique in a Barça shirt; or with Luis Aragonés or Vicente del Bosque for Spain – he wanted to stop the clock, put his foot on the ball, and take a look back.

Any readers wanting a typical footballer's autobiography, we are sorry to disappoint. Don't blame him; the responsibility is ours. But Andrés, as usually happens when he plays, was thinking of others. He wanted the story told of how he went from the concrete playground at his school in La Mancha, where there had never been any tradition of football, to the Camp Nou, to Soccer City, to Wembley and to Stamford Bridge. And he wanted it to be his family, his friends, his coaches, his team-mates and his rivals who told it.

Andrés wanted to play the same role in this book as he plays on the pitch. He picked up the ball and began to play passes and give assists, and he was pleasantly surprised to have details of his own life revealed to him that he had not previously known. He never took his eye off the ball in what was a long game. He was there every step of the way. We spoke with a lot of people and he guided us through all the games, be they Champions League, La Liga, World Cups and Euros, hotel stay-overs, and training sessions. The doors were always open to us; all of them, even the most difficult ones. 'If it's for Andrés, then no problem; just tell me when,' was what we heard time after time. There was no diary that resisted us. If there was no gap at first, then one would soon be found with trips, telephones, mails, WhatsApp messages, all used to find a solution. All methods served our purpose of uncovering testimonies and there were hours and hours of chats that we were privileged to be party to. As much as playing the lead role, Andrés was our producer, our guide as we covered so much new ground.

It has taken us four years, and if it was down to him, we would still not have finished. He always found (and still finds) a new person for us to call or a different story for us to share. This is a new way of looking at a very different player who still has so many layers yet to be discovered – peel one back and another appears. But this is not just a book about a footballer, even though his exciting journey is intertwined with that of Barcelona and of Spain. It's also about Andrés the person – someone who obsesses over perfection and over getting every last detail right. And we mean every last detail. From the typeface of the text, to the colour of the cover of the book that you now hold in your hands, and finding a title for the English language version that he was happy with.

It was not easy, but in the end we came up with *The Artist* which fits the fact that this is the story of the way he has played his life. With creativity, a flourish, and an almost magical appreciation of space and time.

That's why we say it is *his* book in every sense. We would perhaps have done it differently. Perhaps. But it is not our book, it is the book of Andrés. He always wanted others to shine. We had our work cut out making sure that happened, never giving the ball away; his ball, the ball that he had at his feet as a boy in La Mancha and still has at his feet now for Barcelona and for Spain.

Ramón and Marcos

---

*'The obstacles we encounter along the way help us to see life from another perspective and to lift ourselves up once more with even greater strength.'*

*Roman Emperor Marcus Aurelius*

If you google the name Andrés Iniesta and read the material that comes up, you might start believing that you know everything about me.

You will know everything about my life in an instant for sure, you and thousands of other people. Except of course you won't really. There are many things that have not come to light. There are other things that I want to put into context or into a certain order. I believe in the old adage that everyone should become a parent, plant a tree, and write a book. Fortunately, I have a daughter and a son; my football career will always be associated with the tree that grew out of the playground where I used to play as a kid in Fuentealbilla; and so what remains is this book, *The Artist*.

I take things very seriously. If I set my mind to do something, it's because I really feel that it's the right thing to do, not just for the sake of it, or because I think it will reflect well on me. So I have written this story with the same conviction, desire and determination that I feel when I am playing football or caring for my family. I wanted the text 'made to measure'. I wanted it to turn out just as I had visualized it. I wanted the story to have form and substance and not just be a stream of sentiments and memories. And for that I have needed the help of people who know me and who would be able to interpret my feelings; people who know my career, and have been able to express the thoughts that I have been jotting down since the process began back in May 2012.

The book has taken this long because I did not want to give myself deadlines or tie its publication to any fixed point in my career with Barcelona and the Spain team – decisions made for personal, not commercial, reasons.

The experiences that I wanted to reveal needed to be properly understood by those who were going to help me write this book. In Marcos López and Ramon Besa I knew I had two people who I could trust to put this story together; two journalists with a knowledge of my career, both with Barcelona and with Spain, and who know this sport. Not just copy takers or hired writers but trusted professionals. People I knew I could reveal things to, without being shy or afraid, safe in the knowledge that the material would be used properly; and people I knew who would also be accepted by everyone else who contributed to this book.

I don't know anyone better suited for such a big task than Marcos

López who is a great hardworking journalist and a good person. He comple-
ments perfectly Ramon Besa, who is always determined to make sense of
things, to find the tone of the story and a consistent style with the
protagonist. The three of us have combined as a team, working under the
one condition that we would write the book without intermediaries and
that we would not deliver it until it was written in full. Negotiations with
the publishers would be left in the hands of Pere Guardiola and Joel Borrás.
And it has been that way practically until the end when Hachette and
Malpaso bought the rights to the work. We were also lucky to have as our
translators from Spanish to English, Sid Lowe and Pete Jenson, two good
friends; and Malcolm and Julián as the editors in Spanish and Catalan,
whose input has been decisive in the editing and improvement of the
book.

On putting together my story, I am bound to have unwittingly left
somebody out, and there may be readers who complain that there is a
lack of criticism in the book, or that I have left out certain characters. But
I want to make it clear that this is the book that I wanted. It's my book,
and its final composition is mine, not that of my collaborators who I am
sure, in certain given moments, would have modified the story or put their
own different focus on things. I wanted to explain how I see things, or, if
you prefer, how I feel about things, and how the people that I believe
know me well, see me. I have deconstructed my life into parts, into chap-
ters, to make it easier for the reader to follow the thread of the story. This
was never about putting together a novel; it was about constructing a
journalistic record of my life and career.

I have almost nothing to say about the things that, while they might be interesting for some people, I feel, in my case, are well known and already recorded elsewhere. I'm talking about my day-to-day life and my habits. It's well known that I love being with my family, with Anna, with Valeria and Paolo Andrea, and also with my parents, and with my sister, Maribel. I can't go back to the village as often as I would like, but I love spending precious time with my grandparents and with my uncle Andrés, who I go running with before pre-season, and my other uncles, aunts and cousins even though some live as far away as Almeria and Mallorca. I love taking Valeria to and from school, seeing her contagious smile. I love being with my little terror Paolo Andrea. And I love being with Anna. When we can, we try to do something together once a week: we go out for dinner and try different restaurants, go for a walk. We sometimes go to the cinema. Music? Estopa are still my favourite group, because I like their songs and because I like the way they are as people, and beyond that I am in debt to Alex de Guirior, who mixes me music with a little bit of everything – reggaeton, house, Spanish pop – so that I have an eclectic selection at my disposal. And naturally, as a sportsman who likes to look after himself, I like to sleep a little so that I can stay rested.

It was never my intention to write a book about such everyday things, however. I wanted instead to tell of my passion for this game, a passion that I have had since I was a boy. Marcos and Ramon sometimes tell me that I was a little boy without a childhood. Understood in those terms, I wanted to reclaim that childhood by writing about it, trying to show, in the process, that I am very proud of that little boy. There were certain episodes that were not nice or easy to get over, both when I was young and even more so when I was older, such as the months leading up to the

World Cup in South Africa. But I have tried to explain them as sincerely as possible, as I experienced them, without overthinking the right way to record them.

It certainly was not easy going from Fuentealbilla to La Masia. It took me a year to settle, to make my life in the residence, but I got there in the end with my own place at the library, my own room, my own wardrobe, my things, my sweets. I loved the cakes that my parents would bring me, and the sponge cake Jordi Mesalles' grandmother made, and that we would always dip into our chocolate milk at night before bed. And I have some wonderful memories. One which is especially fond for my family is when Joan César Farrés, the director of La Masia, chose me to represent the club in the reception that was given by Pope John Paul II to mark the centenary of FC Barcelona. My mother bought me a new suit, as if it was my first communion.

I also have the need from time to time to go to Fuentealbilla. That's where home is, *my* home. A large portion of my family are there, the neighbours, our vineyard, and the people from the village who have lived there all their lives and seen me grow up. I like to remember where I come from as much as I like to say that I am also now from here in Barcelona. I like to delve into my feelings sometimes. A person should know how to take care of who they are, and of the people they hold close: Anna, my children, my parents, my sister Maribel. We should know how to look out for the people we have around us so as not to feel alone, even though we all take refuge in a little solitude from time to time.

I'm not quite the silent figure people think I am. It's not true that I have never had a row or never been involved in a shouting match. People who know me have even accused me of being overbearing at times and of trying to organize their lives. But I feel good when people say that I know how to bring the family together and find the right people for the right jobs. I am very stubborn, and I naturally rebel against anyone who tells me I cannot have what I want.

I am also a very appreciative person and I want that to come across in this book. I am grateful to everyone I have worked with in the Spain team and for all that I experienced when starting out at Albacete. I am grateful to my family and to Barça. I am not going to single out directors or presidents. I prefer to express my gratitude to the club as a whole and all the directors who have worked there are reflected in that. The best way for me to show my affection for the club is by honouring the shirt and by being a good team-mate, giving everything on the pitch at all times, and always representing the institution with loyalty and dignity. That's something I feel I have done from the first day, even when I was just a ballboy behind the advertising hoardings that were bigger than me and prevented me from seeing my heroes out on the pitch. Nothing motivates me more than trying to make my club and my country as successful as I possibly can.

I have a deep respect towards my profession. I respect my team-mates and rivals. And I respect the people who watch the game. My dedication is complete and I try to never cheat anyone. I love that the people applaud me; not that they do it out of courtesy, but because they really feel it inside. It's the best feeling any player can have when you know you have given everything and not let anyone down.

This book is also further evidence that I need to express myself, that I need to reaffirm my decisions, as encapsulated in the message that is displayed at the entrance to our home: 'The obstacles that we encounter along the way help us to see life from another perspective and to lift ourselves up once more with even greater strength.' Sometimes we need to unblock ourselves but that is only possible if we first realize that we have a blockage.

My passion for football has always been what has moved me, and I feel it more than ever now that I have the good fortune to be captain and can enjoy the testimonies of people who have helped me enjoy life, who have bent over backwards so that I could dedicate myself to what I love doing, being who I wanted to be, in the best team in the world. It's a privilege. There is nothing better than to carry out your work, be recognized for it, and then thanked for it too. That is priceless. We have won so many trophies, even managed two trebles in six years, and we want to win much more. As incredible as it seems, the desire for success is unchanged.

Marcos and Ramon have often asked me for the purposes of the book to explain to them what it feels like when I have six or seven opponents surrounding me. Or they have asked me if my way of playing the game resembles Roger Federer's way – the speed and synchronicity of his movements. And what really makes me blush is when they say that in just one move they can see reflected in me so many of the qualities a player would need to be considered complete: the speed of decision making; the quality of pass; the ability to apply the brakes, to accelerate, to pause; the use of the first touch to take me away from opponents; or the ability to change direction. I don't know what to say. I would rather these things be spoken about by other people.

Of course I believe it is necessary to have good technique, to be intuitive, to know how to find the gaps and to able to take the team with you when you attack – a clear sign that you have your team-mates' confidence and that you also have the adversary on the retreat. There are those who say my secret was in the first 10 metres of ground I cover when I begin a move. Others say I have sacrificed the goal-scoring knack I had when I was a kid, for the ability to cover as much of the field as I do. I don't know. As I have already said, I just do what comes naturally to me. If I was born all over again, I would play the same way. When I go out on to the pitch I more or less know how I am going to fit into the game, I have an immediate feel for the pace of the match and how it will flow. Sometimes I even get a feeling for what is going to happen during a game on the day before. I visualize it and then it happens that way. Or I do things completely intuitively, never having thought of them before. My brain works very quickly. My mother says that sometimes it works so quickly it will explode – that's a very Luján characteristic.

The Iniesta-Lujáns are tenacious and austere people. We are workers and ultimately sport is like life: it's about never giving up, and fighting every day for what is yours, while remaining true to your principles. I wanted to remind myself of that in this book. To see the years that I have spent growing as a person and a professional recorded in the pages of a book that speaks with the voices of those who have helped me along the way and with the complicity of those who have been judges of my work and my day-to-day existence, such as Marcos and Ramon.

I want to give my most sincere thanks to everyone who in one way or another has given their time during the four years it has taken to put this book together. I have never claimed to be 'World Heritage', as manager Luis Enrique once referred to me (much as I will never be able to thank him enough for the definition). I don't need any individual awards that I don't have. Nor do I feel the need to have to assert myself any more. I feel just fine as I am, in Barcelona, in Fuentealbilla, playing for Barça or the Spanish team, in Catalonia or in La Mancha, in Spain, or anywhere.

I consider myself a citizen of the world who is lucky enough to enjoy people's affection. And it is to those people that I want to tell this story; the story that doesn't appear in the pages of Google. My life as told by me and those who know me best. I hope you enjoy the way I have done it. It would make me very happy for people to derive pleasure from reading this book as much as they enjoy watching me play. I can say that in its compilation, I have put the same amount of interest and dedication into it as when I am out on the pitch in the beautiful shirt of Barcelona or Spain. That, at least, has been my intention.

Thank you.
Andrés

FIRST HALF

On the field

## THE ABYSS

'I felt like I was in freefall, like everything had gone dark. I went to find the doctor: "I can't take any more."'

*Andrés Iniesta, summer of 2009*

'We searched for something that would explain it, that might justify the way he was feeling. But there wasn't a simple answer.'

*Dr Ricard Pruna, Head of Medicine at Barcelona FC*

It's not a question of need. I want to tell my story.

The idea is a nice one. To tell my story, to see the things I have experienced, my life, brought together in a book. It's a way of showing my gratitude towards the people who have marked my life, who have been there forever. I am the kind of person who needs company. I need people

3

around me to be able to express myself. So that they can help me to be who I am.

There are a thousand ways to start this book, because there have been lots of moments, when they happened, that I thought were the most important I had experienced. I am sure that as I start to look back on all of them, to remember them, other things will come to mind. And I will think I was wrong to do it this way. But I have chosen to begin with one of the most recent moments, maybe because somehow it's always there, it never goes away.

I want to begin with the worst moment. It's not a matter of days, or months, or a year; it's an undefined period in my life. Nor can I divide things up by victories or defeats in matches I played; no, this is about that moment when I couldn't see any light at the end of the tunnel, when I could see no path to follow, because I lost confidence in Andrés.

It was like I was on the edge, somewhere I'd never been before, never experienced. Confidence had driven my career. I always felt confident in myself, in my ability. Confidence was always there. So when it deserted me, I felt vulnerable, like the victim of something that terrified me, that I couldn't cope with. I felt a kind of fatalism. There's nothing in life harder than the feeling that you are no longer you. It's frightening.

● ● ●

The worst moments always follow the best ones. In good times, pessimists warn that there are bad times ahead. Andrés had a glorious summer in 2009, even if achieving what he achieved had been, in his words, 'hard, tense, the demands ever greater'. It had ended so well, in a unique and historic treble. In 2009, Barcelona won the league, the cup and the Champions League. But then? . . . 'Then, suddenly, without really knowing why, I started to feel bad,' he says. 'One day, I wasn't right. Then the next. And the next. They did all these tests and they all came back fine. But somehow, body and mind were not one; it was like they were heading in different directions. You can't find that balance and then the anxiety starts. Your head never rests, and at the same time your body screams at you to look after it, especially that damned thigh muscle that had threatened the Champions League final in Rome and become even worse afterwards. You're constantly going over things in your head. You wonder why you feel so bad, even as you're trying to convince yourself that you're actually enjoying your holiday; or at least act as if you are.

'It grows, the problem snowballs,' Andrés continues. 'You're not right, not well, but the people around you don't understand it, because the Andrés they know isn't this Andrés; they can't see that somehow you're empty on the inside. It's very hard.'

The summer passed, badly. Then came pre-season training, which always begins with a medical. It's routine when a player is looking after himself, when he feels fine. It's routine for Andrés normally. 'But in the first session, I hurt myself a bit. It was logical really, after going through the summer feeling so under pressure, tense, weighed down by everything. It was impossible for the muscle to be in the right condition after a summer like that. The scans they ran in the medical were fine, but the muscle wasn't strong enough and I went through pre-season injured, spending a fortnight training alone in the USA. Just me and Emili Ricart, the Barcelona physio.'

No one knew that Andrés was suffering so much, just as no one knew how he had suffered when he was little at Barcelona's youth team academy La Masia, so far from home. He only told people years later. 'I keep everything in. I don't like to burden others with my problems; I deal with them on my own. But there comes a time when there's no other way. There were training sessions that I couldn't finish because of this strange feeling I had.'

In the final few days of pre-season things seemed to be improving, as if the solution was within reach. The change seemed to be coming. 'I hadn't played a single game since the Champions League final in Rome and that first treble three months earlier. I hadn't been able to train with the first team once during that fortnight in the USA, but then one day the doctors, at last, thought they had discovered the cause of the problem. And then the work began. I was getting closer to a return, things were progressing, the medicine was helping.

'It was then that I heard . . . the worst news imaginable.

'Carles Puyol came and found me to tell me that Ivan de la Peña had called him with the news.

"Dani's dead."

"What? Are you sure?"

'I froze. I couldn't understand it. I didn't know what to do, what to think. I couldn't believe it. Dani, my friend Dani, had died. How? Why? This couldn't be . . .'

Andrés and Daniel Jarque, the central defender at Barcelona's city rivals Espanyol, had been through a lot together. They had played together in the Spanish national team's youth system; they had shared journeys together to their clubs' training grounds in Barcelona. They were friends, close. They had been since they were kids; they had shared so much.

And now Dani had died, victim of a heart attack during pre-season in Italy for Espanyol.

'The next few days were awful,' Andrés says. 'I felt like I was in freefall, like everything had gone dark. I went to find the doctor: "I can't take any more."'

Andrés doesn't know what to call it: not depression, exactly, not illness either, not really, but an unease. It was like nothing was right.

'I don't know how to explain it,' he says. 'But I learnt then that when your body and mind are vulnerable, you feel like anything can happen to you, that you're capable of doing something very damaging. Of doing anything, really. I don't know if this sounds too strong, if it's the right way of expressing it, but I felt like, somehow, I came to "understand" how people can be driven to madness, into doing something crazy, completely out of character.'

Iniesta found protection and consolation in his family. 'My parents, my wife Anna, everyone . . . without them I would never have recovered, felt right again. I owe them so much. I would like to think I would do the same for them, of course, but you never know what would happen in a situation like that until you live it.'

The family supported him, but they alone were not enough. Iniesta needed professional help, someone to listen.

'Sometimes it's enough just to be able to explain to someone how you feel, what's happening to you, and for them to listen and understand. I found that with the Barcelona medical specialists, Pepe, Bruguera and Imma.'

Pepe was the first to help open his eyes. 'I can't take any more,' Andrés told Doctor Pruna, medical head at Barcelona. 'Can you get someone to come and see me?' That same afternoon, Pepe arrived at his home. A few days later, Imma. And she was the one who recommended that Andrés go to see Doctor Bruguera.

'My life is what it is, and that is the way I had always approached it. *This is the way things are, deal with it yourself.* All the things that have happened to me, the way I have always dealt with problems, in the good times and the bad: it's just the way I was brought up, I suppose. The way I am.'

Iniesta kept things to himself, took it all on and kept it all in. Until one day, everything broke down. 'It was like my body said: "That's it, no more . . . you've spent years listening to everyone else, pleasing them, now it's time to listen to me, time to give me your time. To give time to yourself." I had always felt like I could take it all on, all my life, like some sort of superman. I couldn't explain why it was that I now felt empty inside, with no sense of hope or drive or desire. I couldn't explain why nothing seemed to make me feel happy. You might be wondering: "What's he talking about? He has everything: he plays for Barcelona, for Spain, he's got money, he's won it all, everyone admires him, people respect him." You might think that; I ask myself that too. And I know it's impossible for some people to understand. But I felt empty. And if you're empty, you need to somehow get that energy back, to recharge, find something to power you. If not, you're dead.'

●  ●  ●

It should have been the happiest summer of Iniesta's life. He'd come from winning a treble with Barcelona, he was reaching his peak as a player.

Instead, it was hell. There was no comfort, no escape. The holiday didn't help, nor did the memories of that historic 2008–09 season: not the goal at Stamford Bridge, not winning the league or the cup final. He hadn't played in that, in fact: a broken nose had kept him out. Maybe even then there was something there; not on the surface, but there. Even as Barcelona won the treble, even though he kept on playing as if nothing had happened, there were those who had noticed something wrong. Andrés was not Andrés.

One day Sesi, one of his best friends, was watching a training session on the old pitch that used to stand next to La Masia, alongside the Camp Nou. Halfway through the session, his phone rang. José Antonio, Iniesta's father, was at the other end.

'He's not right; something's up.'

'Relax, José Antonio, he's still out there training.'

'How can I relax? He's the only one in the family who's not happy. This isn't right.'

Though he appeared calm, Sesi was worried too, ever since a family lunch one day in Cadaqués, when Iniesta's wife Anna had noticed something was wrong.

'What's the matter?' she asked Andrés.

The table fell silent.

'Nothing, nothing. I'm fine, I'm fine . . .'

But round that table, they knew that he wasn't fine. Sesi, Anna, his parents . . . all of them could see that something wasn't right.

He needed professional help, and that was where the club's psychologist Imma Puig came in. 'With Imma, I found a space, someone with whom I could share everything,' says Andrés. 'There are people you can talk to and people you can't. With her, I could. I let it all out, pretty much everything from the day I was born. And she helped me so much. I remember that if we had an appointment at six, I would be there ten minutes before, ready. That tells you that I was getting something from the sessions, that it was good for me to share things with her; and, of course, that I had a lot to share.

'She helped me to understand, to improve, and above all she helped me learn how to choose. Sometimes you don't realize what you're doing. None of us do. You do things automatically, because you have to. You just keep going day after day after day . . . until one day you can't keep going any more. She helped me understand that and became an important part of my life. She was vital in me being able to move on.'

Andrés was looking for some way to break free, looking everywhere. Searching.

He doesn't name names or places, but he came to know every inch of this dark tunnel in which he had found himself, of this place where he had become trapped, as if he was living in limbo. Most had no idea what he was going through. In the dressing room at Barcelona, only a very few friends knew and they tried to give him all the support and the space he needed to come through it, without pressuring him, without crowding him, aware of the size of the mountain that stood before him. Outside the dressing room, practically no one knew what he was going through.

Two worlds, two Andréses. On the surface, a smile, artificial, a mask. On the inside, concern. A search for absolution that could not be found. How was he going to emerge from this? How was he going to escape this place, this dark unknown place, where he had ended up?

• • •

'It was difficult, really difficult,' says Emili Ricart, the Barcelona physio-therapist who is also Andrés' friend. 'Time has passed, but the pain of that summer of 2009 is still there. He told me, "Jarque died, and it all came out." A moment of anxiety in which everything came together: the injury, pressure, the sadness ... in the end, your head isn't completely right. Although people don't believe it, your brain affects your muscles too. Your body starts to break down. Your muscles give up, or tear. And Andrés starts to have that sensation that does so much damage to sportsmen: the feeling that he is vulnerable, that he's on the verge of breaking, that he can't be fixed. "I'm made of glass," he said to me one day. It was like he thought he would never be right, that he would never be fully fit again.'

Emili's words are well chosen. Iniesta breaks on the outside and breaks on the inside. 'He was thinner than normal, he wasn't right. He was working harder than ever before, but there was just no way forward. And that torments you, of course. He needed help to be himself again. How did he come out of it in the end? With will, energy, determination, by making every day part of a countdown. I'm sure there are many sportsmen who would not have overcome what Andrés did.'

Although he felt alone, Andrés was fortunate to have the support of his people, that circle of family and friends who always stood by him, who gave him the foundations he needed to rebuild. 'Of course, we feared that it could all fall apart, that it could be the end,' Emili says. 'We all thought that. But no one said it. His family and friends are close, and they helped him through those dark days. One day, during a recovery session in one of the physio rooms, treating one of those damned muscular injuries that just wouldn't go away, he told me about Rafa Nadal, the tennis player. Nadal was going through a terrible time with injuries and a loss of confidence. And Andrés said to me: "Emili, I was listening to Nadal talk and I knew exactly what he meant: it's the same for me."'

Emili, more psychologist than physiotherapist, fell silent for a moment. He remembers telling Andrés what he always told him: that you have to respect your biological clock, always. 'You can't hurry nature. He respected that, for sure, but he didn't have a clock. There was no model to follow, he was in a different place. There was no pre-ordained plan to get fit, no clear guidelines. He was so broken . . .'

Iniesta hurt, and not just physically. That pain had brought him here; lifting him out again was not easy.

'Andrés is very close to his roots; to his home, to his people. He has lived through everything with them and those ties are strong. He struggles with them. Those ties are never broken and never will be. He cannot help that. And he worries about all of them.'

He worried about them so much that somewhere along the way he forgot to worry about himself. And inside, it all came together in a perfect storm.

● ● ●

'Andrés went through a very difficult spell,' says former team-mate Bojan Krkic. He too is careful with his words, careful about how he describes those dark corners of an experience that no one really knows except the person going through it. But if anyone understands, or can come close to understanding, it is Bojan. The former Barcelona striker had been through something similar.

'It was my first year in the first team at the Camp Nou,' he says. 'Just about the time when I got called up by Luis Aragonés in 2008. And I started to suffer anxiety attacks.' Like Andrés, Bojan came through Barcelona's La Masia youth system. Andrés was six years older; to Bojan he was a giant. He admired him and saw him as an idol, as someone who had everything he aspired to. They barely spoke: both are shy. There was something that connected them, but in silence.

'So it surprised me when one day after training Andrés said to me: "Bojan, I need to talk to you." And when Andrés says that, you know something strange is going on. He explained to me, briefly, what was happening to him. As he went on, I could see that it was very similar to what happened to me. I felt like we were sharing something; these aren't the kind of issues you talk about with everyone. And I understood immediately. It was like I was reliving everything I had been through. Everything I still lived with: the scars were there still. And he wanted to share it with me. I know that what he told me are things that you normally don't mention to anyone, apart from your family. It's so bad, so unpleasant, so painful, that you keep it to yourself. You don't want others to know; you don't want to burden them with it, or for them to suffer too. But in the end, you hurt yourself even more by doing that.'

In the corner of the dressing room, Andrés and Bojan sat alone, talking. 'There came a moment when we realized: we were living the same thing. We felt the same way. We knew that we were going through the same anguish, that we felt that there was no way out.' Andrés talked, Bojan listened. 'I thought to myself: "I'm not going to let Andrés go through something like this." There I was talking to my idol, to someone who had won the European Championships and the Champions League, and he had opened up his heart to me. That tells you something about him, about his humility and his sensitivity. He called on me. He was the one who said he wanted to talk to me. And I wanted to help him in any way I could.'

From that moment, the relationship between Andrés and Bojan changed. 'We talked more and more often. I felt comfortable talking to him and he felt the same with me. It was almost like therapy, for both of us. And we grew close, we knew each other better. We helped each other. Andrés was heading into a difficult year with everything that happened, with injuries, the fear that he wouldn't make the World Cup. He had gone into the final of the Champions League on the edge, not really fit. He was fragile.'

Bojan recalls the first time he met Andrés. 'It was in Egypt, in a friendly. I had never trained with the first team before, so that day was like a door opening on a dream. It's curious really: for the first-team players, going to Egypt to play a friendly was a pain. For me, it was a wonderful experience. We had got to the stadium three hours before the game and it was already packed. I remember that I was very nervous. During the warm-up, Andrés came over to me and said: "Relax, don't worry." I don't know why, I still can't really explain it, but I remember that those few words gave me a real sense of energy. I can still see that moment in my mind's eye, right down to the training top we were wearing to warm up in. It was red.'

It was April 2007 and Bojan was 16. He made his debut and he scored. 'It was a huge moment for me,' he says. 'I played that game, went back to the youth team for the rest of the season and in the summer I was called up to do pre-season with the first team.' Fast forward two years and it would be a very different Andrés from the one Bojan had first met. An Andrés that people were worried about, especially Carles Puyol, the Barcelona captain.

● ● ●

Puyol was the one who told Andrés about Dani Jarque's death. Amidst his own grief, there was concern for Andrés. He feared for his friend's reaction. It was Puyol too who called on Raúl Martinez, the national team physio, to seek out some hope, some solution, along with Emili.

'Andrés takes it all on board, loading the pressure on himself, keeping it all inside,' Puyol says. 'Maybe that's why he gets injured so often. Sometimes you think you can handle everything, but you can't. He'd say to me: "It's not fair, Puyi, my calf's gone! Why does this keep happening? Shit. Just when I was at my best. Why?"'

'I went four months without playing,' Andrés says. 'It seemed never ending. It felt like forever. It was very hard. All these questions and no answers. That sense that I just wasn't progressing at all. It goes on and on. Medicine, treatment, tests, day after day. I would try to train with the team, but I wouldn't be able to finish the session because I felt so bad. But I kept on. Somehow, somewhere inside, I told myself that it was another step. When I finally returned against Dynamo Kiev in September, it was four months and two days since the [Champions League] final in Rome. I could only play the first half. Why? Because I couldn't last any longer, I couldn't cope. I felt like my head was going to explode. I had very strange sensations. I don't really know how to explain them, but there must be people who have been through similar things who can explain it, who understand what I mean. I knew that playing at all was a small step forward, though. And I also knew that however small it was, it was important. Bit by bit, I started to feel better; for the first time, I felt like I might get back to normal.'

But nothing was normal.

● ● ●

'Andrés, you decide, okay? The moment something doesn't feel right, you go. Don't ask for permission, just walk. Okay? Leave. Don't worry about the training session. As soon as something feels wrong, stop. It's fine. You're what matters; you and only you.'

Pep Guardiola's message was clear, delivered not by a coach but by a friend. 'If you don't feel right, don't push it, don't worry, don't carry on, don't even think about it: go. Please.'

And he did, too. There were countless sessions when they hadn't even been out there for ten minutes and Andrés was already on his way back to the dressing room. He didn't even need to look at Pep. And Pep didn't even need to look at him. There were no words and no need for them either. He was there, and then he had gone, as if he had been swallowed up.

'You always want people around you to be okay, to be happy and healthy; you want them to be comfortable, not to have any problems,' says Andrés. 'But you never really think that it might be you who is not right. You always think those kinds of things won't happen to you. But no one is immune. You think it's something that happens to other people. Until it happens to you. And it happened to me.'

'Andrés is very, very sensitive,' says Guardiola. 'There are times when things go wrong; that's life. But his wife, his kids, his family, pulled him out of it. We were there to help him in any way we could, but he was strong too. All we wanted was to help, to make sure he knew that we were there if he needed us.'

But Andrés doesn't seek that help, instead he turns in on himself. 'He's like me. When he does that there is no way of reaching him,' his close friend and former team-mate Victor Valdés says. 'His physical problems, on top of that anxiety, were what really did for him. All those injuries made his day-to-day routine awful, giving him the sense that he just couldn't get on with his life. Everything was wrong, strange. He was destroyed. I could see it.'

Valdés had been with Andrés virtually every step of their careers, ever since they met at La Masia. Now Andrés would ask his friend why this was happening to him, what was going on, how could this be: 'I just don't understand it.'

The same question was repeated over and over. To Valdés, to Puyol, to Bojan, to Emili, to Raúl . . . but no one knew. They had no idea what was happening. 'Inside my head, right in there,' Andrés says . . .

He had no idea either.

●　●　●

Barcelona doctor Ricard Pruna knew there wasn't a straightforward medical explanation for Iniesta's problems. 'Those were extremely delicate moments, the worst I have seen Andrés go through,' Pruna says. 'He came to realize how vulnerable we all are when the head is not right. It doesn't matter if you're a footballer, or whatever, you reach a point where you would give it all up just to feel okay again, to be "normal", in control; to feel strong and to be at ease with yourself. To *be* yourself. Yes, normal. That's the word.

'Andrés was struggling, his problems were personal, and he came to me for help. He wanted a medical explanation. And we did tests, analysis, everything we could. We searched for something that would explain it, that might justify the way he was feeling. But there wasn't a simple answer. Bit by bit, the human, personal explanation came to the fore. The realization that this happens to people. And when it did, that started to give Andrés some strength.

'It wasn't tests he needed,' Pruna continues. 'What he needed was harmony, balance. And slowly he found that. Slowly he was able to be what he is now. And, no, I don't mean the footballer. I mean the person.'

After months and months of suffering in silence, months when from the outside people thought he must be the happiest man on earth, Iniesta finally found that balance, some harmony. Without the support of people like Pepe, Imma and Bruguera, he might have been lost forever.

## FUENTEALBILLA

'We saw him in the trials and after five minutes we said: "Take that little kid off; we've seen enough."'

Balo, Albacete coach

He was barely eight years old: this scrawny little kid, white and thin like a piece of cotton thread. He always had the face of the perfect, innocent child, some said. Others glimpsed a thousand masks: an ability to adapt to his surroundings and to every moment, always guided by the ball and by the game, but guiding it too, in control; always there, in every corner of the field. That day the 'field' was a rough gravel pitch, his game a trial. There were hundreds of kids being watched, judged, their futures decided, yet he played as if he was still out on *his* field: the concrete playground of his school in Fuentealbilla where he could always be found.

Day after day, he was there. Until night came and the light went. 'I spent hours playing, especially after school,' Iniesta says. 'What a shame there were no floodlights back then. When it went dark, I had to go. Sometimes, my mum or my grandmother would come and find me. If there had been floodlights, like there are now, I'd never have left.'

Little did he know that there alongside his school – less than a hundred metres from the Bar Luján that his mum, Mari, ran while his dad, José Antonio, was organizing the teams of bricklayers who worked in the area – a story was being written. Little did any of them know. Not the family, nor the friends who shared those games with him; still his friends now.

Abelardo, nickname 'El Sastre' (the tailor), can still see that small figure walking towards his house. 'I was four years older than him. Andrés was six, I was ten, but he was three or four times better than me,' he says. 'My relationship with Andrés was based on football. Football, football and more football. There was nothing else in our lives. He would come to my house every day with a ball under his arm. The only ball we had. It was more a lump than a ball, but it would do.

'He would come and get me to play. And if he didn't come and get me, I'd go to Bar Luján to look for him. From there we'd head to the playground at the school, kicking the ball all the way there. Then we'd play as long as we could, until someone came to get us. Usually his grandmother. She'd get him and take him off. But as I was older, I'd walk home on my own. There was no other "pitch" in Fuentealbilla at the time.'

A pitch turned basketball court was marked out on the school playground with a huge tree in one of the corners. 'I don't know why but the tree is the thing I always remember; it's always there in my mind,' Abelardo adds. 'My parents told me there used to be a pond there, and the tree. And then they built the playground. Julián [another childhood friend], Andrés and I spent all our time there, all day playing with the ball. We'd take penalties, practise lobs, we had everything we needed.'

Everything was the ball and the ball was everything. 'How I'd love to find that ball again,' he says. 'Hard, rubber, the surface worn away, the colour gone.'

'I'm not even sure if it *was* white,' Julián admits. 'I don't remember any more. But I can still see Andrés walking down the road kicking that ball. Even now, every time I see him, that's the image that comes to me. He was like Oliver Atom in the cartoon *Oliver and Benji*. The ball never left him; he always had it on him.'

For Julián, nicknamed 'Peto', the same scene was repeated daily after school. 'He'd arrive at my door with a sandwich in one hand and the ball in the other . . .

'"Let's go and take some shots."

'"Okay, Andrés," I'd reply.'

Then off they went to find Abelardo, the first *tridente* of Andrés Iniesta's football career. Julián lived just behind Bar Luján. He still does.

He says: 'We invented games, free-kick competitions, penalties . . . we spent hours out there on the playground. When we needed a goalkeeper, we got one of the little kids to join in. There was always someone about. Andrés was one of the smallest, of course, but he didn't count as a little one. He always played on our team. He was too good to play with kids his own age. He got bored. The other kids his age were only there to fill in in goal or to make up the defensive wall for our free-kick competitions. Not Andrés; Andrés was different.

'We'd spend some nights out in the town with the ball too,' Julián continues. 'The problem came when the ball flew over a wall or went into someone's front yard.'

Then someone had to go and get it. And it's not as if the neighbours were impressed. Abelardo or Julián would go while Andrés waited. He was the youngest, after all. 'You should have seen the faces of the neighbours . . . but in the end they always handed it back to us, even if they were furious. "Here's your damned ball."'

Damned? Blessed. Especially for Andrés.

'It's true,' Julián admits. 'The ball was almost always his. He was the one that turned up with it under his arm . . . and in the end, he even managed to make half-decent players out of us. Not half as good as him, but not bad. We spent so much time with him that something had to rub off. We were among the better players in town.'

Abelardo adds: 'He used to play against older kids. He hardly came up to their waist most of the time, but he could do anything he wanted with the ball. He could be up against the best, and biggest, kid in town and he would leave him on the floor.'

Even when the sun went down, they had a pitch of their own. 'There was a backroom at Bar Luján and we'd organize the last game in there,' Abelardo says. 'Our parents would be eating in the bar while we were in the back with a ball of some screwed-up paper. One of us would be on the floor, playing in goal while the other two tried to get it past him. It got quite competitive; we'd end up sweating.'

At weekends Julián, Abelardo and Andrés 'signed' another player: Manu, who was Andrés' cousin. He it was who alerted the world to the fact that something extraordinary was happening on the streets of an anonymous town in La Mancha whose name most people didn't even wish to remember.

●　●　●

'Andrés had already been recommended to us by his cousin, Manu de Manuel, who was playing for Albacete at the time,' recalls Víctor Hernández, one of Iniesta's first coaches at Albacete, the club where he would begin his career proper.

The story starts with Pedro Camacho, the brother of the former Spain coach José Antonio Camacho, one of Real Madrid's great players, an icon at the club. Pedro had been Dani's coach at Atlético Ibañes. 'Dani' was José Antonio Iniesta, Andrés' dad and, by his own admission, 'an Athletic fan back then'. He was nicknamed after Dani Ruiz Bazán, the Athletic Bilbao striker from the Seventies and Eighties. 'He [José Antonio] wasn't as good as his son, but he could play a bit, a central midfielder who was a star in *Preferente* and *Tercera*,' says his former coach, Pedro.

José Antonio hoped his son would make it where he could not. But to start with, he couldn't even get him a trial. José Antonio had read an advert in the local paper, announcing that there would be trials at Albacete. But when he got there with his son they were turned away. 'He's too small,' they said and he was. Just seven years old. Too young and too little.

So his father turned to Pedro and asked him to open a door somewhere.

The door he opened eventually led onto the Federation pitch; only it wasn't a pitch, not a full-sized one anyway. Instead, it led to a seven-a-side gravel pitch, with no dressing rooms. So they changed in the dressing rooms that belonged to another pitch not far away.

So Pedro had given in. José Antonio was pleased; so was Manu. 'You won't regret it: he's genuinely good,' Manu said, over and over. He wasn't wrong. 'I kept telling them that until they saw him for themselves, they wouldn't realize how good he was.'

That day they did. That day José Antonio took the car, an old Ford Orion, and drove Andrés the 46 kilometres to Albacete. There were lots of kids. The men watching them, judging them, were Ginés Meléndez, in charge of the youth system at the time, coaches Andrés Hernández, his son Víctor, and Balo.

'We watched him at the trial and after five minutes we said: "Take that little kid off; we've seen enough,"' Balo says.

Balo reckons it wasn't even five minutes. It didn't matter either way. 'It didn't take him long; we were convinced. After everything we had been told and with what we had just seen, that was more than enough. It was wonderful to watch him: so small, the ball at his feet, bigger than he was. Why did we take him off so soon? Because we were so sure and we had to use that time to watch the other kids, the ones we had doubts about. There were no doubts with Andrés.

'Andrés played in the middle and once he got the ball there was no way of getting it off him. It was impossible. Pretty much like it is now, in fact,' says Balo. He could barely believe his eyes that cold morning.

'There was no need to see any more; we'd seen it all,' says Víctor.

'He was different to all the rest,' says Pedro.

He remembers the conversation with José Antonio: '"Don't worry," I said, "I'll look after the little kids' team. He'll be with me." And in those first games, after a fifteen-minute warm-up, Andrés would pick the ball up, dribble past everyone and score. Day after day, until one day I went up to him. "You have to *pass* it to your team-mates, too. Give it to them as well, okay?"'

And that's what he did. The ball was not only his. He shared it with the other boys and girls. There was just one problem. When they picked the teams, everyone wanted to be on Andrés' side. They knew they'd win that way. They wanted to train with him too. As for him, he barely opened his mouth. His lips were sealed.

'I was one of the worst,' recalls Mario, who met Andrés that very first day. 'There were twelve of us I think, more or less, and I was about the tenth best. Andrés was the best, of course. The captain eventually. Everyone wanted him to be their partner in training and we'd all crowd round him going on at him. Quiet as he is, he just stood there, not saying anything. Eventually he said: "I'll go with Mario." He was looking for one of the weaker kids so that he could help them out. That's what I think. He could have chosen better players; don't ask me why he chose me otherwise.'

Mario and Andrés are still friends. 'He was from Fuentealbilla, I was from Albacete. I didn't know him at all. But that first day he scored two and I scored two. It was easy really. We just waited for the goal-kicks on the edge of the area. We were eight years old and the goalkeepers couldn't kick it that far; it kept dropping to us. Andrés would get it, play it to me and . . . goal!'

It finished 4–1 and every time Mario sees Andrés, the same image comes to mind. 'Remember those enormous red shorts?' Andrés says.

There was another recurring image back then. The midday session would be just starting in Albacete when, at the last minute, they'd see this small figure appear, in boots and kit. 'The things he had to go through to get there . . . ,' Mario says. 'His dad was working on building sites and couldn't always bring him. We had no problem because we lived in Albacete; we'd leave school, go to training, and then head back to school. He couldn't do that. He had much further to go and he was always just a little late for training.'

En route in the car, he'd get changed. On the way back, he'd devour the sandwich his mother Mari had made for him and the carton of juice. It was lunchtime, after all. He'd leave as quickly as he came.

'Why did we train at midday? Basically because there were no pitches available later on: all the other age groups were using them,' Mario says. 'And because Balo, the coach, worked in the casino in Albacete. Andrés would turn up with his boots already on, getting out of the car in full kit.'

Every Tuesday and Thursday, the Mario–Andrés partnership was perfected. But at weekends, they didn't often play together as Mario wasn't a starter. And it's not like they had the chance to talk much either: one lived in Albacete, the other in Fuentealbilla. They only saw each other on the training pitch. Andrés wasn't much of a talker, anyway.

Bit by bit, people took notice of Manu's cousin. How could they not? He was tiny but he still stood head and shoulders above the rest. 'This kid's amazing!' they told Víctor. 'What a player!' It was the same every game. 'He did things that just weren't normal. With both feet, he was incredible. Can you teach that? I'd love to say yes, that it was down to me,' Víctor says. 'But, no, you can't teach that. It came from within. It was fantastic to see him play.'

From that first day, there was a strange sensation that took over them. 'It wasn't just me, it was all of us,' Pedro Camacho confesses. 'This little kid was incredible, although none of us imagined he would go so far. For his age, he was a blessing. But it was like he didn't fit, like we didn't know where he had come from or what to do with him ... he was like an extra-terrestrial.'

Word gets around quick in Albacete. 'No one could compete with us; we won every game,' remembers Víctor with pride. That was Albacete's Under-10s team: Andrés and his amigos. Bruno, an inside left; José Carlos, the goalkeeper; Mario; Carlitos Pérez, who ended up playing in the Slovakian first division after Rafa Benítez had signed him for Valencia only for him to never make a debut at the Mestalla; and 'Chapi', named after Barcelona full-back Chapi Ferrer, real name José David, who never stopped running up and down the wing, tough, aggressive, just like the original. Not only that: he was a Barcelona fan too (he's even more of one now, of course) and even looked a little like Ferrer; he still does, what with both of them having lost their hair since then. 'If I hadn't been a Barcelona fan I wouldn't have let them call me Chapi,' he says.

He needn't have worried with Andrés. 'Everyone called me Chapi except him,' he says. 'I don't know why. Maybe he was embarrassed. He was the only one who called me José. I always played as a full-back. I ended up at a team called Gineta in Tercera División, I got married and, well, you know . . .'

That day, Chapi knew. They all did. 'The day of the trial, I looked at

Andrés and thought: "Where did he come from?!" There were two hundred kids there that day and he stood out a mile.

'I remember he didn't say much but he made you laugh. He was just as pale then as he is now. And there was nothing of him. Every shirt he wore was way too big.

'The other thing was that although he didn't say anything, he had a huge personality on the pitch. It was quite incredible. He used to carry the team on his shoulders. He wasn't frightened of anything. He took the penalties.

'Andrés never complained to the ref, he didn't get angry and he was very clear about what he wanted. I shared a room with him when we went to the Brunete tournament. I remember one time I began messing about, leaping on the beds, making a racket, running about the hotel, playing with the kids from the other teams, until he turned to me and said: "José, pull the shutters down and turn the lights off, please! We've got a game tomorrow. Go to sleep now! We have to rest." He was acting like a professional already.'

A professional, but still a kid. They all were: kids, born in 1984, just enjoying playing football. From school to the pitch and back again.

'Back then the school day was split in two, so they'd leave at midday,' Víctor says. 'Andrés would leave school clutching the sandwich his mum had made for him, and head to Albacete. We would train at 12.30 or a little later, until 2. There was no other time we could do it, and no other pitches we could use.' Sometimes Andrés would stop to change at Manu's house.

'He was allowed to leave class a little bit early,' Balo recalls. 'He would then make up for it in the afternoon. But, my God, it was an effort for his family.'

They would arrive, watch him train, then drive all the way back. One hundred kilometres in three hours, twice a week. They'd take it in turns to drive, his dad and his granddad, but Andrés was always the same, quietly sitting there with his chorizo sandwich and a fruit juice.

'Andrés was a quiet kid. He didn't even say hello when he arrived or goodbye when he left. We played games every Saturday, not competitive games, just for fun. He was little and skilful, very skilful, he could hide the ball from you better than anyone. He can't have weighed more than forty kilos. I don't think I ever had a conversation with him,' reveals Juanón, his coach at the Salesiano school in Albacete.

Balo remembers one Friday, which was the day the coaches used to meet to discuss the kids in the youth system across all age groups. 'They said "*Madre mía*, Balo! Just wait until you work with Andrés next year." I hadn't seen him play yet, apart from in that original trial, because my age group played at the same time . . . I still had that to look forward to.'

They had told Balo so much about Andrés that he decided that he wanted to see for himself. He didn't tell anyone, but he headed incognito to Andrés' next session. And this time he got lucky: 'I got there and I went to stand in one corner.' Balo didn't want to get in the way; he didn't want anyone to even notice him. Away from the parents, away from the friends and families, he stood alone watching. It turned out, they were right: he *was* good.

'*Madre mía*,' he said to himself. 'Next year's going to be great!'

Every time Andrés touched the ball he felt luckier; this was the kid he was going to work with next season. When Ginés eventually saw him, Balo turned to his boss and said: 'Whatever else you do, don't sack me before next year!'

●  ●  ●

Balo enjoyed that year. 'I remember Andrés had this centre parting in his hair that was so clear, so straight that you'd think someone had dropped an axe, blade-first on his head,' he recalls. 'He didn't look much like a footballer. Not at all, in fact.

'It was an incredible year,' Balo continues. 'Round here loads of people know me because I played at Albacete. I'd be walking down the street and they'd ask: "When are you playing? Saturday? Sunday? What time?" The ground was full every week. It was like it was the Carlos Belmonte, Albacete's ground. It didn't matter who they were playing against; no one even asked. They wanted to see Andrés. Word had got around: "Balo's got this kid playing in his team who's incredible . . ."'

It was a phrase that got repeated often, all over Albacete. Soon, Andrés was 'famous'.

'The referees started to say to Balo: "Take him off for a bit to even things up,"' Bruno Moral, another member of that team says. 'I heard it with my own ears. You'd watch him play and he was just too good. It all looked so easy for him.

'That's been his problem, I think. He does everything so simply and it all looks so easy, so effortless that we don't realize how hard it is. We think we can do it too. No chance! It's like playing on the PlayStation. He had, still has, this kind of peripheral vision that means he can always see a way out. I don't know how he does it. Up in the stands you can see it, sure, but down there on the pitch . . . down there? No way. Only he finds a way. It looks like he's walking at times, you watch him and think that he always does the same thing, but there's still no way of stopping him. At times you would think: "The ball's run away from him a bit there, he's tripped a little, it's not quite under control . . ." but that was never true. He would change pace and leave you trailing. He fools you. Every time.

'There are times in a game when you're a kid and you feel under pressure because you don't know what to do with the ball Easy: give it to Andrés, problem solved. He never lost it. Whenever the ball burnt our feet, we gave it to him. He would make the right decision, give the right pass every time. He would let us restart any move, begin again. And it destroyed opponents. They would come and pressure him, two or three of them chasing him, but he would turn and, somehow, you never really knew how, come out of there with the ball at his feet. So much for pressure! What makes him great is that what he did with us as kids he still does now, in a World Cup final or a Champions League final.

'Everyone talks about his goal in the World Cup final and rightly so. But forget the goal and watch the game. Really watch it. He moved five metres further back, exactly as he used to do with us; he asked for the ball, he started to play one-twos and began enjoying himself. And from there he controlled the game. He tricks you every time. It looks like he's not strong, but look at his lower body strength. He looks like he's not quick, but look at the way he pulls away from people. It looks like . . . forget what it looks like! Don't trust appearances; Andrés catches you out every time. Andrés didn't look like a footballer and look where he is now.'

The pity is that Bruno couldn't be there with him. In the end, he abandoned football. 'I reached the Albacete first-team squad at the age of sixteen,' he says. 'But I felt a bit burnt out. I never made my debut. There were changes in the boardroom, all sorts of issues, things happening off the pitch . . . I went somewhere else and didn't even get paid for the first three months. I played behind the forwards, like Andrés. It used to be me passing the ball to him; now it's him passing it to Neymar, Messi . . . hahahaha!

'I remember a tournament in Santander against a Racing side that had Jonatan Valle. Every journey we did was like an odyssey for Andrés. He'd get sick, miss his family, start vomiting. The first day there was this skills competition and he had to pull out because when he arrived he felt awful and was puking up.

'Luckily, he recovered in time to play the tournament itself. Seven-a-side, although it didn't go to plan. They'd sent us this letter beforehand telling us that we couldn't use boots with studs. We had to use Astroturf trainers with rubber soles. If I remember rightly, Andrés bought these blue Umbros but they were too big for him and he had to stuff them with cotton wool to get them to fit. And when we got there the pitch was grass anyway. The other team turned up in studs. They knew, of course. We lost 5–4 and Andrés scored all four. The following year we went back and won the tournament but he had joined Barcelona by then. We made sure he knew: "You had to leave for us to be any good!"'

● ● ●

José Carlos was the Albacete goalkeeper and he has a special souvenir from back then. 'I've still got the letters that Andrés sent me from La Masia, after he had joined Barcelona,' he says. 'There was no text messaging back then and Andrés loved to write. We're not talking quick notes; these were six or seven pages long, proper letters. Sometimes I'd call La Masia too and ask to speak to him. We'd spend ages telling each other stories. Every now and again, I look at those letters, you know. I get a bit emotional sometimes.

'What did he write about? A bit of everything, about life in Barcelona. "Today we played Castelldefels and won 40–0. You know what, José? They make life easy for you here: when you get to the dressing room everything's all laid out. You don't need to worry about a thing . . ." It wasn't always so positive, though. "José, this is tough. I miss my family a lot. Really, a lot. It's hard." Of course it was hard. I don't know if I would have coped.'

Every hour was a battle; and with every hour that passed at La Masia, those days in Fuentealbilla and in Albacete appeared happier. Andrés looked back fondly, more fondly than ever before. He missed it. That pitch, that playground. Those days.

'I look back on my childhood with happiness and nostalgia,' Andrés says. 'I spent hours on the school playground, the games were endless. At the end of morning classes, if there was no training at Albacete, I'd join Julián and Abelardo playing games that we'd make up. We'd almost always be up against kids who were three or four years older than us. The game was simple: five penalties, five free-kicks, and five long shots, from the middle of the pitch with the goalkeeper off his line.

'I loved that, just as I loved those long summers playing five-a-side football, matches that seemed to go on forever. You had to gather together a decent team because if they scored, you had to leave the pitch: it was winner stays on and we wanted to play. You didn't want to be standing at the side getting cold. I enjoyed that so much.

'It was always the same kids playing and the opposition were always older than us. It was better that way. Then there were the tournaments they set up during the village fiestas in August. We had a great team. And we took it very seriously; we wanted to beat everyone, even if they were bigger than us. We were very motivated; we'd even do team get-togethers before the game. Madness. My cousin and I would write it all down: the score, the teams, who got the goals, what happened. We did pre-season, made signings, we even made some kids go on trial for the team . . . like a mini professional team. And it was so much fun! I'll always remember those moments really fondly; they'll always be part of me.'

Then there were the 'home' games. Literally. 'The living room at my house was a stadium too,' recalls Manu. 'We'd make a ball with socks to try to keep the noise down and not annoy the neighbours too much.'

The main thing was not breaking anything. 'When Albacete's first team had games, we were expected to go. But sometimes we were enjoying playing amongst ourselves so much that we'd look for excuses not to go so that we could carry on. "Oh, I've got stomach ache" . . . "my head hurts" . . . "We should probably stay home, just in case."'

It worked every time. Well, almost. And so it went, a childhood spent together; the kids from Fuentealbilla. Until one day, football interrupted. Serious football. The move to Barcelona.

There were many from his local town that looked on disapprovingly at the family's support of Andrés' football career and the long trips to La Masia.

'It might seem strange but some people thought we were stupid, that we were mad. Of course we were,' says Andrés. 'My dad was mad to believe that one day his son could be a footballer. And so was my mum: "How can you put up with this?" they asked her.

'But with what? What does it matter if you don't get there in the end? What have you lost trying? What would it have mattered if one day I had to go home, back to the town for good, knowing that I hadn't been lucky enough to make it? None of that matters if you're doing what you want to do, what you think you have to do, when you've got hope and enthusiasm, when you believe in something. What does it matter if you're doing what you love and doing it with all your heart?'

That little kid believed in himself; he was sure he would make it. He wasn't sure where, but he was convinced that for him life was a game of football, just as it had always been. Nor though did he allow himself to be carried along by those who, far from criticizing, tried to climb on board, like a mini-court surrounding him, a mobile circus that followed him round La Mancha.

Andrés did make it. And every step he took amazed his coaches. 'I was an old-fashioned central midfielder. A number 5, defensive, a destroyer. Whenever I got the ball, I just wanted to give it back again. That's how I saw football. And then I saw Andrés . . . he knew what to do, always. I didn't need to tell him anything,' says Catali, one of his coaches at Albacete. 'Even before he got the ball, he knew what was going on around him. I'd tell the kids: "Before you receive the ball, lift your head up, look around, see what's there . . ." I didn't tell Andrés that; I didn't have to. I watch him now and he still amazes me. The ball hasn't arrived yet, but he knows what's going to happen next; he knows who's there, who's not and above all, what to do.

'When he plays for Barcelona or for Spain, I watch him closely. "How the hell did he do that?!" You don't know how he can see the play, let alone make it.'

Catali still can't work it out. Just like Víctor, Juanón and Balo, his other Albacete coaches, can't. They followed him then and they follow him now and still he surprises them. The kid who allowed them to travel round Albacete province like they were Pelé's Brazil. 'We won it all. Locally, provincially . . . everything. There was such a difference between us and the rest. People would say: "What a team Catali has!"' the coach recalls. 'Not because of me, but because the kids were so good. There was Andrés of course and four or five others who were also very good. Some are lucky, some make it, others don't have the dedication. That's life.

'I made Andrés captain. In footballing terms, he was the leader. I like seeing him wearing the armband now; even talking back to the referee. He never did that with us. It was hard enough to get him to say anything to us, how was he going to say anything to the ref?!'

Catali's team flew. And he was always there with a word of caution. 'If you think you're the best, if you get cocky, you won't get anything.'

No chance of cockiness with the family Andrés had. Modest, hard-working, they gave their all. 'My parents often did not have enough to pay the bills but they found the money to buy me some Adidas Predator boots when they came out. Why? So that their son could have the best boots around. What did it matter to them if they couldn't pay the next month's rent when their boy was happy playing football in his new boots?' Andrés says.

He doesn't wear Adidas any more. He's been with Nike for years now. It's funny how life goes. It's a decade since the American brand saw what Pedro, Víctor, Juanón, Balo, and Catali saw . . .

'So much of what has happened is down to my parents,' Andrés says. 'Back then I didn't know if I would make it as a professional. You're young, a lot can happen. You live in a small town. If you're from a small town, you know how things work. My parents had to put up with a lot. More than people imagine. It's not easy to hear people talking about you, to see people looking at you and judging you. I know that and I'm grateful for it. Thank you. You were proven right.'

So thanks to José Antonio and Mari. And Manu, he said it. He knew.

'My cousin can play, you know. He's good, very good. You should see him.'

## BRUNETE

---

> *'Speak to my dad, please. Speak to my dad.'*
> *Andrés to Albert Benaiges, the coach*

One of Albert Benaiges' huge arms wrapped itself around the shoulders of little Andrés Iniesta.

It was 1996 and Iniesta was playing for Albacete in a seven-a-side tournament in Brunete, on the outskirts of Madrid. The Torneo de Brunete, in its third season, featured junior teams from clubs in the Spanish first division and was where many future stars came to people's attention. Albacete were not even meant to be in the tournament that year but had got in because both Celta Vigo and Sevilla had been relegated after going into administration. That allowed the boys from La Mancha to play in the Los Arcos stadium in what was at the time the game of their lives.

After his tournament debut, Andrés was approached by Albert Benaiges, the long-time football scout, coach and later coordinator of La Masia, Barcelona's world-renowned youth training academy. Benaiges wanted to congratulate the 12-year-old but Iniesta, more evasive than shy – as if he was at the tournament *incognito* – hardly spoke a word.

The tournament that year had a higher profile than ever thanks to the efforts of promoter Carmelo Zubiaur and journalist José Ramon de la Morena, who were working on the popular late-night radio show *El Larguero* for the national station Cadena SER. Alfredo Relaño, who was in charge at Canal+ TV at the time, had also helped promote the tournament.

'Speak to my dad, please. Speak to my dad,' repeated Andrés every time they asked him if he would like to play for a big team like the Barça side represented by Benaiges. De la Morena will never forget the scene that played out after every game, with Benaiges looking for Andrés.

'No, I never spoke to his father,' recalls Benaiges. 'There was no way I could walk up to him dressed in my Barcelona tracksuit. Everyone would have realized that we wanted to sign him.'

At first, he did not even know the name of his latest find. 'The boy wearing the number 5 really stood out . . . for his exquisite technique but also for his surprising intelligence,' says Benaiges on seeing Iniesta play for the first time.

'I sent Mr Fàbregas, who was Barça's club official at the tournament, to speak with the father. He was wearing a jacket and tie but nobody knew who he was representing. "Look, that man there is the father. Go and speak to him and tell him that we want to sign his son."'

Iniesta's Albacete, usually wearing white but sometimes red, progressed to the semi-finals of the competition where they were beaten by a Racing Santander side inspired by Jonatan Valle, who was one of the sensations of the tournament that year.

'Brunete? Ah, what memories,' says Valle. 'We beat Fernando Torres' Atlético Madrid in the quarter-finals 3–1 and in the semi-finals we beat Andrés' Albacete 4–2. I scored three goals. That was probably my last ever hat-trick.

'Everything worked out perfectly. We played a 3-2-1 formation and I was the midfielder behind the striker, like Bakero in the Barça team of that era. I had a great time. Then I had offers from Barça, Madrid, Ajax and Arsenal, but I stayed at Racing.'

Things had moved very fast for Valle, who was training with the first team at Racing Santander when he was barely 14 years old. He made his debut in the Copa del Rey, at just 16, and two years later he was already a first-team squad member in the first division.

But Radomir Antic, a former manager of Real Madrid and Barcelona, and at the time in charge of Atlético, was more interested in Andrés, for all the seductive quality of Jonatan Valle.

Andrés was not difficult to spot. He was the captain so he wore the armband. He had worn his hair short the year before because of a bet he'd had with his cousin Manu. He had wanted to look like the 'Little Buda', Iván de la Peña, who was lighting up the Camp Nou at the time. Not many could pull off the look, neither with the hair nor the football. In 1996, Iniesta's haircut drew less attention but everyone noticed the football.

'We believed we could win it,' says Andrés. 'We were very excited but we had to settle for third place. I was named as the player of the tournament. So for me and for Albacete, it was a very important tournament.'

Jonatan Valle recalls: 'It was between Andrés and me. He took the best player award from me by just one vote, if I remember correctly. And he took the prize too which was a trip to PortAventura amusement park – if you see him, tell him that he owes me and my kids a day out!' Jonatan's football career never took off and he ended up training with the Spanish FA's unemployed players' team, burnt out by that early success. He started but never really finished an alternative sporting career as a boxer. Back then at Brunete, he was side by side with Iniesta as the promised paradise of a professional career seemed to await them both.

'He went to Barcelona. I could have gone too, but I decided to stay with my mother,' says Valle. 'Andrés was a lot more relaxed than me. He always stood out. You only had to see him touch the ball once and you could tell he was different.

'I have had my moments in football like most players, but he has always been there. He is the best Spanish midfield player that I can ever remember seeing. I would even say the best of all time. What most surprised me at Brunete was that *pause* that he had. It is the same one he has now. It is something that the rest of us do not possess. I remember how we used to play when we were representing Spain at boys' level. There was always one player who you knew you could give the ball to and he would know what to do with it. Andrés was that player. He would always make the right decision. If Andrés had the ball, you could always say to yourself, "Relax, everything will be okay."

'He has always had that gift. I think it comes from how he is as a person. The rest of us are tense, pressured and nervous. If he has to bring the ball under control very quickly, then he does it. But he always seems to have more time than everyone else. That is the difference between a good player and a genius.

'He never panics and always plays the right pass. It's an honour for me to have been a very small part of his story. Sometimes I tell my children, "I have played with this beast."'

José Carlos, now a policeman but back then the goalkeeper Albacete recruited a week before the tournament started, remembers: 'My mother went to Brunete without a change of clothes. Everyone thought that we would be knocked out after the first game. We went without luggage and with no hotel room. I went to school with Mario every day and one day he said to me: "We need a keeper, do you want to come?" We had very little time to train together. I was certainly the last to arrive. I will never forget the goals Jonatan scored against me, but nothing compares with what we faced against Madrid in the quarter-finals.'

Albacete were meant to have no hope in the Brunete tournament, and yet here they were up against the mighty Real Madrid. 'I loved it,' says Albacete's left-winger at the time, Carlos, or 'Karlitos' as he was known to his team-mates. 'We were there for a variety of reasons but mainly because of him [Andrés]. He was the player who ran the team from one end of the pitch to the other. And as the only left-footed player in the team, I had a wonderful time playing alongside him. He kept on playing us into great positions. He was a joy to watch even at that age. The pitches were reduced size and Andrés just made everything look so simple.

'We were four or five rungs above all the rest. The day we played Madrid, they had designated us a pitch with no stands around it, but as it was Madrid and Lorenzo Sanz [Madrid chairman] and Radomir Antic [Atlético coach] were going to be watching, they put us on the best pitch with stands and everything. Madrid really suffered against us. And yes, I remember my parents went to Brunete imagining it would just be a day trip! They had to go out and buy new underwear because we went so far and had to stay for so long.'

Parental excitement was at fever pitch by the time of the Madrid game. 'We had a great time in the group stage and then came Madrid in the knockout rounds. Our parents could not believe it,' enthuses Karlitos. 'But it was deserved. We were one of the teams that played the best football as a group and we had this one beast of a player on our team. Not even Madrid were going to frighten us. It went to penalties. Remi, another of the captains, took the first one, then Andrés and the third and final one was mine. I was terrified as I approached the ball. They had just missed one.'

'It was Madrid's captain and he didn't miss it, I saved it,' interrupts the goalkeeper José Carlos. 'We had a great team and we were flying on the wings of our captain. We were a band of brothers. I am still in contact with my team-mates, each one now with his own life. We are united by that tournament and it was a fabulous time – pure football, the innocence of sport.'

Sixteen years later, José Carlos would receive a very special phone call from the president of Albacete. 'Andrés wants you to make the inauguration speech for the new training complex,' he said. It was to be given the name 'Andrés Iniesta' and José Carlos had a small part to play in the ceremony. He was shaking with the emotion of it all; it wasn't just Andrés, his old team-mate alongside him, but Spanish football legend Iniesta.

'You see Andrés more than the rest of us,' he began, 'but none of us have changed that much. Some have a little more weight and a little less hair, and others instead of arriving in their grandfather's old Ford Orion have come in a BMW. But we are still as together as ever. Those who could come today, as much as those who could not, all want to give you a hug, a really big hug. From all of us, from the old team who played together on the dirt pitch of the Federation. Welcome home, Andrés.'

The words were enough to make Iniesta bow his head slightly, lost in memories of his childhood. After crouching down together for the photograph and jokes such as 'You're going to split your trousers' and 'My knees have gone', it was time for a final message from Andrés. 'Albacete is a club with roots and its roots are in its youth academy. And it was in that youth academy where it all started for me,' he said, remembering once more that penalty shoot-out against Madrid.

It is true that José Carlos made the all-important save. It is also true that it was only going to count if Karlitos could put away his spot-kick and he did. Three penalties, three goals that helped changed the life of Andrés.

'It's strange but during that tournament no-one called him by his name,' reveals De la Morena. "Have you seen Albacete's number 5? Watch what he does with the ball." He was not Andrés, and certainly not Iniesta. He was simply the Albacete number 5.' The radio presenter has that Albacete number 5 shirt safely stored in his home, given to him as a gift by Andrés.

Iniesta's coach at Albacete, Victor, says, 'In the quarter-finals we beat Madrid and in the semi-finals we were beating Racing 2–1 at the break, but we ended up losing the match 4–2. The team was good enough to win the tournament.'

Andrés says, 'I never thought it would serve as a stepping stone to a first division team. I never even thought we would get as far as the semi-finals. I just went to Brunete to have a good time.'

According to De la Morena, the most stand-out player of the tournament was Jonatan Valle. 'He would juggle with the ball and he reminded many of Rabadan, a boy who had dominated the previous year's tournament with Madrid. Andrés caught the eye but not as much as Jonatan. People were fascinated by this kid from Racing who scored Maradona-style goals.

'But it was Atlético coach Antic who put everyone in their place with a couple of observations I can still remember. "None of you have any idea, no idea at all. The best player is the Albacete number 5! The number 5!" I can remember thinking, "Well, maybe he's right." I started concentrating more on the number 5 from Albacete. And of course, Antic knew what he was talking about. The Albacete number 5 ended up playing for Spain and the other boy never got to play in the first division. He said it so convincingly too. "Look at him, he never makes a mistake, never gives the ball away, every decision is the right one."

'In the next game, Albacete knocked out Madrid and that was tough for the tournament in some ways because everyone wanted Madrid to reach the final. "Look, look, he [Andrés] never disputes a single decision," Antic said to me. "He just concentrates on the game. He is the best by a long way."

'Racing ended up being champions and then it was down to the business of picking the best player of the tournament. After listening to Antic,

I was now convinced it was Andrés. We had the meeting to decide and everyone agreed that it should be Iniesta. I went to look for him at the Hotel Alcalá de Madrid, where the boys competing in the tournament were staying. I arrived and I found him sitting on a bench, his legs barely reaching the ground, and in tears.

'"But what is wrong, Andrés?" I asked him.

'"Albacete have been relegated to the second division; they have gone down," he said.'

De la Morena put Iniesta and Jonatan Valle in the car and took them to the radio studios of Cadena SER where they began the interview for the programme *El Larguero*.

'Your father, Jonatan. What does he do?' asked De la Morena.

'My father is head of a ministry,' replied Jonatan.

It was now Andrés' turn. 'Your father Andrés, what does he do?'

'My father is a bricklayer,' replied Iniesta, 'but he will stop doing that when I make it as a player. Maybe he'll become a construction magnate, I don't know, but I want to bring him down from the scaffolding.'

The conversation did not stop there. It was past midnight and Andrés and Jonatan were still chatting away. Albacete coach Víctor was there too as a stand-in father for Andrés that night. 'Don't worry, I will be there the whole time with you. You just answer what you want to answer. Don't worry about anything,' he said to Iniesta to help him overcome the nerves of what was his first interview, one played out to over a million listeners.

'Now Jonatan, what do you think you are worth?' De la Morena asked the boy from Racing.

'Five hundred million [pesetas],' came the reply.

'And you Andrés?

There was silence. The presenter waited impatiently. 'He looked terrified,' De la Morena remembers. Víctor intervened, afraid that the startled youngster was not going to say anything. He whispered into his ear, 'You say that you are worth one thousand million. Tell him, tell him.'

The boy from Fuentealbilla did not respond immediately but eventually gave his answer. He said, as his coach had told him to say, 'Me, one thousand million.'

● ● ●

'You know, that day I was in Brunete and I was listening to the radio,' says Santi Cazorla, who went unnoticed at the tournament but was inspired by the little midfielder from Albacete and his timid debut radio appearance. 'That was the first time I got to know of Andrés. I never spoke to him, but I heard him on *El Larguero* with Joserra [De la Morena].

'I was at Oviedo back then, but they were not giving me much playing time and they were going to get rid of me because they thought I was too small. We all saw at Brunete that Andrés had something different. I didn't even know his name at the time, but he stood out alongside Jonatan Valle, Fernando Torres and Diego León.'

Even though he had always been a humble boy, Andrés couldn't help but feel important in front of the microphone, already well aware of the nice things being said about him by Antic. He was also buoyed by the praise from Benaiges who had approached him after the final, put an arm around his shoulder and said, 'If you want to come to La Masia, you know where we are.' Andrés repeated the same words as before. 'Speak to my dad, please. Speak to my dad.'

Destiny had another surprise in store for him, as Iniesta recalls. 'The player of the tournament was given a day trip to PortAventura with his family, and as the theme park was close to Barcelona, we all went to La Masia to see how they worked and what they did there. It was an important visit, before later taking the big leap towards Barça.'

Andrés did not know it then but Barça had watched him before the Brunete tournament. Someone had alerted Oriol Tort to him. The high priest and legendary talent scout of La Masia had been told that Albacete had an extraordinary young player. Tort had called his friend Mani. 'Please go and check out this kid that I am hearing such good things about.' So Mani, as Germán Vara is known, an experienced former Betis scout who was now Barça's man in Andalucía, set off for a seven-a-side tournament about to take place in Plasencia.

'I wrote the first scouting report on Iniesta,' says Mani.' Some say I'm responsible for the club signing him, but it was actually a Dutch scout who saw him at Albacete and told Tort about him. He then sent me to watch him in Plasencia.'

No sooner had he started to watch him than Mani told Tort: 'I would sign him right now. He is small and probably doesn't weigh more than thirty kilos, but he reads the game brilliantly.' And that was despite the fact that, as Mani remembers, Andrés 'did not start the tournament that well'. By the end of the tournament he had been awarded the best player award, just as would happen weeks later at Brunete. 'He played then just as he does now,' says Mani.

The same physique, the same quality, the same seductive football – only then it was for the Castilla–La Mancha representative team. There in Plasencia they lost to Extremadura, courtesy of a solitary goal from Jorge Troiteiro, who would become one of Andrés' best friends in La Masia. The championship was won by Cataluña who beat Castilla y León 2–1 in the final. The gathered coaches and scouts, however, went away with the name of Andrés on their lips; the boy from La Mancha who danced with the ball and whose dream was to bring his father down from the scaffolding.

● ● ●

The key to success in football lies in detecting talent, knowing when someone is born to do something. For many years, Barcelona had someone whose ability for doing just that served the needs of Cesar Luis Menotti, Terry Venables and Johan Cruyff. He was Oriol Tort, the man they called the 'Professor'.

The expert eye of the professor worked once more in the case of Iniesta, or at least the expert eye of his trusted friend Mani who gave him such a glowing report that Tort never even went to Albacete to see for himself. Tort was always someone who could take one look and know whether he was watching a player or not.

Jaume Olivé, head of youth football at Barça, recalls: 'The professor used to say: "It is the first impression that counts, because afterwards the more you see a player the more defects you see. You have to go back to your thoughts when you first saw him. Did you think: He has something, I like him."'

Oriol Tort would watch the young players but all the coaches and scouts were watching Oriol. It would be enough to see how he finished his smoking to know if he had just witnessed a new talent: if the end of the cigarette burned bright red and there had been a deep inhalation, then you could be sure he was watching a star in the making. No one understood him better than Olivé. They were a fine team when it came to sharing opinions and then making sure everything was recorded in print on an old typewriter.

Tort used to joke, in the less sophisticated days of La Masia when they asked if he was going to stay at the club, that the continued presence of the archaic machine meant he was sticking around too.

'Professor, have they renewed your contract?' they would ask.

'Well, my chair and the old typewriter haven't been taken away,' he would reply.

It was a sign that, verbally at least, his future was assured. In his early years at Barça, Tort was a pharmaceuticals salesman by day. He and Olivé were among many coaches who alternated between their day jobs and training the young players in Barcelona's youth system. A group of volunteers like Pujol, Carmona or Ursicinio, whose reward was not financial but to be found in the joy of discovering a player who in time would become a member of the first team, and with any luck a really special one – a Guardiola, a Xavi, or an Iniesta.

'My life changed at Brunete,' says Iniesta, and he is right, but without Tort's call to Mani the tournament would never have taken him to La Masia.

'I want to dwell on something for a moment,' says Andrés to close his memories of Brunete. 'I know that he has had a tough time over this, even though he has never said anything to me. There are a lot of people who talk out of turn about De la Morena. It's not about whether or not you like his radio programme, although it is also true that he has been at the top of his profession for many years now. It's just that I wish people were not so hypocritical.

'I hear people say: "You always make time to speak to De la Morena and not to us." That hurts me. We are talking about someone who has been following me since I was twelve years old, back when no one knew who I was. It is easy to be forgotten once you hit fourteen, fifteen, sixteen years of age. De la Morena was at Brunete and he never forgot about me. And whenever I have been criticized, and he thought the criticism was unfair, he stuck by me.

'When I was not playing and he thought I deserved to be in the team, he would say so. And when people stick up for you, then they earn your respect and your affection. It would have been easy to go along with what the majority were saying about me without making waves. He didn't have to defend me. But he did. And he never asked me for anything in return. I never asked anything from him and he never asked anything from me. You do things just because you believe they are right and that is how he has behaved with me.

'I'm not saying that everyone else treated me badly, not at all. I have always tried to be respectful and polite and give my time to as many people as possible. I'm talking about certain isolated incidents. It's just something that I feel strongly about. There are certain opinions and things that get said that you always remember and I will never forget "Joserra". He was there for me when nobody else was.'

## LA MASIA

'It's true, I spent the worst day of my life in La Masia.'

*Andrés*

*It sounds like a contradiction but it's the truth. That's the way I felt that day and it's still how I feel about it, as if no time has passed since. I felt a sense of abandonment and loss, as if something deep inside me had been ripped out. It was one of the most difficult moments of my life. I wanted to be at La Masia. I knew it was the best thing for me and for my future. But I had to go through the very bitter experience of separating from my family, of not seeing them every day or feeling them close to me. It was tough. It was my decision to do it, but it was so hard.*

● ● ●

The calm and serenity of Andrés' story are abruptly interrupted by his memories of that first night at La Masia in September 1996. He had arrived there because suddenly one day, without warning, he had asked his father José Antonio: 'Dad, can you still call them?'

Andrés: 'It was a few days after the deadline Barcelona had given us to decide. I thought it was no longer going to be possible, but Mr Tort told us that they would make an exception and wait for us, be it this year or the next. We arrived just in time for that year. At no time had my father or anyone in my family told me that I had to go to Barcelona. I remember my first day was 16 September. School had almost started and so had the football. It was a very late decision, but it was the right decision.'

It may have been the right decision but nothing about it was going to be easy, for Andrés or his family.

José Antonio: 'Why have you decided now that you want to go? Why now?'

Andrés: 'I've changed my mind. I'm in the right frame of mind now. I've thought about it a lot and I think we should go.'

José Antonio: 'When he said: "Dad, let's go now," I felt something inside me asking: "Why is he saying this now?"'

Andrés: 'Because I am sure that it is what you want. I can't take this away from you, after all that you have done for me.'

On the one hand, José Antonio was happy; but he was also worried: 'I was the one that wanted it more, for him. But I was also the one suffering the most.'

Nothing about Andrés' decision was going to be easy, either at home in Albacete or away in Barcelona. Andrés: 'I don't want to offend anyone or air any dirty laundry, but I want to express how the situation was at Albacete just before I went to Barcelona. I don't hold a grudge against anyone. I am always grateful to the people that have helped me and to the places where I have belonged. But there is a certain attitude that I do not like. I got the feeling that inside the club they wanted to make me, and especially my family, out to be the bad guys. They said some really silly things to mislead people. I had to go two weeks without being able to play for Barça because the paperwork was not finished. Really, I don't have the slightest reproach against them. And up to a certain point, I can even understand their disappointment that one of their young players was leaving. But in life it is not necessary to harm anyone. I just did what I thought was the best thing for me and what 99 per cent of people would have done in my situation.'

When the Iniesta family arrived at La Masia, his parents spoke with Señor Farrés, who was in charge of the residence. Andrés, slightly detached from everything that was about to happen to him, walked around the corridors of the old and symbolic building that had housed so many childhood dreams over the years. He was not about to take this journey alone.

Andrés: 'I remember José, who was the Under-17 goalkeeper at the time. He had massive feet and I think I probably came up to his waist. He showed me around La Masia, bit by bit so that I could get to know it. "Here you

have a dorm; here you have another dorm; here you have the library, Andrés."
He was talking, but I couldn't stop crying. Tears, tears and more tears. I was
there in body, but my head and my spirit were still with my family.'

His parents were still below in the entrance to La Masia, speaking with
Señor Farrés, while he was going up and down the stairs. 'José was showing
me around the house as if it mattered to me,' he says now, remembering
those first few minutes in his new and strange home.

'Come on, Andrés,' José Bermúdez, the imposing goalkeeper, remembers
telling the new recruit as he towered over the small boy. 'He was pale,
tiny and sad. I had the feeling that he was thinking: where are my parents
leaving me? I can still remember the moment very clearly. I am not
surprised that he does not remember my surname.

'He was very frail, really slight. Up to my waist? I think that's probably
right, but Jorge [Troiteiro] was even smaller than Andrés. We were all in
the hall when they arrived. I was seventeen years old and they were both
twelve. If it was hard for us, then just imagine what it was like for Andrés.
You go through so many moments of loneliness. Andrés was very shy; Jorge
was a lot more extrovert, a lot more talkative, he was always the one who
led the conversation. I liked Andrés from the start. He was so polite and
well spoken, but very delicate and sensitive.'

●  ●  ●

'We left him in La Masia and we went back to the hotel to sleep,' remembers Andrés' father, José Antonio. He was so near and yet so far – perhaps
200 metres, 300 maximum. One Barcelona street – Maternity Street –

separated Andrés from his father, mother Mari and his grandfather on his mother's side. After José Antonio went up the stairs of La Masia for the final time, leading his little boy to the bunk-bed he shared with Jorge Troiteiro, and returned to the hotel, the Iniesta-Luján family were also about to experience a traumatic night.

With the gates of La Masia now closed, the three of them made for their rooms in the Hotel Rallye and went their separate ways without exchanging so much as a word. They had very little to say. But José Antonio did not last very long in his room, such was the pressure he was feeling. He got into the lift and went down to the cafeteria of the hotel where he found Andrés' grandfather also unable to sleep.

'I thought I was going to die, there was no oxygen in the room. It was horrible. I had an anxiety attack,' says Andrés' father, remembering the volcano of emotions he felt that night. 'I had started to pack so that we could go back to the village, but I could not go without my little boy. If it had not been for his mum, I would have brought him home. His mum made the biggest sacrifice. Mari always said to me: "If he goes and he is successful, then I will have been without him for six or seven years."' Mari was losing him. José Antonio was losing him. Maribel, his sister, was losing him. Andrés was losing them all.

'You know what? I'm going to go back to La Masia and I am going to get the little one! I can't stand it any more,' José Antonio told his father-in-law, convinced that he would find the perfect accomplice and that together they would be able to conquer the indestructible will of Mari. Andrés' grandfather stretched his hand out to José Antonio, with Mari still oblivious to the plan being cooked up. She would soon find out, however.

'Mari, I'm taking him back. I'm going to La Masia right now and I'm going to get him out of there! And we are going home.' The torn voice of José Antonio resounded around the hotel that sat just 50 metres from the giant Camp Nou stadium. But Mari, the strong and steadfast mother, intervened. She did so using very few words – as is typical of the Luján family – but in a way that made it clear it would be impossible for anyone, even her own husband, to change her mind.

'If you take him you are selfish,' said Mari to her distraught husband. 'You are not thinking of him, José Antonio. You have to think about him too. At least give him the opportunity to try it. We have not come this far to not even try.'

When Mari was at her weakest, she made herself strong; or at least stronger than Andrés dad. They had made the journey; they had to at least resist this first temptation to turn around. The four of them in one little corner of Barcelona, at the foot of that great temple of football, the Camp Nou, had no choice but to suffer.

● ● ●

Andrés: 'I was sat at the dining-room table during my first dinner at La Masia and I could not stop crying. Obviously, I could not eat anything.'

Across the street Andrés' dad was also going without his dinner. And his grandfather and his mother were the same. But Mari made sure that if she was crying, she was crying inside. No one saw so much as a solitary tear from her that night. For a then-anonymous football-mad family from Albacete, that evening in Barcelona there was no supper and there was no sleep.

'I don't know if the worst night was the first one or the following evening,' Andrés says. 'I knew my parents were close by at least. I knew they were just a few metres away in that hotel. But I knew that sooner or later they would have to get back in the family car and head home to the village. They had to get back to work. They could not stay with me.'

Little did he know that would be the case sooner rather than later. They were about to leave their son in Barcelona.

Andrés: 'The next morning, I had to go to school. They were waiting for me at the gates of La Masia to accompany me along with Jorge Troiteiro, my new classmate from Mérida, who was the same age as me.'

No one spoke about what they had gone through the night before. They all greeted each other as if nothing had happened; as if they were all in the village and Andrés was just going to the local school. They were all in Barcelona but they wanted to pretend they were still in Fuentealbilla.

'We went to school and they kissed me goodbye,' says Andrés.

Andrés and Jorge got themselves into school and into a routine that would be theirs for many years, but what he was not prepared for was what would happen at the end of that first school day.

'I thought that on the way out of class in the afternoon, they would be there waiting for me,' says Andrés. 'But when I ventured back out there was nobody.' There was no José Antonio, no Mari, and no grandfather. Suddenly, apart from Jorge, he was all alone.

'Now looking back, I think it was absolutely the right decision, because we saved ourselves that teary definitive goodbye that would have been terrible.

'I'm okay with it now; but back then I wasn't. Now I understand it; before I just felt a sense of neglect, as if I had been almost totally abandoned.'

● ● ●

'It's hard to believe because I had only been there a week more than Andrés, but the truth is I was already used to it,' explains Jorge Troiteiro, the boy who accompanied him to Luis Vives school. 'You have to understand what this change meant for us. We stopped being children overnight. When I was ten or eleven years old, everything at home was done for me and I imagine it was the same for Andrés. Your parents dress you, your parents take you to school, your parents go everywhere with you and pretty much do everything for you.

'At La Masia, we would come out of school and nobody would be waiting for us. Nobody. We were twelve years old. We had to grow up fast and not every boy is prepared for that. We went from being children to living in a much bigger family – the family of La Masia – that until recently we did not even know existed. Suddenly, you have new brothers and because we were the youngest they helped us with everything. They looked after us, but . . .' Troiteiro cannot finish what he is saying, transported back to those lonely days when only the late arrival of Andrés lifted his spirits. For Andrés on the other hand, coming out of school and seeing that there was no one there to meet him meant that in an instant, without any period of adaptation, he understood the new world he was now in.

Maybe the realization came in the car on the way from Fuentealbilla to Barcelona when three generations of the family – three adults and one child – sat in silence as they drove into the unknown.

Andrés: 'I remember when we stopped to eat in Tortosa and nobody ate anything. It was like we knew "the end" was getting closer.' The end. That is how they all viewed it. 'We knew there was no going back. And with that stop for food, we were already in Catalonia, so it really felt as though we could not turn around. When someone spoke, it was to say something that really made no sense. Or it was to start a conversation that would then go nowhere. No one could stand the pain that we knew we were going to feel. But we had to bear it.

'I never had any lunch in Tortosa and I had no dinner in La Masia.'

Looking back now from his perspective as a father himself, Andrés can appreciate more what his family felt that day. 'Before, I only thought about how I experienced it; what I went through or what I felt inside in La Masia. I could try to imagine what it must have been like for my parents and my grandfather, but until you are a parent yourself you cannot really understand what they were going through at the time. You cannot understand what they were suffering, or what my sister was going through. Now that I am a dad, I know that I'm dying inside if I have to spend so much as one day without seeing Valeria or Paolo Andrea, or if I cannot see Anna. To not be able to touch my little girl or my little boy, to not be able to touch them for just one day, I can now imagine how my parents felt having to leave me in La Masia. Even now, I really prefer not to think about it.'

They left knowing they would only be visiting once a month from then on. The life of that 12-year-old boy had changed completely. 'It was weeks, or maybe even months, before the situation came to feel normal and I got used to it.

'At first I found it difficult to eat,' says Andrés. 'I did not want to speak to them on the phone, because it meant I would cry and cry. But you get used to things in the end, because you think about why you are there and what you are trying to achieve. I wanted to be there. And as bad as it got sometimes, there was no way that I wanted to go home. I had to stay and see through my ambition of being in La Masia and becoming a Barça player.'

This kind of stubbornness is very common in the Luján family. His mum was headstrong that dramatic night when José Antonio threatened to break down the door no sooner had Andrés gone inside Barça's elite academy for the first time. And her son was headstrong too when he was holding back the tears in those early days, lost in the corridors of the 300-year-old La Masia de Can Planas.

Andrés: 'When my parents came to see me, it seemed small consolation, it really did. They made the trip on the Friday because they had to wait for my sister to finish school. They would arrive in Barcelona about eight or nine o'clock at night. Of course, I was waiting for them with everything prepared. I would be at the door so we could go straight out with no delay. We would have dinner in the bar next to the hotel and then we would go back to their room and all climb inside the same bed and sleep together. We did everything together. It's a great memory!

'Then on the Saturday after I had played a match, we would have the afternoon free. We would go to the cinema or go for a walk in Barcelona, but by then I would already be thinking that it would soon be night and that the time for them to leave was getting closer and closer. There was no way to stop it. Time flew and there was no way for me to control it. In the beginning they would come every month, then it was every fifteen days.

'I knew that after lunch on Sunday they had to set off again for the village. They had to be there to help my uncles and my grandfathers with the bar. In Fuentealbilla people would go out to have dinner on Sunday nights and my parents had to get back about seven or eight o'clock, no later. That meant they had to leave Barcelona at two or three o'clock at the latest. When the time came, it was always a drama. It felt like they had spent so little time with me.'

The wait before they visited again would be carefully counted. 'I would cross off the days in my school diary. I would count down the days until Christmas or Easter, or until the summer holidays. That was how I got by month after month. I have always been very family-orientated, but those days I spent in La Masia have made me even more so for the rest of my life.

'I love the fact that I have a really strong link with my family. I can still remember the first trip that my parents made to Barcelona. They had a blue Ford Orion. They told me that they would arrive at about eight o'clock in the evening more or less. I was waiting for them from seven o'clock. Where would I wait for them? Sitting on the wall by the ramp that leads into La Masia, where else? I would be watching every car that drove past to see if it was theirs. And what kind of luck did they have that day? When they were only a few kilometres away, the car broke down on the motorway and they had to call a rescue service to bring them in the rest of the way to Barcelona.

'Aside from the inconvenience, it meant I lost hours of time with them. They had to pay around 30,000 pesetas and they had to ask Señor Farrés, the director of La Masia, to lend it to them. The poor things had been saving all month to be with me and that happens to them on their first visit.'

Then it was a case of everyone back to their everyday lives. Andrés' father went back to the scaffolding, his mother went back to work behind the bar, and he went back to La Masia. He put on a brave face in front of José Antonio. 'Look Dad, I think I can stick this for one year, but for two I'm not so sure. I will get through it somehow.'

Deep down, Iniesta knew that he had to overcome his fears and tears. 'The canal that runs through our village is not deep enough to hold the tears my grandson cried,' remembers Andrés Luján, the fourth passenger in the blue Ford Orion that travelled in silence to Catalunya. 'It was something that you wouldn't want anyone to experience. Too many tears; too many . . . .'

Andrés was left all alone. He stayed in La Masia from the age of twelve through to seventeen. They were five long years, but nothing compared to that first night when even the old stones of La Masia seemed to be crying out for the little boy from La Mancha.

PAPÁ

'I wanted my son to be what I would have liked to be: a footballer.'

José Antonio, Andrés' father

Andrés Iniesta might just be a footballer today because José Antonio wasn't.
No one put more effort into Barcelona's captain becoming a professional
than his father, the man who, when he played, was nicknamed Dani, after
the skilful, crafty winger who played for Athletic Club Bilbao. José Antonio
risked the stability of his family and his own professional life for Andrés,
always hanging on every move and every moment of his son's career, from
the day he first took him for trials at Albacete to Barcelona, always
wondering if the coaches there looked at his son the way that he did.
Every summer, the same feeling, the same doubts, the same hopes.

'From the first day that Andrés joined Barcelona, I got used to living with that uncertainty, with not knowing what would happen to Andrés the following season, even when he signed his first professional contract,' José Antonio says. 'What if he doesn't stay? What if they don't want him? What if . . . ? The same questions always arose, however much you thought he was getting better by the season. To start with, when I took him to those trials, I thought that things could go well for him. But I didn't know. It was like playing the lottery. You're never sure, you never quite bring yourself to believe that it *will* happen, but you never lose hope. I was always very cautious, maybe too cautious. I have always seen the tough, competitive side of football, how hard it is to make it. I never joined in when people said: "He'll make it, for sure." I never said that. I had hope, of course. I hoped that my son might become what I never managed to become: a footballer. And that hope, that idea, dominated my life; it became what sustained me.'

Not everyone in Fuentealbilla saw it in the same way. But whenever anyone doubted Andrés' commitment to a career in football, José Antonio gave the same answer: 'What do you want him to be? A footballer? A bullfighter? A waiter? No one had an answer for that, they just shot me bad looks. I'm sure they thought that this little lad only said he wanted to be a footballer because I said so, not because he actually wanted to. It was my passion, it's true, and would take him to games anywhere, any time, but it was his passion too, from a very young age. At first, I just watched him; then I saw that he was good; then, later on, I would correct parts of his game after each match. He stood out from the start.'

Andrés knew that when he got in the car after a game, he would have to answer the questions his father fired at him and listen to his appraisal of the way he had played. 'Always for his own good,' José Antonio says. 'He was lucky: he loved football, it was deep inside him, even more than it was in me, and he was always very intelligent. He knew, not least because I always reminded him of it, that whatever I told him he had to listen to his coach. I kept saying to him: "Remember, Andrés, the manager is always in charge. You can be as good as you like, but if you do the opposite of what he tells you, it's no good. Understand?" I have never been the kind of father who pesters his son if he doesn't share his manager's ideas, filling his mind with the notion that the coach is wrong. I was his dad and his coach, sure, but I always had the same basic message: "If your coach says white and your father says black, it's white."'

For a long time, José Antonio was father, coach, consultant and manager. It wasn't always easy for the family to understand. One example was when Barcelona were interested in signing him after the Brunete tournament. 'They spoke to me on the Sunday at the tournament, then on the Monday Oriol Tort called me and I made the proposal to Andrés, telling him that he had the chance to go to Barcelona. He said no, but I insisted: "Andrés, opportunities like this are there to be taken; this chance might not come round again." But he was determined: "No, Dad. I want to stay here in the town with everyone; I'm happy here. I'm not going." I had no choice but to ring Mr Tort and tell him: "Look, I'm sorry, but at the moment he's not going. Not this year, anyway." Andrés did pre-season with Albacete and in the meantime I kept on at him; every journey the conversation would be the same. I'd say: "If you say no, then it's a no. But you should think carefully about this, Andrés. They might not call you again." And that's the way it went every day for two months, until one day he said: "Dad, could you call Mr Tort?"

'Because he had been named the best player at Brunete, they gave him a trip to PortAventura theme park,' José Antonio continues. 'I had already said no to him signing for Albacete and we set off for Tarragona, where PortAventura is. It was September, school had started and so had the season, so I asked Tort: "Is there still a place available?" "Of course," he said. "There's always a place for Andrés." So we headed straight from PortAventura to Barcelona. They showed us around and they took me up on my suggestion that he should play a game with some of the kids from La Masia. I wanted to know that he could do it, to be reassured. We went back home afterwards and a few days later Andrés said to me: "Dad, I want to go there. Can I still go to Barcelona? Could you ring them, please?"'

The roles were reversed. Now it was the son who was convinced, while his father began to warn him of the downside. 'I said to him: "Remember that if you go, it's not for a couple of months; you'll have to be there for a year at least." And he responded: "Yes, a year's fine. I'll last a year, I promise." He'd taken that first step. *He* had taken it, even if he wanted to please me, because Andrés always thinks of others more than he thinks of himself. He did that as a kid and he still does now that he's a father himself. I'm sure he must have said to himself: "If I don't go, I'll be letting down my dad; if he says the train only comes by once, he means it." He was very brave. Very. I don't know how many twelve-year-old boys would have done something like that. I would have given my right arm for him to go to Barcelona, because I wanted him to play for the best club possible. But the decision was his.'

It's hard to decide who found it harder: Andrés or José Antonio. Both suffered, both hung on the other's words, both were under pressure. José Antonio thought about his son . . . and his son, the footballer. His son, the footballer for Barcelona.

There were days, starting with that very first day at Barcelona, when José Antonio thought about driving over there and taking his son back, bringing him home to Fuentealbilla. Mari, his wife, convinced him not to, but she watched him suffer so much that she almost gave in too. 'There was a moment, a couple of weeks in, in which I said to her: "If it carries on like this, Mari, I'll go and get him and bring him home. You're going to end up with depression."

'It was hard. We would go and see him at weekends and every time we said goodbye it was torture. Mari was losing her son, she couldn't sleep, she'd go and sit in Andrés' empty room. I tend to shrug off things like that and I kept telling her: "It'll be alright . . . It's no different to any other kid. It's like a schoolboy who gets bad grades. If he went to Murcia to study, he wouldn't be here either. And I'll tell you something: if he stays here, at the bar, one morning at six o'clock, he'll get up and leave and he'll have a spliff in his hand. That's what happens to everyone here. If he's there, you know he is being looked after, you know he is studying, he's playing football. I don't know what's better: you decide. If he's lucky, if things go well, it could actually bring the family together forever."

'One of the best things about Andrés is that he sees everything through the family,' says José Antonio. 'When there's tension, he lightens the atmosphere; when there are problems, he solves them. All of us revolve around him, everything does. He's always aware of every little detail, always determined that we have everything we need; he takes on other people's problems as if they were his own. When I get up every morning, there's a message there waiting for me already on the phone: "Dad, how are you?" If I had another son, I don't know what I would do; if I would do it all the same. I never wanted Andrés to suffer then and I don't want him to now either.'

It wasn't easy for Andrés to deal with his footballing father. Andrés would never say so, of course, but his father admits it. A single example will do: 'One day I went too far . . . much, much too far,' José Antonio remembers. 'It was his first year at La Masía. His coach, Ursicinio López, wasn't there and so Roca took over for a few games. Andrés was twelve, going on thirteen. I went to Barcelona with Mari that weekend, just for a couple of days, and I saw Andrés play. I went mad. Watching him, he was like a hen, just standing there in the middle while all its chicks run around it. After the game, we picked Andrés up and when we got to the hotel I said to Mari: "Get out a minute, I want to talk to Andrés on my own." I couldn't get it out my head; I still couldn't believe what I had seen: he didn't run, he barely moved, it wasn't him. And I started on him . . .

'I was very unfair on him. Why did I have to do that? There was no need. The thing is, I get very emotional. What had happened on the pitch wasn't even his fault. Far from it. I realized that later, reflected on it, and said sorry. I was selfish. But that day after we had the chat we ended up in tears: I was bawling my eyes out and he was just there quietly, trying not to cry, probably thinking: "Why's my dad saying this to me?"

'When I saw him like that, I didn't know what to do. I felt awful. I didn't know whether to take back what I had said or what . . . and then of course I ended up arguing with Mari. Andrés was so little. With time he saw that what I said to him was for his own good. I was always very direct, always straight with him. I wanted him to learn. He knows that I always insisted that to be a footballer you have to work hard, you have to be honest. Talent comes naturally, but all the rest has to be worked on. If you don't work, you make life harder for your team-mates. There are eleven of you on the pitch, not one. He knows that. But I know that I went too far that day. Much, much too far.'

José Antonio Iniesta wants people to know that his intentions were good; that was just the way he is – a bricklayer who earned a living working from sun up to sun down, day after day, on the building sites of Fuentealbilla, hours spent up scaffolding. A man who, he says, 'risked everything for Andrés'.

'I have been lucky because everything turned out well,' he says. 'If it hadn't, I don't know what would have become of me. I could have lost everything. The risk was huge, there was a one in a hundred chance of it happening, one in a thousand. He left at the age of twelve. People will ask why we didn't go with him. They did offer me a home in Barcelona, and work for my wife and I, but I didn't want to go. "Thanks, but the day I go there it will be to enjoy watching my son play. With a bit of luck, of course. If not, I will stay in my town, working," I said. What was I going to go there for? And if at the end of the year they let Andrés go, then what? I would have lost my job there and here. We would have been a laughing stock. That's not the way you do things. I knew that we would have to make sacrifices for four or five years, that we would have to struggle through, that it would be as if our child had been sent away, taken from us. But anything that is worth chasing is hard.'

●  ●  ●

Andrés soon settled in at La Masía but José Antonio's fears didn't come to an end. Now he worried less about Andrés Iniesta his son and more about Andrés Iniesta the footballer, Barcelona player and Spain player. He had an argument with the director the youth system, Joaquím Rifé, during the European Under-16 championships when Andrés got injured having played well during the tournament and had to go back to Barcelona for treatment.

Negotiations on his first contract with the club were particularly unpleasant. 'They called me to a meeting one night at the Hotel Rallye,' he says, the same hotel where they had stayed on that very first, traumatic night in the city, having left Andrés in tears at La Masía.

Charly Rexach, Joan Lacueva and Rifé were there, the men in charge of youth football. It was supposed to be a secret meeting, but no sooner had I got there that I stumbled across the former Salvadoran footballer 'Magico' González in reception and he said: "They're waiting for you!" I'd just arrived, tired from work and the journey in that damned Ford Orion, the one that did thousands of miles from Albacete to Barcelona and back again, with the windows open because I had no air conditioning and the temperature dial through the roof, terrified that the thing would break down on me halfway there. And I thought: "That's not a good start." The meeting went on and on until I said we should stop going round and round.

'Just write a contract, the way it's supposed to be, put it in front of us, we'll look at it and *then* let's talk!

'I was really worried,' José Antonio continues. He knew that Barcelona had just paid 5,000 million pesetas for the Argentinian striker Javier Saviola and now they didn't appear to want to offer a decent contract to his son. 'He could have gone to Real Madrid whenever he wanted, any time in his career, but he never did. And I never forced him. In fact, no matter what people say, I have never spoken to anybody there. Three times people from Madrid approached us through other people; I never spoke directly to anyone at the club. Carlos Sainz, the rally driver who wanted to be Madrid president, called me but I never answered the phone. I didn't respond to José Antonio Camacho either, when he was Madrid manager. His assistant Pepe Carcelén called me and said: "Would Andrés be prepared to come to Madrid if we paid his buy-out clause?" "No, never!" I said. "Andrés is very happy here and unless things change, he'll stay."

'It is true, though, that there was a day when I said to Jesús Farga, who was in charge of youth football at Barcelona: "He can't stay here after all that's happened with the contract. We're going to go to Madrid!"

Of course, Andrés never joined Madrid; not as a kid, and not as a senior player either, and that was because of Jesús Farga. José Antonio remembers: 'Jesús wanted to sign Andrés. He said: "Don't worry, I will speak to Joan." Joan was Joan Gaspart, the Barcelona president at the time. And three months later, we finally had a contract in front of us. A good one.

'We'd had problems before because I didn't want to just sign the standard contract that all the youth team players sign. I didn't want to know. I still remember Lorenzo Serra Ferrer calling me into his office, sitting me down and saying: "Why hasn't he signed yet?" And I replied: "Have you read the contract? I can't sign a deal that ties a kid down until he's twenty-two or twenty-three." At the end of the meeting, neither of us were happy, but that's life.

'I was on my way back to the car when Mr Tort came over and said: "Don't worry, Mr Iniesta, your son will not be leaving here. I'll make sure of it, if it's the last thing I do! If I have to, I will ring the president, Josep Núñez." That gave me confidence. And two months later, Serra Ferrer gave Andrés a chance in the first team. He had an eye for young players. One day we were watching a youth team game and I had noticed this kid from Andalucía: tall, strong, a big lad. I said to Serra Ferrer: "If only Andrés was a bit bigger! What a pity!" And he said to me: "Make no mistake, José Antonio, he doesn't need to be. He will be one of the great players Spanish football has to offer . . . and that kid? That kid won't get past Segunda B. No chance. Why? Because from the neck up, all he has is air! Andrés might only be 1.72 metres tall but that's 1.72 metres of pure talent and football, even if there are lots of people at Barcelona who don't want to recognize that yet."

'Serra Ferrer was brave enough to promote Andrés to first-team training when he was only sixteen. I couldn't believe it when Andrés told me. He never lies but I still didn't believe it until I saw it on the telly; there he was running out to train with the first team. I know it was Serra Ferrer who told Louis van Gaal about Andrés; they went to the mini stadi to watch a game together and Serra Ferrer told him: "Have a look at the number 10, see if you like him." And then it was Van Gaal who took him up to the first team every day. They both had a huge part to play in Andrés' career.'

● ● ●

Although he can be stubborn, Andrés was always obedient and listened to his father and his coaches. He always respected authority, something that you can still see now, even though these days he has power of his own. 'I think that was one of his great virtues . . . but also one of his defects when it came to getting the status he deserved in football,' José Antonio says. 'But that's the way he is. I was more egotistical, more of a rebel. I wouldn't say he was passive, or submissive, but it is true that he always accepted authority. He accepted decisions that didn't always work in his favour. In the end, it hasn't worked out too badly, though. He has always been very generous and that's unusual in football. I remember that when he was little he used to score lots of goals. He always dribbled well, he would see the move a second before anyone else and he accelerated quickly. He used to get in the box a lot too. At youth team level, he could do everything, he had it all.'

Including scoring goals, but then . . . 'Everything changed when he got to Barcelona B at sixteen and they made him play as a number 4, a deep midfielder like Guardiola, Milla, Xavi, Celades, De la Pena . . . That distanced him from goal,' says José Antonio. 'I remember people telling him he was the new Guardiola. They made him play in a way that didn't entirely suit his characteristics. He never lost the ball and he anticipated well, but he was no longer giving the final pass or scoring goals. He had to play for others. And when Van Gaal called him up to the first team, he had Rivaldo, Kluivert and Riquelme there. It's not easy for a seventeen-year-old kid to

train with players like that and still less for a kid like hi
obedient. Others get full of themselves and don't pass the ball, not
to Rivaldo. And then the year after that, Eto'o and Ronaldinho arrived. He
was at their service, always thinking of others more than himself.'

José Antonio thinks that Andrés doesn't play the same way for Barcelona as he does for Spain, as if somehow with Spain he feels like more of a protagonist, less like a player who is there to assist others. More of a star. And that's the way his dad likes to see him play: 'He has more freedom, it's a different way of playing. And once in a while he scores too, just to remind everyone that he can do that as well, you know,' he jokes. 'I still remember that 2–1 win against Chile at the 2010 World Cup, and the goal against Paraguay after one of those runs he's so good at, going past player after player. They tried to knock him over at least three times but he kept on going, eventually giving it to Pedro, who hit the post before Villa followed up. He played well at that World Cup, and after a difficult season too. Mind you, he's always good for Spain. Luis Aragonés and Del Bosque have always trusted in him and given him so much confidence. And players feel that.'

Maybe the coach that most trusted in Andrés was Guardiola. 'I will never be able to thank him enough, as a father, for all he did,' José Antonio says. 'Never. Not just when it came to football, but everything: as a person. At the hardest moments, he was there for Andrés, helping him find a way out.'

## THE WISE ONE

*'I knew by then who Andrés was. Everyone at Barça knew who he was.'*

*Lionel Messi*

I'm still not sure what happened. The day I was supposed to make my debut for the Barça Under-13s, I overslept. The previous night I had slept in the older boys' dorm and we were talking for a long time. I don't remember what time I went to bed but it was late, very late. I slept right through my alarm clock. I never heard a thing.

It was a good job that we were playing in the mini-stadium which is close to La Masia, because if not I don't know what would have happened. I remember that they came to wake me up and without having any breakfast I went straight to the dressing room. We played against the 'Cinco Copas

*Peña' team and we won 8–0 and I scored four goals. Yes, I used to score goals you know. That was my official debut with the Barcelona youth academy. It wasn't bad. But imagine oversleeping ahead of my first match. Considering how shy I am, you can imagine how timidly I walked into that dressing room knowing that I was late.*

● ● ●

Ursicinio López, a true craftsman of La Masia, did not know what had happened. The game was about to start and Andrés had still not arrived. He could imagine all sorts of things but not this – he had never overslept. Just in time, the little boy from La Mancha arrived to slip on the Barça shirt for the first time ever. No sooner had the game begun than he started to dance with the ball at his feet, putting his very special stamp on the way the team played right from his first match.

'He played with that mix of sobriety and delicacy that he has always had,' says Ursicinio. 'Although he did not like the idea of it, he was the star of the team. He played in midfield but linked play with the forwards and was very much in the style of a young Luis Suárez.' Ursicinio refers to the Spanish Suárez – the only Spaniard to ever win the Balon D'Or, in 1960.

Suárez was the Galician who triumphed in Barcelona but never won the European Cup he deserved – losing the final in Bern to Bela Guttman's Benfica 3–2. He would later get universal acclaim with Inter Milan where he lifted two European Cups. Andrés had something of 'Luisito', as Ursicinio calls him. An elegant player who grew up kicking an improvised cloth ball around the streets of La Coruña, succeeded by one who did much the same on the streets of Fuentealbilla.

'Andrés had that ability to arrive in the box; he could play the final pass, he scored goals, and above all he participated in the incredible way the team played,' says Ursicinio. 'Andrés played as a number 10, although he would end up as a number 4 and a number 6 and a number 8,' says Ursicinio, remembering the numbers used by Johan Cruyff, who had arrived at Barça as coach in 1988, eight years before Iniesta. The number 10 was at that time the left-sided midfielder (the position Iniesta plays for Barcelona today). The number 6 played behind the strikers (Bakero at that time). The number 4 was the central midfielder (Guardiola first; later Xavi; and now Busquets) and the number 8 was worn by the right-sided midfielder (Eusebio). Everything was influenced by Cruyff's Dream Team – the side that changed the way we looked at modern football.

'In the Under-13s, we played 3-4-3 with a midfield diamond. But Andrés used to be wherever the ball was. I think really it was the ball calling to him: "Come over here please, Andrés." That is the way it was in that first game for Andrés, still with his eyes red from sleep and that slightly embarrassed look on his face for having arrived late.

'He had that ability to give and go,' explains Ursicinio. 'He could go past an opponent, or two or three. He did it with such ease that you watched him and imagined you could do the same. He had, and still has, a very clear conception of football and he had the technical ability to put that vision of how the game should be played into practice. He was hugely superior to his rivals. If he has that superiority now, then just imagine what it was like when he was a boy.'

Ursicinio had known what to expect because Oriol Tort had told him that he had a 'real pearl' coming his way from Albacete. 'One day before he arrived, the "Professor" came to see me and he said to me: "You are going to get this boy who we have signed from the Brunete tournament. Yes, the one that Benaiges saw. Madrid wanted to sign him too, but he wanted to come to us."'

Concise as he always was, the professor did not want to build the boy up with too many words to Ursicinio, in whom he had complete faith. Although Tort was a man driven by enthusiasm, he did not want to raise expectations too much. But if the good eye of Mani, his trusted friend in Andalucía, was to be believed, then there was no room for any doubts.

'He's all yours,' Tort said to Ursicinio.

'Everything looked really easy for him. He got away from people so smoothly, he could see where his team-mates were, and he could see the right pass to play. If he could do the same things at a higher age level, then there would be no problem. "He'll get there," we used to say when we watched him playing. The only possible problem was a physical one. We did not know if his slight frame would be able to resist what he was going to come up against further down the line,' admitted Ursicinio, unaware at the time that this problem had already been solved 500 kilometres from Barcelona.

Abelardo and Julian, Andrés' friends from Fuentealbilla, four and five years older than him, had cracked the code long before. His age was not going to be a problem and neither was his physique. If he had 'survived' the hard unforgiving pitches of the village, how was he not going to cope with the green carpets of the Barcelona training pitches?

'It's true that even in this respect he tricks you – even with his physique,' says Ursicinio. 'Because you see him barely filling his shirt and he looks as if a strong gust of wind would blow him away. He appears so frail and yet he stands up to the physical test of every game without a single problem. He is at the heart of things from the first kick to the last, as if he never gets tired ever. Sometimes I would say to myself: "With all the running he has put in during the first half, he is not going to last five minutes in the second period!" But he did last. His rhythm never dropped. He always played the same way.' It was the same surprising resistance that the young boy showed on his debut, arriving late and going straight out on to the pitch with no breakfast, to score four goals.

'Sometimes when we were on the gravel pitch that used to be next to the Camp Nou, and which is now a car park, Olivé would come up to me and say: "How is the Wise One playing today?"'

Ursicinio would happily laugh back: 'See for yourself, Olivé. He's playing as well as always, doing his own thing.' The wise one – Andrés – was doing things in training that were incredible. 'We should be paying them to be here watching this instead of them paying us,' Ursicinio used to joke with his assistant, Joaquin.

When Ursicinio had Andrés in the Under-13s, it was as if he had one of his heroes in front of his eyes. He was the boy from La Mancha, but he was also the boy from Galicia and the little Catalan lad: it was Andrés, Suárez and Fusté all in one.

He used to cover so much of the pitch and he knew how to hide the ball from the opposition. 'Sometimes I lost sight of it myself,' says Ursicinio. 'We used to practise striking the ball with the left foot, which was his weaker, but there are some players who somehow manage to make sure the ball always seems to arrive on their stronger foot. That was the case with Andrés and his right foot. As for his heading, I don't think I ever saw him head it. He used his head for other things. Look at the way he defends, for example. He does it by positioning himself so well, and whenever he had a one on one he would always come away with the ball. He did not go on long runs hunting possession down, but his intuition meant he was capable of being in the right place at the right time to steal the ball away when no one was expecting him to. He did that all the time with us.'

The coach admits he had very little personal dealings with Andrés, who he saw only in the dressing room and then on the pitch. While the coach of the Under-13s worked every day from eight o'clock in the morning until three o'clock in the afternoon, Andrés was at the Luis Vives school with his friend Jorge Troiteiro.

● ● ●

'We were the youngest and the best looked after at La Masia,' Troiteiro says. 'I arrived a week before Andrés and they were very difficult days for me. That is why when he turned up I was really happy to have his company and it meant I was not the youngest any more. Puyol, Reina, Motta, Arteta – they were all older than us. It might not seem like it, but a week was a very long time in La Masia. I was more used to it than Andrés. And anyway I was more daring, more outgoing and more talkative. He was the shy one; he still is.

'We slept in the same bunk-bed in La Masia. At first they put us in the same room as the basketball players. There were five or six of them and just two of us. Andrés slept on the bottom bunk and I slept on top. And we had Puyol who kept an eye on us at all times. Puyol and Victor Valdés both made sure that no one laid a finger on us. They really looked after us. They protected us.

'He always looked pale; he nearly always had red eyes and he was just very white. He looked sad but at the time I could not understand how he was suffering inside,' reveals Puyol. 'I was the happiest guy in the world because they had chosen me to play at Barça and I was in La Masia. What more could I ask for? Nothing, absolutely nothing. But Andrés was still a very young boy. At the time, I could not understand what he was feeling. For me, it was a case of having arrived exactly where I had always wanted to be.

'He wanted to be there as well, but he was suffering like nobody could imagine. Everyone is different. For example, I never called anyone on the telephone, I never went home in four months and nobody came to see me. But I was really happy with things that way,' says the former Barça captain who was too busy trying to prove people wrong.

Ever since Puyol had abandoned the dirt pitches of La Pobla de Segur, there were doubts that he would make it. 'I am going to prove to you that I can play for Barça,' he repeated to himself time and again. He felt no pressure, just a very strong belief in his own ability to overcome. He had needed a month (the longest trial in Barça's history, Puyol confesses) to convince the coaches to open the doors of La Masia to him.

Every morning he would wake up in Ramón Sostres' house, now his and Andrés' agent. He did so with that infinite energy that he brought with him from La Pobla. This is someone who started off as a goalkeeper and ended up as one of the most legendary central defenders in the world; to do that he had to knock down all obstacles in his path. And so night and day, the 12-year-old and the 18-year-old both went in search of a golden future at Barça, one armed with brilliant technique, the other with an unbreakable will. One with courage, and the other with a tremendous emotional burden to carry.

'One day,' says Ursicinio, 'while I was coaching the Under-18s, Joan Martinéz Vilaseca, who coached the Under-19s, came over and said to me: "We are going to a school in Tarragona to play a game, and a boy we are watching will be there. He is from Lleida." That boy was Puyol.

'He played on the right wing, and he was already very powerful physically,' he remembers. 'In time he would acquire the necessary technique to go with his other attributes. What did I tell him? I gave my opinion based on what I saw that day and they signed him. Afterwards those great physical qualities were matched by his technique and he improved beyond all expectation thanks also to that extraordinary willpower and determination that he always had. With so much enthusiasm, it was impossible that he would not eventually succeed. But I would also say that he was the only exception to something that Pujolet always used to say to us.'

When the boys came to La Masia, there was a phrase of Pujolet's that, while not written down anywhere, was universally accepted. 'Pujolet' is not to be confused with the man who would captain Barça under both Rijkaard and Guardiola. Lluís Pujol is a famous forward from the Sixties who debuted for Barça aged 17 and who ended up as a scout at the club under the orders of Professor Tort.

'Pujolet always said to us: "I want players who know how to play." Andrés was one of those. For me, the arrival of Cruyff was a real blessing for those boys. In that era, strong, tall, physically powerful players were all the rage. But when Cruyff arrived everything changed. Look at the case of Luis Milla. When Barça wanted to sign him everyone said: "There is nothing to him, he has no strength. If you loosen the belt on his trousers they will fall down." Everyone looked on him with suspicion but Jaume Olivé, one of the coordinators of La Masia at that time, took a very serious line with Josep Mussons, who was the vice-president at the club and said: "This one is worth a million pesetas. If you sign here, the boy will stay."'

Milla stayed at Barça and went on to play in the Camp Nou before joining Madrid and leaving another famous Cruyff phrase to posterity. 'Let him go! It doesn't matter,' said the Dutch manager back in 1990. He then asked: 'Who is the best in the youth system in his position?' 'Guardiola,' they told him. So Johan went to watch the best La Masia had at the Mini Estadi where the Barcelona youth teams played.

He arrived after the game had started so as not to arouse suspicion, sat in the most discreet place possible and looked down at the pitch to see that Guardiola was not even playing. 'If he is the best, then why is he not playing?' he asked angrily. 'There is nothing to him, he is too light-weight,' they told him.

That same year, in December 1990, Guardiola made his debut in the Camp Nou, following in the path of Milla, but only after hearing a phrase that he would never forget: 'You played more slowly than my grandmother,' Johan said to Pep after he had given him his debut in a friendly in Banyoles in May 1989. But he was taking the same path later taken by Xavi and finally by Iniesta – players who seemed to have no place in modern football but ended up dominating the game.

●　●　●

Andrés Iniesta arrived at Barcelona in 1996; Lionel Messi in 2000. Curiously, Andrés arrived on 16 September and Leo on 17 September. Four years and one day's difference between two players who would eventually coincide for over a decade in the Barça team that would rewrite the club's history.

'No, I was never at La Masia with Andrés,' says Messi who travelled at lightning speed through the various levels of youth football at Barcelona until he made his debut aged just 17, much like Andrés; child prodigies the pair of them.

'I never lived there because at first I was with my parents in a hotel in Plaza España, then we found an apartment,' he adds. 'Later, when my mother and my brother and sister went back to Rosario, I stayed here alone with Jorge my dad. Some days I went there to eat or to chat with a friend, and I knew by then who Andrés was. Everyone at Barça knew who he was.'

In many ways, both Iniesta and Messi were fortunate to have joined Barcelona after Johan Cruyff and his assistant Toni Bruins had introduced Total Football to the Camp Nou. 'When Cruyff came on the scene, the club's football was revolutionized,' says Ursicinio. 'It seemed more complicated, but in reality it was actually easier. Toni Bruins put a whiteboard up and started to draw passing drills and he said to us: "This is positional play, the essence is in the first time pass; two touches at most, do you understand?" We all looked at each other until somebody, I don't remember who, said: "Is that it?" And Bruins, with his basic Spanish because he had just arrived in the country, said: "Yes, it's everything. Football is simple. You divide the pitch up into triangles and the key is to always have the ball and to create superiority."'

Little could Cruyff and Bruins have realized that the Total Football they had brought to Barcelona in 1988 would end up being improved, overtaken, and raised to a new sublime level by Barça. In Andrés' case, there was not much to teach him. It was more a case of enhancing the few things that were not already in his genetic make-up.

'Sometimes I think about that clinical eye that Cruyff had,' says Ursicinio. 'It's true that he had much more besides. But that ability to be one step ahead of things, I have only seen that with Johan. Andrés was where he was because of the way "El Flaco" looked at football. There are some players that you need to show things to, but not Andrés. He already had it all inside of him.'

● ● ●

This was no longer the era of Cruyff, of course. When Andrés arrived that philosophy was no longer at the forefront, but the great man's ideas were still alive at Barça despite the ups and downs that rocked the club. It was the 1996–97 season and the era of Sir Bobby Robson, and of José Mourinho, first as his translator and then as his assistant. It was also the era of Ronaldo, the extra-terrestrial centre-forward parking his spaceship on the pitches of all La Liga's top-flight clubs.

It was the Barça that almost won everything but that lost the league in the final breath because their star player was in Brazil, called up by his national side. It was also the Barça of Guardiola, Andrés' childhood hero, alongside Figo, Luis Enrique, Stoichkov, Blanc and Popescu. The little boy from La Mancha could turn his gaze towards the small pitch next to the stadium, the one that did not even have the correct official dimensions, and see his heroes. That training pitch situated between the Camp Nou and La Masia does not exist anymore. The fence Andrés clambered up remains but the pitch is now a concrete parking lot. The goalmouths have been ripped up, all traces of where it all began having been erased forever.

When Andrés had days off he would find himself even more trapped in the routine of tears, devoured by loneliness. Ursicinio remembers that Albert Benaiges, a guy who loves football, took him to the cinema with his son to free him from the monotony.

'It's true we went to the cinema, but we also used those free afternoons to go to the park, those ones with the big pools of sponge balls so he could have some fun,' says Benaiges, the coach who signed him for Barça after the Brunete tournament.

'And when his parents could not come one weekend to see him, well, I took him home to my mother. There he played for hours and hours with my adopted son Samuel. They are nothing like one another. Samuel is black and came from Brazil; Andrés is the palest shade of pale. My son does not like football; Andrés, however, can't live without football. They just did not go together at all, but they spent the whole day in each other's company,' remembers Benaiges.

Jorge Troiteiro remembers the afternoons with Benaiges that helped kill the boredom that tortured them on those days off. 'We were also invited to lunch by Benaiges. And he took us to a place where they sold Horchata because he loved it.'

José, the goalkeeper who received Andrés when he first arrived, evokes what life was like behind those old stone walls. 'In La Masia, your bed is your home. Well, your bed and your table. You have everything there,' he says. 'We spent a lot of hours at home, in other words, in bed. Or we would go from room to room talking with the others. Inside La Masia, there were no separate age groups. We would talk forever, but nearly always from our beds.' Perhaps that is why Andrés overslept the night before his debut with Ursicinio.

'What did we do? Well, we would go out into the garden at the back of La Masia where we would play endless games of football if the weather was good. We were in our own world. The ball would go where it shouldn't and we would be told off, especially by Juan, one of the security guards. Because he was one of the newest there, he was very strict; nothing got past him. Ferri, another of the security guards, messed around with us a little bit more. And Andrés, just like Jorge, because he was the youngest, was the most spoiled.

'Even Juan would mess around with those two. If it was us, we would get in big trouble every time. They got away with a lot more. The ball would roll away to every corner of La Masia, it was great fun. The hairs on the back of my neck stand up just thinking about those times,' says José.

'We were never apart,' says Jorge Troiteiro. 'We went everywhere together: to school, to the dining room, to the dorm, to the bunk-beds, everywhere. When they told us that we had to go to sleep, we would get one more game going on the landing of the sleeping quarters. The doorways to the bedrooms were the goals and we used tennis balls, so as to not make too much noise. Although when one of the security guards appeared, Ferri or Juan, they would always say the same thing to us: "Go to sleep, now!"'

Jorge in the top bunk and Andrés in the bottom bunk – off to school every morning and with nobody to meet them when they came out. That was how it was day after day, with just a small green telephone cabin, situated at the entrance to La Masia by the kitchen, connecting them to the outside world.

Sometimes parents would prefer not to ring their sons so as not to awaken more homesickness. It was better to let the pain of separation lie dormant rather than provoke more tears. 'When they called me, I would cry,' says Troiteiro, and all the boys were the same.

'I knew the number to La Masia by heart; I can still remember it now from all the times I called Andrés,' says Manu, the cousin who first announced the existence of the little genius of Fuentealbilla, and who was then heartbroken to have lost him.

● ● ●

'No, I did not cry. And I never saw him cry either, but they told me he did. It is true that I arrived two years after Andrés. I arrived here right in the middle of August,' explains Jordi Mesalles, former Barcelona player and a friend of Andrés in those days.

'I came from a village in Lleida and for me to get here was a really big thing. I remember having written things at home with drawings that my mum still has that say: "My dream is to be in La Masia." I was overjoyed to have made it. No sooner had I arrived than I was training with Andrés' team and playing alongside Troiteiro, Rubén and Lanzarote. When the other boys went home or their families came to visit them, I was left feeling very lonely in La Masia. I can remember thinking at the time: "This is hard, really hard,"' says Mesalles, who would soon find out that Andrés was suffering too.

'From the second week onwards, we started to hang around together,' says Mesalles who began his immersion into La Masia under the guidance of Andrés. 'We walked from La Masia to the training pitch three, "the sandpaper pitch" as we called it because every time you went down you really hurt yourself on that tough artificial grass. There were four teams training at once on that pitch. Each group had their own corner.

'We were both the same in the way we lived day to day. We were both very relaxed about things. We were comfortable in our rooms, or watching the television, and we were among the few boys who used the library at La Masia. And it was a good one too, although you would not have guessed from how empty it often was. We were homely boys, happy with very little. If we were just chatting about football then we were happy,' he says, as he begins to remember stories that go far beyond just the football.

Jorge Troiteiro recalls: 'Víctor came to see us one day and he said: "I'm leaving." We were all so surprised. I cried a lot that night, because he was like a brother to me and Andrés. I remember telling him: "Look, Víctor I want to give you this cross and chain so that if you don't come back you will have something to remember me by."'

The Víctor in question was Barcelona's record-breaking goalkeeper Víctor Valdes. 'In the end, everything was sorted out and Víctor stayed with us. He never gave me the chain back but that was fine. It was his, I gave it to him forever,' says Troiteiro, room-mate, team-mate and friend for life.

Friendships formed a big part of the young players' time at La Masia. 'We would share our secrets and the food parcels that arrived from home,' remembers Mesalles. 'My parents would bring sweets and crisps from Lleida, things that we liked. We had our own hiding place in our locker at La Masia. We had a locker and cabinet with two drawers – one for the top bunk and one for the bottom bunk. The thing I liked most about La Masia was that it was like a family. We all knew each other from the oldest to the youngest. We used to queue for the telephone – we had to because although there were two cabins only one worked, so we had to be patient and to remember to ask the cooks or the security guards for change, or face an even longer wait. It was like the Big Brother house, but it was much nicer because we shared everything. If you arrived last to the dining room, then you got the last steak, the one that looked the worst and that everybody else had left, but I have only good memories. It was a great experience.

'We were together twenty-four hours a day and so we formed some great friendships. In the end your neighbour, whether you like it or not, ends up becoming your confidant, and you become his.' Jordi is still friends with Andrés, and, from time to time, still a confidant too.

FIRST TEAM

*'Where can he play? Andrés can play anywhere; he's a genius.'*
Lorenzo Serra Ferrer to Louis van Gaal

The boys were there in their usual place, watching Van Gaal's Barcelona: the Dutch contingent of Cocu, Overmars, the De Boer brothers, and Bogarde, alongside Guardiola, Figo, Luis Enrique. 'We would sit between the north end and the side stand, across from the main stand, not far from the corner flag. We'd all be there.' Jordi Mesalles still gets emotional when he remembers those days, even if he never got the chance to be a ballboy like his friends Andrés and Jorge Troiteiro.

Troiteiro remembers it well: 'It was a derby against Espanyol and we didn't have a great time of it. People kept throwing lighters and things onto the pitch and we were only little, and in their line of fire. We were positioned just behind the advertising boards and we had to stand on tip toes to be able to see over them. We hardly saw the game.'

These were the kids who had come from all over Catalonia and Spain, hoping that one day it would be them out there on the pitch. 'I watched Cocu. Andrés loved Michael Laudrup but he had gone to Real Madrid by then and so it was Guardiola he followed; he couldn't take his eyes off of him,' Mesalles says.

They didn't know it yet, but they would get their first experience of that field sooner rather than later, when the prestigious Nike Cup, a kind of Under-15 club world championships, was held at the Camp Nou. Barcelona made the final there, with Andrés, Troiteiro, Jordi, Rubén . . . Their coach was Ángel Pedraza, who had become the first La Masia graduate to play for the first team, when the club's legendary former player and coach Laszlo Kubala called him up for a UEFA Cup game in September 1980.

'It was incredible to play that final at the Camp Nou,' Mesalles says. 'The main stand was full; there must have been 20,000 people there. We were used to sitting in that corner over the other side watching the first team; now, suddenly, here we were out on the pitch, with people watching *us*. When we arrived at the stadium, we didn't even know which way to go to get to the dressing room. There seemed to be tunnels everywhere, long passageways. You go in, you change and then you start walking. Then suddenly the pitch is there in front of you. The place looks immense. You think: "We can't play out there, it's too big. We're only small."

'You dreamed of playing out there but somehow you never really imagined it. From sitting in the corner, you suddenly feel like a first-team player. Of course, we didn't want to waste that opportunity; we wanted to win that final. All those people we watched were watching us. I remember that Van Gaal was there that day, Guardiola, Figo, the president Núñez . . .'

The final began badly. 'We were playing the Argentinian side Rosario Central. We'd beaten them heavily in the group stage, but we went a goal down quite early in the final. I suppose that was down to the tension and everything that game meant to us. The stadium, the pitch, it all felt immense. It was like it never ended.

'Gilberto, a really strong, powerful Brazilian kid we had, played up front; Troiteiro played on the wing; Andrés played in the centre of midfield; I played to the side of him,' Mesalles continues. 'We really struggled until Andrés moved up to play behind our forward. He had always scored a lot of goals, even if that might surprise people these days, and we needed him further up the pitch. He used to get into the area a lot, arriving at just the right time. We had him and Troiteiro behind Gilberto. Troiteiro was spectacular, so strong. And on the other wing we had Alfi. Andrés was the one bringing it all together, moving the team. We played 3-4-3, Cruyff style. I think all the Barcelona youth teams did; I remember watching the Juvenil A for example with Arteta, Valdés, Reina, Nano and Trashorras playing that same system. It was a risky strategy, very bold, very attacking, but enjoyable to play, although you needed a lot of energy because it forced you to cover so much ground. What it gave you was a man over in midfield, where you could control the game, and allowed you to attack in numbers. We had almost all of the ball. And that was how we turned that final round.

'Alfi scored the equalizer off a free-kick from Andrés, then Andrés scored the winner after a great move from Gilberto, who pulled the ball back for him. When he scored, his boot flew off. I remember that while we were trying to celebrate the goal, he was trying to find his boot. It was the golden goal, an incredible way to end it. It was a very Andrés kind of goal: arriving from deeper, in that line behind the strikers, to score.'

After the final, Pep Guardiola handed the trophy to Andrés, chosen as man of the match that day. Then there was that nod towards destiny. 'In ten years' time, I'll be up in the stands watching you play at the Camp Nou,' Guardiola told him. He was right, but for two things: it would be nine years and Pep wasn't up in the stands, he was down on the bench as Iniesta's coach. The same Iniesta who had been moulded by Pedraza, managed through a key moment of his career, when he captivated everyone in that Cadete B team.

'Ángel Pedraza is one of the best coaches I have had,' Mesalles says. 'He loved teaching and training. He explained everything to us, he got the very best out of us. He used to have conversations with me that left me reflecting deeply on football and on life. He was always honest and up front and that's something a player appreciates, even when he is just a kid. He gave so much to us; we learnt a huge amount from him.'

His impact on Andrés was as big, his educational role never forgotten. 'He was such a good person,' Andrés recalls. 'The day before he passed away, I went to the hospital to see him and say goodbye. There are moments in life that you can never really grasp, never fully understand. We lived so much together; we won that tournament together but it was more than that. He was a wonderful person. I like to remember him the way he was, full of vitality, energy. A good man.' The day that Pedraza passed away in 2011, the victim of cancer aged 48, Iniesta played at Riazor against Deportivo. Barcelona won 4–0 with a goal from Iniesta; they were still in the stadium when they found out that one of those anonymous heroes of La Masia had succumbed to illness. 'If I had known, I would have dedicated that goal to him,' Iniesta says.

'Andrés stands out for his intelligence and class; he is the leader of the side, the axis. He controls the pace of the game and has great technique,' Pedraza had told *El Mundo Deportivo*. Andrés hadn't even reached 16 years of age yet.

●  ●  ●

Together, Jordi Mesalles and Andrés won the Nike Cup at the Camp Nou in Barcelona's centenary year. Yet people had been talking about Andrés even before that success. Carlos Martínez, who would later become one of Iniesta's best friends, knew about him already. He was in Barcelona's youth system as well and word got round about the little magician. 'Andrés was two years older than me. Everyone talked about him and Troiteiro, but I'd never met him,' says the forward who was born in Mataró, just like Andrés' wife Anna. 'I didn't meet him until almost ten years later and football had nothing to do with it. I was studying law at Barcelona University with Anna and he turned up one day to see her.

'He said: "Hello, I'm Andrés."

'Yeah, yeah, I think I recognize you.'

Carlos didn't know that was the start of a long friendship. A competitive one, too, as anyone who has seen them play board games against each other can testify. 'We're like little kids in adults' bodies,' Carlos says. 'And we trust each other completely: we tell each other everything; we trust each other with our secrets.'

Pep Alomar was the coach of Barcelona's Cadete A team, the man who inherited Pedraza's side, one that had been moulded according to the principles laid down by Johan Cruyff and Oriol Tort. 'Pedraza did a splendid job with those boys,' Alomar says. 'He had an incredible team, full of talent, but that was a complex period for them; a time of physical and emotional change, when their bodies are developing and changing, when their hormones are too. The formative work done at the age of fifteen has a huge impact on the development of a player, and he managed that superbly.'

Alomar worked closely with Lorenzo Serra Ferrer, the coach who had designed the structure of the club's youth system. He continues: 'At the time, Barcelona followed an ideal expressed by Rinus Michels and Stefan Kovacs and implanted by Cruyff, but also took on board some of the ideas and methods of Europe's best centres of excellence, from Ajax to Clairefontaine and Coverciano.

'I remember Andrés would come to the office we had in the stadium most afternoons and ask if we would let him use the phone to call his parents who were back in Albacete. There were no mobiles back then. He was a quiet kid, very polite, and he never missed a day of school. Every year we'd do marks to find out who the best team-mate in the dressing room was. Andrés won it every time, of course.'

At the end of that season, Alomar left the Cadete A team to become assistant to the first-team manager Lorenzo Serra Ferrer. Both of them had Andrés on their radar.

'He had the greatest talent I've seen in a player,' Alomar says. 'When he was at Cadete level, he played with the same tactical awareness and intelligence that you see now. It's innate: he reads the game better than anyone, he executes every move quickly and makes no mistakes. He played as a number 4 but he could perform in any other position. In that 3-4-3 we played it was incredible watching him, the way that he would arrive in the area to finish. I'd ask him: "Where do you want to play, Andrés?" He'd reply: "Wherever you tell me to play, *míster*." He was good with both feet, he turned very quickly, and he processed everything extremely quickly, always coming up with the right option. Can that be coached? Yes . . . and no. If your "processor" is good, like Andrés', you'll always encounter better solutions and quicker too.'

Serra Ferrer would stroll over to pitch three as often as he could to see the kids play. He didn't need telling about Andrés; he could see for himself. And everyone was talking about him, about this kid that Jaume Olivé called 'El sabio', the wise one.

'When he took over the first team, Lorenzo was clear that he wanted Andrés to learn from the great players, the teachers, that we had in the first team at the time: Guardiola and Xavi. That was the best thing for his development, so he brought Andrés up,' Alomar says.

'No, I didn't discover anything,' says Serra Ferrer. 'Andrés was a genius, a natural phenomenon as a player and a person. I never had any doubt.'

Carlos Naval, a Barcelona club official and the embodiment of the club over so many years, remembers it well. 'I called La Masia and said: "Tell

Andrés that tomorrow he's training with the first team,"' he says.

'I thought it was a joke,' Andrés admits. He walked from La Masia to the main gate of the stadium, barely 300 metres. There, he stopped. He didn't dare go past that barrier. The security guard didn't know who this shy kid was, but Andrés got lucky. At just that moment, Luis Enrique was driving in and he recognized Andrés. 'Get in,' he said. 'I'll take you down to the dressing room.' And so it began.

'I wanted him to join the first-team squad for lots of reasons, but above all as a reward for his behaviour, for his leadership, for his attitude towards his team-mates,' Serra Ferrer says. 'He never had any problems with his school work, he was always the first one in every morning and he never missed a class. He would be there waiting for the bus, while there were others that the bus had to wait for.

'I remember Guardiola was very happy that Iniesta joined us that day, Rivaldo too. Imagine what it must be like for a kid to go into a dressing room like that with so many stars in it. So the message was simple: "Relax, Andrés. Just do what you know and that's it. Just enjoy this, okay?" Then when we went out onto that training pitch next to La Masia, he took it all in his stride, so naturally. If he had to speed the game up, he did. If he had to slow it down, he did. He surprised everyone. The only thing he didn't do was take the session himself. The players were looking at him, not at me. He was a star, but he did it all so naturally, so humbly. He understood the game and the Barcelona philosophy. There was no way it could go wrong. He knew that he would succeed.'

Iniesta didn't let anyone down, especially not Louis van Gaal, the coach who would give him his debut and definitively opened the door to him.

Van Gaal spoke to Serra Ferrer first before giving Iniesta his debut, but it was not as if he needed much convincing.

Serra Ferrer recalls the conversation: 'Van Gaal asked me: "Where can he play?" I said Andrés can play anywhere. As a central midfielder, dictating the game; as an *interior* on either side of that; behind the forward; as a number 10. And if one day you need someone to bring the ball out cleanly from the back, you could even play him at full-back, although he's not going to be so defensively tough, of course.'

● ● ●

The journey was not as easy as it might seem, though. Iniesta was training with the first team and playing in the youth teams, making progress through the ranks, but there were moments when he might have thought he wouldn't make it, when his progression slowed. Especially when he was playing for Barcelona B. That was hard, despite the fact that he arrived there having just enjoyed almost the perfect year with the Juvenil A under Juan Carlos 'Chechu' Pérez Rojo – the coach who himself had been named the second best *juvenil*, after Diego Maradona, at the Under-19 World Cup in Japan in 1979.

'I remember Guardiola coming to one of our training sessions,' Rojo says. '"Hey, Chechu, they tell me you've got a kid who's very good . . . the little pale one, right?" We were on pitch three and Pep sat and watched the whole session. At the end of it he said to me: "This kid is better than me."

'I also remember a game we played in Mallorca once. It was incredibly hot and in virtually the last minute of the first half, we had Dani the full-back sent off. I was on my way back to the dressing room at the old Sitjar ground there, going up those narrow stairs thinking to myself: "What do I tell the players now?" We were 1–0 down, we were a player down . . . I was thinking: "This lot are going to stick four past us today." But then the second half began and Andrés appeared. It was spectacular. Incredible, really. I'm not even sure where he was playing. In theory, he was a *media punta*, behind the forwards. But he was everywhere. I remember him appearing on the wing and me asking Rafel Magrinyà, my assistant: "Should I say something to him?" "Not a word!" he said. "Leave him to it." He was right. We won the game 2–1, with a man down, and Andrés was everywhere.

'Afterwards the Mallorca coach Tomeu Llompart asked me: "Who's that kid?" Then he said: "If you're looking for someone to replace Pep Guardiola, you've found him." He wasn't wrong,' says Rojo. 'The thing that struck me most about Andrés was how clearly he saw the game. He was sixteen that day and he was playing against *juveniles*, kids of eighteen or nineteen. He read the game so well, he knew how to change the pace of the match. When we were under pressure, he took responsibility: "Give me the ball." It was barely believable how this kid, who looked small and weak, took control; the way he positioned himself, the ease with which he did everything.'

Not that Rojo had Iniesta for long; Serra Ferrer had plans for his development and he was soon moved up to Barcelona B. Josep María Gonzalvo was his coach with the B team. 'The first time I saw him, I fell for him,' he says. 'I'm not sure when it was, probably when he was still playing at *infantil* level, well before he came up to the B team. One day, Serra Ferrer called me and said: "Andrés has to move up to the B team right away." It was the 2000–01 season. At first I refused. Why? Because I wanted to protect him physically. I thought at that age he was vulnerable, that moving up would not be good for him. I argued with Serra Ferrer, but in the end I accepted it. Serra was my boss, after all, and I'm still grateful that he had at least listened to me. It wasn't easy for Andrés to make that step up, either. After we had spoken, Serra Ferrer said to me: "Okay, go and see Andrés and tell him yourself."'

Gonzalvo headed over to the bedrooms opposite La Masia, built into the back wall of the Camp Nou itself. 'I knocked on the door and Andrés opened it. I was struck by what I saw inside. There were figures of saints all over the place, like it was a mini chapel. "Andrés, you're coming up to the B team." He was surprised, he didn't expect it. I told him not to worry about anything, that we would be there to help him out. I told him that he would play as a number 4, a position in which La Masia had produced a lot of talented players – Milla, Guardiola, Xavi – who I had coached the year before. But when Andrés played a little further forward, on either side of the midfield diamond, he was spectacular so I played him with Thiago Motta, almost if they were a partnership but with Andrés having the freedom to play further up.'

There were bad moments, Gonzalvo says. 'But it is also true that he progressed quickly and adapted well to each new challenge. Apart from his talent, what I liked most about him was his humility. Whenever you corrected him, he took it the right way: as something positive, as a lesson to learn. He was always keen to help. That Barcelona included Valdés, Arteta, Motta, Trashorras, a fantastic collection of players . . .'

Not an easy team to manage, though. Here was a group of ambitious kids who could see the Camp Nou closer than ever before. There were huge differences in salaries between some of them and egos, too. Big egos. In December, Barcelona B were top of the table in Spain's Second Division B, but on the inside all was not well and they collapsed, finishing tenth. Some players earned ten times as much as others, and everyone knew that. 'Andrés was in that group of players, the modest ones earning less,' Gonzalvo recalls. He admits that the step up from child to adult wasn't easy; the players were taking a step into a world they didn't really know.

'Andrés making it wasn't really a surprise with the talent he has. But the fact that he improved every year shows what kind of mentality and attitude he has. In the circumstances, he could have gone under or developed bad habits; bad influences could have carried him along. But he didn't. His attitude was good, very similar to Carles Puyol. They seem to be very different on the outside but, in reality, they're very alike. More so than they realize themselves. Andrés is more of a rebel, more of a fighter, than people think. That toughness, that edge and competitiveness, doesn't come to the surface but it is there. He has his moments; he grits his teeth and fights, even if people don't see that. I think he needs that. Some people's character comes out through shouting or standing out; Andrés is different. With him, you see it in the way he plays, the way he constantly overcomes the obstacles placed in his way. He does it all with the ball at his feet; that's where his personality shines through.'

'No one discovered Andrés; he discovered himself, he's that good,' says Quique Costas, Iniesta's last coach before he made the step up to the first team under Van Gaal. Yet few remember that Charly Rexach had the chance to call him up, to be the coach who gave Iniesta his debut, and he didn't take it. His first game with the senior side came as an unused sub. Barcelona were playing Espanyol in the city derby at Montjuic. Xavi was suspended and Gerard López was injured. It was December 2001. Rexach talked publicly about what a good player Iniesta was: 'He is another one in that line that includes Milla, Guardiola and Xavi,' he said. 'He knows how to escape the pressure he is put under, he has vision, he gets into the opposition's box, and he's always well positioned.' Costas added: 'Barcelona's fans can rest assured that if he plays, he will play very well. He's focused and technically very good.'

But Iniesta didn't play a minute. Rexach chose to play without a number 4 and instead played Christanval, a tall, muscular French defender in midfield alongside Philippe Cocu. Espanyol won 2–0 with two goals from Raúl Tamudo, and Rexach didn't even use all three subs. Andrés watched it all from the bench. He would have been the second youngest player to make his Barcelona debut. Ten months and seven days later, Luis Van Gaal did what Charly Rexach had not and handed Iniesta his first Barcelona game.

● ● ●

'Louis van Gaal was a key person in that long chain of coaches that I'd had since the Infantil B team, with Ursicinio all the way to the first team,' Iniesta says. 'I remember that we had just finished the season with Barcelona B and before going off on holiday Van Gaal called and said he wanted me to do pre-season with the first team. That same summer I had the Under-19 European Championships so I couldn't be there for the start of pre-season. I didn't know what to do. I thought to myself: "If I go to the Euros and

I'm not there at the start of pre-season with Barcelona, it might damage my chances . . ." But Van Gaal said to me: "Go, and when you come back you'll train with us." That was a great gesture on his part. I came back and trained with the first team, but played with the B team still until my debut in Bruges.'

Van Gaal believed in him, just as Serra Ferrer had. As Carlos Naval recalls: 'Van Gaal said to him: "There's the pitch, it's yours: play!"' And he played from the start, all 90 minutes, with the number 34 on his back. Barcelona won 1–0, with Riquleme scoring. It was 29 October 2002.

'Van Gaal always had a lot of faith in young players,' Iniesta says. 'I know he's different, that he has his way of seeing and doing things, but he will always have a place in my heart. I owe him a lot and I'm very grateful. The situation at the club was very difficult at the time, very delicate in lots of ways, but he always trusted in us, in the kids from the youth system. Not just me. I made my debut in October and then in January, when his job was on the line, I played all six games as a starter. I was only eighteen! He left Riquelme on the bench and played me instead. That was because he trusted in us. The proof of that is that after he lost his job, first Toño de la Cruz and then Radi Antic took over. I didn't play for either of them. And the same happened in the first season with Frank Rijkaard. So, I appreciate what Van Gaal did: he was important for me. He was more demanding, tougher, than anyone but he treated all the players the same way. It didn't matter if you were eighteen or twenty-eight. If you performed, you played.

'I still remember what he said to me in Bruges, when I made my debut: "Go out there and enjoy it. Do what you know best: play football."'

## FRANK

'Frank, you should speak to Andrés . . .'

*Txiki Begiristain, Paris, May 2006*

Smoke rose slowly from Frank's cigar. If paradise exists, he was there; or as close as you can be. Frank might have been a semi-secret smoker, hiding in corners to puff away, but few knew how to savour a cigar quite like him. That night, more than ever before, saw him quietly retreating into a peaceful, satisfied little world.

He had arrived at the Camp Nou almost by accident, an improvised solution after a period of self-destruction. But Frank Rijkaard had the tact, the calm and the character necessary to survive at a club that was on the road to perdition. To lead it to glory, in fact. With him Barcelona flew, as if riding on Ronaldinho's smile. The journey took him here, to his own private paradise: a moment alone amidst the partying to enjoy a Cuban cigar. Heaven.

Relaxed, he sat back and enjoyed his greatest moment as a coach: it was just two hours since he and his Barcelona team had won the European Cup, only the second in the club's history. The smoke swirled and he looked back on every moment of the journey, never forgetting where they had come from. Like Barcelona, he had crossed the desert. It was the club's sporting director Txiki Begiristain, advised by Johan Cruyff, who first put forward Rijkaard's name as a potential manager, despite the fact that his last job had ended with relegation at Sparta Rotterdam in Holland. And now here he was: a European champion.

There was a large crowd in that Parisian disco, up in the Bois de Boulogne. Almost a thousand people, listening to Lluis Llach's 'L'Estaca'. They also listened to Joan Laporta, the president who oversaw Barcelona's revival, sing tracks by Sopa de Cabra and watched him let loose on the dance floor, feeling like the King of the World. From Wembley 1992 to Paris 2006, the pioneers were there too: the 'Dream Team', who won the club's first European Cup, joining those who would build the greatest decade in the club's history. There were a lot of people celebrating the re-conquest of a cup that had once seemed cursed for Barcelona. But Frank was alone, as if stretching out on the back seat of a Rolls Royce rather than in a Parisian nightclub, the noise outside unable to reach him. Just him and his cigar. Until Txiki approached.

Amidst the celebrations, Txiki had spotted something important. Not just for that night but for the club's future. He'd been thinking about it since the moment before the game when he saw the Barcelona team line-up. Txiki sidled up to Frank.

'Frank, you should speak to Andrés.'

● ● ●

It had all started a few hours before. Txiki had looked at the line-up a couple of times, as if trying to take it in. Iniesta was not starting. He couldn't understand it, just like thousands of Barcelona fans couldn't either. He still can't, in truth. He checked again. No Iniesta. The key player in the quarter-final against Benfica, as a central midfielder, and again in the semi-final against Milan, on the left and behind the strikers, was on the bench.

Rijkaard, more Italian than Dutch when it came to this decision, had gone for Edmílson, Deco and Van Bommel instead. Xavi was not there; he was injured. Iniesta was not there either; he was a sub. The Barcelona style? No sign of it here. The essence of Barcelona? Not much of that either. Just three La Masia players were in the starting XI against Arsenal, and all of them at the back: Valdés, the keeper, Puyol, the captain, and Oleguer at right-back.

If Txiki took it calmly, others didn't. On his way to the game by bus, on the road somewhere in Paris, Iniesta's father José Antonio saw the line-up and could not believe it. He was furious. 'The *chiquillo* [young boy] is not playing?!' he shouted. 'Why not? Why not?' he cast glances at his family, at the other members of the Fuentealbilla supporters' club, until then travelling happily to the game of their lives. The game of Andrés' life.

Not any more. When they got to the ground and looked at the pitch, he was not there.

Mario was on the bus with them, the kid who Iniesta chose to train with back on that gravel pitch years before. He'd been looking forward to this since that text message arrived from Iniesta, a while before the final. 'Hey, pal, would you be able to get to the Champions League final?' *Would I?!* He looked at the message again. Yes, it was Andrés. 'I'd like my oldest friends to be there,' it said. He didn't know he wasn't going to play, of course.

'I went mad, really mad,' Mario says. 'It was incredible. Of course Andrés is a friend of mine, of course. But you don't expect him to be thinking of you in the build-up to the biggest game of his life.

'What did I do? Well, I took three days to reply, for starters. Three days! I was kind of in shock.' Of all his friends from Albacete, Mario was the only one able to escape to Paris for a few days. There he was on the bus, when the message came through. It was hard to watch José Antonio, so upset, so angry. Andrés, his son, wasn't playing.

There were two and a quarter hours to go until kick-off when journalist Gemma Nierga, who had set up at Saint-Denis, began interviewing the players' families for a programme called 'La Ventana' on Cadena SER radio station. Messi's brother spoke: 'I hope he [my brother] plays a few minutes.' Returning from injury and still not fully fit, Messi didn't play a single one. Then it was Andrés' grandfather's turn. 'I never imagined that my grandson would play a European Cup final.' He did, but in the end he had to wait 45 minutes. Nor did Iniesta's grandfather expect him to be left out of the starting XI.

It was, oddly enough, Xavi's brother Óscar who broke the news about Iniesta. He was initially talking about his brother, who had just returned from a long injury. 'Xavi has spoken to the manager and he told him that he will not be in the starting XI; the players who have been playing regularly recently will be there instead.' Xavi did not play a single minute. Those who had been playing regularly? Gemma Nierga took that to mean Deco, Van Bommel and Iniesta. But Óscar knew differently. Frank and his assistant Henk Ten Cate had other ideas. 'No,' Óscar revealed. 'Iniesta's not playing either. It'll be Deco, Edmílson and Van Bommel.'

So now everyone knew. What Rijkaard could not imagine was that his team would struggle in the first half, with Sol Campbell's header leaving his original plan in pieces. He saw that Barcelona were unable to dominate the game, not even against ten men following the 18th-minute sending-off of Arsenal goalkeeper Jens Lehmann. They did not have control, and they did not have the ball. Only Valdés, agile and strong, kept them in it.

On the sidelines, Barcelona's guardians grew desperate. Not even having an extra man helped: Arsenal were in the lead, Barcelona were not playing well, and the 1–0 half-time scoreline could have been worse. Even Iniesta's team-mates were surprised. Striker Samuel Eto'o recalls, 'When we were losing in Paris, I remember going over to the bench and saying to Ten Cate: "Can Andrés come on?" He said: "We're thinking about it." And we all know what happened when he did.'

Eventually Iniesta was introduced at the start of the second half, arriving to bring a ray of light to Barça. Xavi sat on the bench and watched, sad that he could not enjoy it with his friend. At least he knew that with Andrés out there, it would be different. 'Andrés has been playing very well;

this Champions League and his call-up for the World Cup show that. He deserves it; he's a great guy,' Xavi said that night.

'The pain of not being in the starting XI for that final went away a long time ago,' Iniesta says. 'I don't even like to think of it as something to overcome any more. Because it's my team, my club, and I was delighted to win the European Cup. But on a personal level, it was one of the hardest moments I have experienced.'

The pain had gone. But that doesn't mean he understood it. Not then, not now, not ever. 'If I'm honest, I already suspected something. People didn't realize, but I did. The last league game we played before the final was in Seville and I was on the bench. Van Bommel was too.' The difference was that Iniesta came on and played in a team packed with non first-teamers – Jorquera, Belletti, Rodri, Sylvinho, Guily, Gabri, Motta, Larsson, Montanés, Maxi López, Ezquerro – while Van Bommel stayed sat in his tracksuit, reserved for a final that was only four days away.

'Why did I have that doubt?' says Iniesta. 'Because in all that time since I had got into the team, there were things that meant I didn't have the sense that the coach trusted in me entirely. I hadn't always been a starter and I didn't play consistently. I wasn't convinced; I had doubts.' The fact that he didn't start in Seville but did come on in an unimportant 3–2 defeat only increased those doubts. Barcelona had already won the league; that game, that line-up, was a hint that something strange might happen in Paris. Still, Iniesta clung to the fact that he had played so well in Lisbon and Milan. 'That was where that glimmer of hope, the optimism, came from: in the quarters against Benfica and in the semis against Milan, I had played very well. So there was hope . . .'

In the absence of Xavi, he had taken on a different role: a dominant one. There was a time, long gone now, when Iniesta played like a Sergio Busquets. Or maybe it's the other way round: maybe Busquets watched Iniesta. In Lisbon, Iniesta played as a deep central midfielder, with Van Bommel and Edmílson either side of him. He led one magnificent move, from one end of the field to the other, dribbling round players with the ease of a father going round his tiny son. In Milan, by contrast, he played on the left of a midfield three, supported by Edmílson and Van Bommel. They provided the legs, the muscle; he provided the football. By the end of the game he had been moved to the number 10 position behind Eto'o and Maxi López when Rijkaard reinforced the midfield with Motta. That was the night when a moment's genius from Ronaldinho and astuteness from Guily took them to Paris, with a 1–0 win. 'Iniesta was Barcelona's free spirit, along with Ronaldinho. He's like a snake, silently attacking. How can you beat this untouchable little devil?' *L'Equipe* asked the following day.

The little devil had a hope. And a doubt. Remember the change? When the clock reached an hour in any game, Rijkaard almost always did the same thing. Same minute, same change, like a robot. Somewhere between 60 and 70 minutes, Iniesta would go on and replace Guily. In 11 of the 18 games when the Frenchman was taken off that season, an hour had gone. And Iniesta would go on. The number 24, Andrés' number at the time, only started 25 of the 57 games under Rijkaard. In the end, doubt defeated hope.

Andrés says, 'When he named the team for the final and I saw that I was not in it, I remember the feeling was a strange one. Like I had been cheated, like something had been taken away from me. I didn't understand.

I felt like I didn't deserve to be on the bench, but . . . once again, I had to accept it. Look ahead, not back. Forget the pain I was feeling at that moment. From what I heard, lots of other people felt the same way I did. They couldn't understand it either. It's not for me to decide if I deserved to play in the final, but that day I felt that I did.'

Defeated, hurt, emotionally low, Andrés decided that day his response would come on the pitch.

'I have always been strong. Stronger than people realize. At that moment, once I knew that I was not in the team, I focused on my only desire. I just wanted the chance to get out on the pitch and help my team-mates to win the final. I really, really wanted to play and play well. All the more so with the way the game went . . .' He watched from the bench: Lehmann's sending-off, Henry's chances, and Campbell's goal – the only person who could beat Valdés. When it came time to go on, his pain, his father's pain, drove him on.

If that decision can be summed up in one image, it's that of José Antonio. All those hours, all the pain, the distance, the sacrifice, summed up. 'The *chiquillo* isn't playing, he's not playing . . .' Iniesta can see it, uses it as motivation, all the more so as the final is not going the way they wanted.

'I don't really remember anything the manager said to me at half-time,' Iniesta admits. 'And I don't think I would have heard it properly either. I think at times like that, with all the emotion, the tactics wash over you. It's just: this is a Champions League final and we have to win it. I felt like I had been denied forty-five minutes to do that.

'I was determined to prove the manager wrong.'

●  ●  ●

Edmílson is taken off. The little devil is on for the second half. Barcelona are suddenly transformed. Then Larsson and Belletti appear off the bench. Thierry Henry told his Arsenal team don't yet know what's coming. 'Not a day goes by without me thinking about that final against Barcelona in 2006,' Henry told BarcaTV. 'Why? Because Arsenal had never won the final, they'd never even been there. They haven't been back, either. I was playing at home, barely thirty kilometres from where I was born. My entire family was in the stadium. And on top of it all, everyone was talking about how I could be leaving for Barcelona the following season. So it was a strange day for me. Both teams deserved to be in the final. The best team won, but . . . .'

Henry could hardly finish his sentence, tortured by the memory. 'There's a thought that always goes round my head. What if it had been eleven against eleven? Okay, so Guily scores, but the goalkeeper isn't sent off. It's 1–0, but eleven versus eleven . . .' Henry paused, as if going through it all again. As if he was watching that moment when Guily goes through and Lehmann comes out, all in slow motion. 'I remember that we played well for an hour, even though we were down to ten. But then after an hour Barcelona, with the way that they keep the ball and use it, make it hard for you. It gets more and more difficult.'

Henry remembered Valdés, who saved everything brilliantly. Long shots, one-on-ones, efforts from point-blank range. Whatever they threw at him ended in Víctor's hands. 'It's true,' he said. 'but it is Andrés who really makes the difference. When he comes on, everything changes. We could defend Edmílson and Van Bommel, but Andrés . . .'

His tone was one of resignation, impotence. 'When he gets the ball, and goes, turns, stops, goes again . . . after an hour, you can't follow him any more. There were only ten of us; I had to be a number 9 and a number 10; playing up front but also helping the midfield. We couldn't do it any more. Andrés killed me. He would turn and every time he got the ball, he would be away, too quickly for me. We all know the story of Larsson and Belletti. Sure, I know. But the person who really killed me was Andrés.'

The 'assassin' got what he wanted and proved his manager wrong. 'The happiness was immense,' says Andrés. His team had triumphed at the very end, 2–1, with goals from Eto'o and substitute Belletti, both assisted by the other substitute Larsson. 'At the end, it was perfect. But if it hadn't been for my friend Víctor . . .'

## BROTHERS

*'Andrés has a special aura about him; his success was forged through silent tears.'*

*Víctor Valdés, Andrés' 'brother'*

'The first time I met Andrés, we ended up arguing,' Víctor Valdés says. 'We didn't know each other at all. He had arrived at La Masia aged twelve, and he was young, small, quiet, reserved. You could see from the start that he was the kind of person whose trust you would need to earn. He was that kind of character. Like me, in fact. Maybe that's why we got angry with each other. We spent a couple of days refusing to talk to one another after that. It's not a happy memory.'

It wasn't exactly common for Andrés to fall out with people. No one can remember a bad word from him, never mind bad behaviour. There were no confrontations with staff or team-mates, not with anyone. Except Víctor Valdés, and Valdés ended up Andrés' best friend, his 'brother'.

Víctor is two years older than Iniesta. He knew La Masia inside out when this little kid from Fuentealbilla turned up, with the season already well underway. 'Although he didn't say anything about how I had treated him that first day, I could see that he was upset. I accepted the fact that the argument had been my fault. I hurt too. I have a heart. And from that moment on, I had to look after him because I had got it wrong to start with. It was like I wanted to make it up to him. Things like that happen when someone new arrives, when you've been there for a year, finding your place, and when, although it might not look like it, he has a person-ality like yours. There's a clash from the start. I tried to make amends, because I felt guilty.'

Since then Víctor and Andrés, Andrés and Víctor, made their way through life and football together, hand in hand.

'Andrés and I are like brothers,' Víctor says. 'We could go months without talking and it still wouldn't change our relationship. Those who know me well, and he is one of them, understand that I don't need to be constantly surrounded by my friends. Andrés is a bit like that. He needs his space too. And we have always respected that space.

'I used to go and watch him play. He was in the Cadete team and I was in Infantil. "Come and see us play, please," Jorge Troiteiro would say. So we did. He and Andrés were the smallest kids at La Masia. We would go and watch them on the Astroturf pitch next to the Mini Estadi, sitting on a stone wall. Andrés already stood out for his intelligence, for everything he could do with the ball, and because of that personality he has on the pitch. There's always been a special aura around him. He was a kid who everyone loved and respected. It was hard not to love him, with the ball and without it too. With the ball, he improves everyone around him. Without it, he's never a problem for anyone.

'Andrés has a kind of light that others don't have, a light that makes him different, unique. Special.'

As they rose through the youth system, surviving that often brutal process of natural selection, Víctor and Andrés became close friends. Troiteiro fell by the wayside, but they continued. Only excellence would do, and they knew it. Eventually, they made it to the first team together. Víctor made his debut under Louis van Gaal on 14 August 2002; Andrés made his under the same manager three months later, on 22 November. They were bad times for Barcelona, but even if few recognized it back then, the foundations were being laid for the future. Van Gaal, clinging to his note-book, his manager's job seemingly always on the line, was not able to enjoy the legacy he left for others. Instead, it would be Frank Rijkaard who brought through the likes of Puyol, Xavi, Valdés and Iniesta, a young gener-ation that combined with new arrivals boasting experience and talent. Barcelona won La Liga in 2004–05 with Ronaldinho and Van Gaal's kids, Víctor and Andrés among them.

Víctor and Andrés had started to wonder where football might take them. 'On the way back from Levante, where we had just won the league title, I asked Andrés what he wanted to win next,' says Valdes. 'Back then, Madrid's galácticos were the team everyone wanted to emulate, the team to beat. But we had won the league. So I asked him: "What do we want to win, you and I? How many league titles do you want, Andrés?"

'I'll never forget his answer: *six* leagues titles and *three* European Cups. Six because Pep Guardiola, who he was a big fan of, had won six titles; and three European trophies to match Madrid since 1998.'

Valdés adds, 'When I took the decision to leave Barcelona, he said to me: "You can't go now. We're nearly there. We're just one league title away. Don't go, Víctor. Stay." That sixth league title looked on, we were on course to win it, but then I got injured in March . . .

'Andrés, by contrast, has gone well beyond that original promise. When we set that target, it was almost unthinkable. When I look back on it now, I get goosebumps. At the time, it seemed well over the top. But then, you've got to ask, haven't you? And we got it all.'

The first of those three European Cups came in Paris, a journey that ran from 2006 to 2011 and took in Rome in 2009 and London two years later.

'Winning in Paris was destiny,' Valdés says. 'Frank got the substitutions right. Everything changed when Andrés came on in the second half. He carried the team, taking all the responsibility on his shoulders, and we came back to win.'

Rijkaard had started with Andrés on the bench and with his hopes in Valdés' hands. There was no better place for them. Valdés had been attacked and criticized from all sides, but the dressing room backed him and so did the manager. And in Paris, he was outstanding. Decisive. 'We couldn't let that final escape us, not after everything that happened,' he says. 'I'll never forget that moment, our first European Cup. The first of three for me and Andrés. We could hardly believe it.'

Ask them about that final and Valdés recalls the way that Iniesta played, while Iniesta recalls the way that Valdés played. Andrés and Victor, brothers. Víctor rescued his side, one on one with Thierry Henry, but it is his friend he remembers: 'Andrés killed them,' he says.

'In my mind there is no game, no night, like Paris. Two friends winning the European Cup together. When the whistle went, I threw myself to the ground in gratitude, unable to believe it was real. Then I ran like mad towards Frank, ready to embrace him. Only he and I know what we went through that year. He treated me like he was my father. "Relax, Víctor, you'll play all the way through to the final, whatever happens," he told me. And I did. So I ran to thank him. Then I went looking for my friend; I wanted to share this moment with my "brother". We'd been together for as long as we could remember: La Masia, the bad times, Barcelona B, football, friendships, all those conversations, so many moments . . .'

Paris was hard and they'd had to struggle, all of them. The journey to Rome was tough too, in search of their second European Cup. Never more so than at Stamford Bridge, where millions of hearts were put to the test.

'The truth is that I didn't even know that it was Andrés who had taken the shot,' Víctor says. 'I only realized it was him when I arrived to celebrate with them all, having run all the way from the other end. All seemed to be lost against Chelsea. With Michael Essien's goal, I dived thinking: "I'm going to stop this," but I didn't. It went flying into the top corner. Then Abidal was sent off. Chelsea's players were flying, coming from everywhere. Everything was going wrong. But I kept saying to myself: "There'll be a chance . . . at least one . . . we'll get an opportunity." I looked up at the scoreboard and it said eighty-eight minutes. The game was virtually over when the goal came. Andrés scored and I went mad. Don't ask me why, but I was convinced that something would happen. And it happened. And it was my soul mate. It was unbelievable.'

That third European Cup was a battle in London even more than in Rome. For Iniesta, especially. 'We were crossing and shooting, doing the typical training exercise, when I noticed that Andrés was sitting in a corner of the pitch with Emili Ricart, the physio,' Victor says. 'He'd got injured again and no one could console him. It was like he didn't know anyone, didn't recognize them. It was like talking to a stone. His eyes didn't focus; there was this distant look on his face, as if he didn't understand what the hell was going on.'

It was late in the 2008–09 season and it was not just another injury. Instead, it was the start of the worst time of Iniesta's career, a prolonged period where it seemed he could find no way out. Worse, even, than those early days at La Masia. The World Cup waited at the end of it, but for a long time there were fears that he might not make it there. For a long time, there were fears that he might not make it at all. Andrés would have to fight, and suffer, again.

'Our careers had run in parallel, we'd shared everything, lived inside the same walls, those four bedrooms at La Masia,' says Valdes. 'You're playing for Barcelona and they cater for everything: they give you somewhere to stay, they teach you, they coach you, you're at one of the best clubs in the world, perhaps the best. But, in the end, you're alone. Without your family. You have to get used to it, adapt to the hierarchy, the order. And you have to do it alone.'

When Andrés emerged from the most difficult period in his life, Víctor was there waiting for him. 'I remember in the days before the Spain squad was announced for the 2010 World Cup, he kept sending me messages that were full of optimism, like he knew that there was a chance I would go. Then Vicente del Bosque confirmed it and Andrés sent me a message: "Víctor, you're going to the World Cup." I was happy for myself, of course, but even more so because I was going with Andrés. I knew that I had no chance of playing, that my role there was to be part of the group. But I took it upon myself to play another role too: to be there for Andrés. I thought to myself: "My best friend is in South Africa and he has had a horrible year. I'm here to help him." My attitude was: "Andrés, whatever you need, whatever you want, whatever happens. I'm here. Don't be unhappy any more." And in football, if you work, there's always a reward at the end of it.'

*'Andrés is a master of space and time.'*

*Pep Guardiola, Iniesta's idol and his coach*

Late summer 2008. Barcelona lose 1–0 in Soria against little Numancia on the opening day of the league season. A tough baptism for the debutant coach, Pep Guardiola, made all the harder when the result isn't much better in their second game against Racing Santander, a 1–1 draw at the Camp Nou. Two weeks into Guardiola's career in charge of Barcelona's first team and they still haven't won.

Pressure builds, the criticism is intense. But Guardiola remains steadfast. Sergio Busquets and Pedro Rodríguez, then two virtually unknown players from Tercera División, Spain's fourth tier, are in the team. There are doubts, of course. Concerns.

In the media, it seems that only one voice defends the manager, but at least it is *the* voice: Johan Cruyff. That softens the blow, his authority alone enough to challenge the doomsayers, but still they prophesize doom. 'This Barcelona looks very, very good,' Cruyff writes in his weekly column for *El Periódico de Catalunya*. 'I don't know what game the rest of you watched; the one I watched was unlike any I have seen at the Camp Nou in a long time.' Cruyff, the great ideologue of the Catalan club, its philosopher king, had seen Guardiola coach the B team and was impressed; now he stands against the tide, alone in defending him. 'The worst start to a season in many years. Just one goal scored, and that was a penalty. That's an inescapable truth, numerically speaking,' he admits. 'But in footballing terms, this must be read a different way. And Guardiola is the first to read it differently. He's no novice, lacking expertise, and he is not suicidal. He watches, he sees, he analyses and he takes decisions.'

Guardiola himself agonized over those decisions too. He was holed-up in his Camp Nou office, down in the basement where there was no natural light, going over the situation again and again, rewinding and replaying the videos, re-reading his notes, wondering what to change but convinced of one thing: his idea, Cruyff's idea, had to be maintained. He would persevere, however hard it became. And support was about to come from an unexpected source.

He was still going over it, endlessly, when he heard a knock at the door.

'Come in.'

'Hello, *míster*.'

A small figure poked his head around the door, and spoke calmly.

'Don't worry, *míster*. We'll win it all. We're on the right path. Carry on like this, okay? We're playing brilliantly, we're enjoying training. Please, don't change anything,' said Andrés Iniesta.

Guardiola couldn't believe it.

The request was short, but heartfelt, deep. It caught Guardiola off guard, barely able even to respond. If it was a surprise that anyone should seek him out to say that, it was even more of a surprise that it was Iniesta, usually the silent man. It came as a shock, even more so when Iniesta closed by saying: '¡Vamos de puta madre!'

'De puta madre,' roughly translated as, 'We're in fucking great shape, we're playing bloody brilliantly.'

'This year we're going to steamroller them all,' he added.

And then he closed the door and left.

That's Andrés. He doesn't say much, only what he really has to. It's like scoring goals: he doesn't score often, either. But when it's needed, there he is.

Guardiola will never forget Cruyff defending him in print. And he will never forget Andrés appearing at his door. He'll never forget that they were right, too. At the end of the 2008–09 season, Barcelona had won six titles. All six.

● ● ●

'People usually think that it is the coach who has to raise the spirits of his players; that it is the coach who has to convince his footballers; that it is his job to take the lead all the time,' says Guardiola. 'But that's not always the case. It wasn't the case at the Camp Nou for me, and in my first year at Bayern Munich something similar happened as well. It's not often things like that happen and when they do, they rarely come to light. People always think the coach is the strongest person at a club, the boss, but in truth he's the weakest link. We're there, vulnerable, undermined by those who don't play, by the media, by the fans. They all have the same objective: to undermine the manager.

'You start, you lose at Numancia, you draw with Racing, you just can't get going, you feel watched and you feel alone and then suddenly, there's Andrés telling me not to worry,' Guardiola continues. 'It's hard to imagine, because it's not the kind of thing that happens and because it's Iniesta we're talking about, someone who doesn't find it easy to express his feelings. And after he'd gone, I asked myself: how can people say that coaches should be cold when they make decisions? Impersonal? That's ridiculous! How can I be cold, distant, removed with Andrés? Sorry, no way. Eighty-six per cent of people didn't believe in me [according to an on-line poll]. Lots of people wanted Mourinho. We hadn't won, hadn't got going. And then Andrés comes and says that?! How am I supposed to be cold? It's impossible. Sod that! This goes deeper. This isn't cold, calculated, and nor should it be. There's no doubt: Andrés will play with me, always. Because he's the best. And because things like that don't get forgotten. Why did he come to my office? I don't know.'

Lorenzo Buenaventura is a part of Guardiola's coaching staff, in charge of physical preparation. He has followed Pep from Barcelona to Bayern and from there to Manchester City. He shares this memory with Pep now, offers up an answer too.

'Why? I suppose because that's the way he felt; I suppose because it mattered to him,' he says. 'Andrés doesn't do anything he doesn't truly believe in; he does it because it feels right to him. He's genuine, always.'

Guardiola concedes, 'Maybe he spoke out because he could see that there was a method we were following, that everyone was training well, that we explained to them *why* we did things the way we did, and above all because that was the kind of football that he had been brought up on, ever since he was little.'

'There were other players who sent us little messages,' Buenaventura insists. 'That's true,' Guardiola admits. 'But Andrés' message was powerful. How could I forget that? I can still see him standing there at the door, looking at me. "*De puta madre*." And then he left. I thought: "Well, if Andrés says so . . ."'

Andrés and Cruyff were proven right; Guardiola's decision to maintain that philosophy was vindicated. In week three, Barcelona scored six against Sporting Gijón and never looked back; everything fell into place, it all worked so smoothly. Within a few months, they had become a model to aspire to. Not just because of the results – no one had won a treble in Spain before, still less six trophies from six – but because of the way they played, the way they treated the ball, fans, even opponents. Theirs was a different approach, a way of seeing and expressing football that was embodied by players like Iniesta.

'We never seem to treat Andrés the way we should; we don't seem to recognize him. He's the absolute business as a player,' Guardiola says. 'He never talks about himself, never demands anything, but people who think he's satisfied just to play are wrong. If he thought he could win the Balon d'Or one year, he'd want to win it. Why? Because he'd say to himself: "I'm the best."

'I think Paco defined him perfectly,' Guardiola says. Paco Seirulo was Barcelona's former physical coach, the man from whom Lorenzo Buenaventura learnt; now Guardiola makes Seirulo's description his own. 'Andrés is one of the greats. Why? Because of his mastery of the relation-ship between space and time. He knows where he is at every moment. Even in a midfield where he's surrounded by countless players, he chooses the right path every time. He knows where and when, always. And then he has this very unique ability to pull away. He pulls out, then brakes, then pulls out again, then brakes again. There are very few players like him.

'There are footballers who are very good playing on the outside but don't know what to do inside. Then there are players who are very good inside but don't have the physique, the legs, to go outside. Andrés has the ability to do both. When you're out on the touchline, like a winger, it is easier to play. You see everything: the mess, the crowd, the activity is all inside. When you play inside, you don't see anything in there because so much is happening in such a small space and all around you. You don't know where the opposition is going to come at you from, or how many of them. Great footballers are those who know how to play in both of those environments. Andrés doesn't only have the ability to see everything, to know what to do, but also the talent to execute it; he's able to break through those lines. He sees it and does it.

'I've been a coach for a few years now and I have come to the conclu-sion that a truly good player is always a good player,' Guardiola says. 'It's very hard to teach a bad player to be a good one. You can't really teach someone to dribble. The timing needed to go past someone, that instant in which you catch out your opponent, when you go past him and a new scenario opens up before you . . . Dribbling is, at heart, a trick, a con. It's not speed. It's not physique. It's an art.'

Lorenzo Buenaventura says: 'What happens is that Andrés brakes. That's the key, the most important thing. People say: "Look how quick he is!" No, no, that's not the point. It's not about speed, about how fast he goes; what it's really about is how he stops and when, then, how he gets moving again.'

Guardiola adds: 'Tito Vilanova defined him very well. Tito used to say: "Andrés doesn't run, he glides. He's like an ice hockey player, only without skates on. *Sssswishhh, sssswishhh, sssswishhhh* . . ." That description is evocative, very graphic, and I think it's an accurate one. He goes towards one side as if he was skating, watching everything that's going on around him. Then, suddenly, he turns the other way with that smoothness he has. Yes, that's it, Andrés doesn't run, he glides.'

Guardiola adds: 'Sometimes in life, it's first impressions that count and the first impression I have of Andrés was the day my brother Pere, who was working for Nike at the time, told me about Iniesta. I was still playing for Barcelona myself and he said: "Pep, you've got to come and see this kid." It was before the final of the Nike Cup. I remember getting changed quickly after training and rushing there, dashing to the stadium. And yes, I saw how good he was. I told myself: "This kid will play for Barcelona, for sure . . . he's going to make it." I told myself that, and I told Pere that too.

'On my way out of the ground after that final when Andrés was the best player on the pitch, I came across Santiago Segurola, the football writer. I said to him: "I've just seen something incredible." I had this feeling that what I'd just witnessed was unique. That was my first impression of Andrés.

'But later,' Guardiola admits, 'I came to really value something else Andrés does, something that he had made me see with time: the importance of attacking the centre-backs. No one does it. But watch and you see it. If the central defender has to step out, everything opens up; the whole defence becomes disorganized and spaces appear that weren't there before. It's all about breaking through lines to find space behind them. Open, then find.

'For example, we set up our attack so that Leo Messi could attack the central defenders,' Guardiola explains. 'We had to attack in such a way as to get the ball to Andrés and Leo so that they could attack the central defenders and that opened them up. When we managed that, we knew that we would win the game because Leo scored goals and Andrés gener- ated everything else: dribbling, numerical superiority, the ability to unbalance the game, the final pass, both to the outside and filtered through the middle. He sees it all and he has that gift for dribbling that's so unique to him. That dribbling ability is everything today. And it was Andrés who opened my eyes to the importance of an inside forward or midfielder being able to dribble too. If he dribbles, if he carries the ball and goes at people, everything flows. With time, I saw that.'

At this point in the conversation, Buenaventura offers up another point: there's something else about Andrés that's different. That it took Guardiola a while to see that quality of running at central defenders reinforces it. 'We have a habit in football of idolizing very young players who still haven't really done anything,' Buenaventura says. 'Andrés is the only player who only really got the recognition he deserved from the age of twenty-seven or twenty-eight. There are team-mates of his who now say to you: "Leo is unique, Luis Suárez is brilliant, but Andrés is the best I have played with." It's been a long time coming. Look at what happened with Neymar, for example. He wasn't even twenty yet and they already considered him the best around in Brazil. Andrés, by contrast, has had to wait until he was twenty-seven or twenty-eight for important people in football to recognize him, to say: "This guy's the best." It's strange because a guy with his talent should already be talked about at twenty. Back then people should have already been saying: "This is the guy; no one else, *him*." It's curious. I'm not sure why it's happened like that.'

There's another thing that Lorenzo thinks people took a long time to see. 'People used to ask: "Xavi or Iniesta?" And Pep would say: "Xavi *and* Iniesta." Both of them. Not one or the other. Together, always. People said they couldn't play together. Not true. They shouldn't be played apart.'

●　●　●

Guardiola pictures Iniesta's moment in London, rewinding to the night of the 2009 Champions League final at Stamford Bridge. 'Samuel Eto'o's miscontrol, Essien's scuffed clearance, Leo gets it, Andrés takes a little step back to get the space to shoot . . .' he says. 'And not even Usain Bolt could run like I ran down the touchline. We'd got to the end of the game without having a single shot on target. But you still have faith that something might happen. Everything was going so well after that difficult start to the season. We'd beaten Real Madrid 6–2 three days before. And there we were in the last minute of a European Cup semi-final, waiting, believing, thinking: "Something could still happen." You don't know what it is, but something tells you that we'd get a chance, that we could still score. What I never imagined was that it would be Andrés. You think it might be Samuel,

Leo ... anyone. Even Gerard Piqué, who ended up playing in attack in those situations. Just not Andrés. There were eight Barcelona players in the Chelsea area and someone goes and hits the top corner from outside of it. And it's Andrés Iniesta, of all people.

'You never imagine that it will be Andrés who scores at Stamford Bridge. Or in the World Cup final. You could do a poll: "Who's going to score?" You wouldn't even put Andrés on the list. But he prepares that shirt in honour of Dani Jarque before the World Cup final because he believes that he can score. Don't ask me why, but the greats have something different. Andrés has it. Call it intuition, call it what you like, but he has it. It's not chance that things like that happen to him.'

And it couldn't have happened without Stamford Bridge.

PAIN

*'Pep told us at half-time: "We are playing for Andrés' right leg!"'*
*Carles Puyol, Copa del Rey final 2009*

Mario strained his vocal chords that May evening in 2009. 'I had to go sixty days without raising my voice for fear that I would injure them again,' he says. Mario is Barça through and through, as the club badge tattooed on his arm shows. He went to bed happy the night after Stamford Bridge, delighted, ecstatic, proud and having let out the primal scream of his life when the winning goal went in. When he got up the next morning, however, he noticed a lump in his throat. He was so scared that he went in search of self-diagnosis online and was so worried by what he read that he went straight to find a doctor. He then explained to him exactly what had happened the night of the Chelsea vs Barça game.

'Did you shout very much last night?' the doctor asked him.

'Did I shout very much? No, I shouted *muchisímo*,' was his reply. 'Did you not see the game? Did you not see Iniesta's goal?' the stunned patient asked the doctor, as if everyone in the world had seen it.

The doctor deduced that Mario had damaged his vocal chords, because he shouted so much when Barcelona qualified for the 2009 Champions League final thanks to Iniesta's last-minute goal against Chelsea. 'They had to take some blood from me, make a puncture in me, give me an injection and take away the lump. It was bad, but not as bad as having to watch Eto'o and Messi score the goals that won the final without being able to so much as raise my voice.'

There are so many Barcelona fan stories surrounding that night and that Andrés Iniesta goal. Statistics even indicate that in Barcelona's hospitals the birth rate spiked nine months after the game. Many supporters finished up having lost their voice, though none quite as dramatically as Mario. Andrés put his vocal chords to the test too when he celebrated the shot that beat Petr Cech, before taking off his shirt and setting a new record for the 50 metre dash along the touchline at Stamford Bridge. Coaching assistant Aureli Altimira just beat Pinto, and Bojan was not far behind, in the race to swamp Iniesta in a pile of celebrating Barcelona players.

'We were on the bus, on the way to the stadium,' remembers Bojan. 'And I said to him: "Look, Andrés. If you score a goal, I will give you tickets to the Champions League final."' It was the world in reverse – the striker asking the midfielder if he wouldn't mind scoring the goal that the team needed for them to knock out Chelsea.

The emerging Barcelona of the Guardiola era had just completed its first work of art in the Santiago Bernabéu with that 6–2 win over Real Madrid in La Liga. Now it was in search of its first Champions League final. The semi-final had not been an attractive game, and time was running out for Barcelona who had not managed a single shot on Cech's goal. Standing two metres tall, big hands and an imposing body that filled the goal, he looked like a wall that Barcelona would never get over. Time, what's more, was against them, and in Chelsea's favour.

Despite the urgency of the situation, Barcelona had not given up on their patient passing approach. There had been no desperate long balls hung up in the area. They had not reneged on the style that meant the ball was always to be looked after at the feet of every player in the team. The fans knew it had to be that way too, although not all were as patient as the players carefully moving it from one side of the pitch to the other in search of an opening. It was the patience installed in them by Guardiola; Iniesta knew it and so did Mario.

Tic-tac, tic-tac, tic-tac was the sound of the ball as the team advanced as one, Xavi naturally holding the compass. He it was who found Alves with a pass out to the right. The full-back was in space because Chelsea's players all seemed to be in Cech's area surrounding Piqué, whose aerial ability meant he was now playing as an auxiliary centre-forward. Barça's style does allow for that one concession in situations when they need to score in the last few minutes of a match and are trying to deny space to the opposition goalkeeper.

The cross from Alves was high and curling. It took a long time to come down to Terry who headed it clear as he had done countless other balls into the Chelsea penalty area during his long career. He got there before Piqué and certainly before Bojan, who was crafty and cunning but built more for pouncing on any knockdowns than for getting his head on the end of any crosses.

The greatest antidote to a defender like Terry was a striker like Eto'o. Always on the move he had found space at the back post, but when the ball came to him his touch let him down. He was always better at pulling the trigger to shoot than to restart a move by winning the second ball, and he had perhaps been surprised by the way the ball came off the crown of Terry's head.

'I did not control the ball well,' says the Cameroon striker. 'Not well at all, but it meant that the ball dropped to Leo.'

Time had all but run out for Barça, with the game itself in limbo between Barcelona's attacks and Chelsea's defence. Any error at this point and there would be no time left to make amends and the move itself was panning out to be a succession of errors.

Alves' cross had not been good, nor had Eto'o's control. But then came a mistake from Chelsea too. Essien failed to clear the ball. He had the chance to send it far from the area, but he left it at the feet of Messi instead. Barça's number 10 then took a somewhat unexpected decision, unexpected even by Andrés, who had followed the move up the pitch from Xavi's pass out to Alves and was now on the edge of the area, on the front lawn of Cech's house, as it were, waiting.

Messi tamed the loose ball with the first touch of his left foot; he didn't have a lot of space and he was exhausted having given everything in the titanic struggle. The Argentine took another touch to protect the ball from the imminent blue invasion and then, just before three Chelsea players were on top of him, and just as he was beginning to stumble, he sent the ball with his right foot to the edge of the penalty area.

And there was Andrés – passive spectator as Alves crossed, nervous observer as Bojan jumped with Terry, surprised witness to so many mistakes in the same move, but understanding at the same time that, at this stage of the game, the legs no longer do what the brain tells them to.

'I had stopped there almost out of pure inertia. I was running on empty,' he says. He was about to find the strength to win the game and take a shot that would change his life; a shot that no one had seen before or has seen since.

Chelsea had perhaps thought their defensive work was done. Eto'o had lost the ball and they had swarmed on Messi so it was no longer at his feet. But there was another player wearing that loud yellow jersey now with the ball about 18 or 19 metres from Cech's goal.

He was stood still, as if he was playing another game, one far removed from the frantic semi-final in which he found himself. He possessed in his right leg all the force of 'Barcelonismo, Guardiola would say afterwards. Iniesta had, deceivingly, seemed as still as a waxworks model in the middle of a street demonstration.

The ball reached him from Messi. An instant before being run down by the Chelsea defence, the Argentine had time to lift his head and pick out the option the moment required; resolute and intelligent, even in the 43rd second of the 92nd minute of a semi-final that it seemed Barça were going to lose.

Messi passed the ball to Andrés. And the man from La Mancha drew back his right leg at the same time as planting down his left, so that it was as strong and unshakeable as one of the pillars of the Roman Colosseum that he would visit weeks later. He then launched a missile that would be impossible to intercept, even for Cech.

That powerful right-footed shot had a secret key to it. Michael Ballack bent down and to one side when the ball began to fly, without knowing that his instinctive flinch would doom Chelsea to semi-final defeat. Cech dived a fraction late, no doubt surprised because Chelsea were convinced that Iniesta, unlike Piqué, Bojan and Messi, all neutralized by their defence, was a man for floaters and curlers, not for brute force.

That was the definitive error. 'When Andrés shot, I heard the sound of the ball,' says Eto'o proudly. The ball went over Ballack, Cole and Terry and finally past the outstretched arms of Cech, travelling faster than it had first seemed. It was a bolt of lightning that would take away Marco's voice and the breath of a million Barça fans.

Very few spotted that Andrés had worked a space for himself just before Messi's pass reached him. He had moved slightly forward and then back a few steps to make the shot more comfortable. Some spectators had already dropped their gaze, seeing that Barça forwards Bojan, Eto'o and Messi had all been unable to get a shot or a header on target. 'As soon as he hit it, I began to run to the corner,' says Eto'o. 'Don't ask me why, but I was already running because I could not believe what had just happened.'

Iniesta, in contrast, never looked at anyone, not even Cech. He moved his body forward and then back two or three barely visible steps before dispatching his beloved football into the top corner. 'Of course I have it

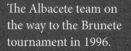
Me and cousin Manu.

Our Bar Luján first team.

The Albacete team on
the way to the Brunete
tournament in 1996.

Aged 12, outside La Masia with
my grandparents. I cried a lot
in the early days.

Puyi and I were together from the start. Posing with the 2006 Champions League Trophy after beating Arsenal in Paris.

Joy for my long-time friend Fernando after scoring the goal against Germany to crown us 2008 European Champions.

Stamford Bridge, Champions League semi-final 2009 and the goal
I will remember forever. We were in paradise.

'Relax, Andrés, everything will be OK.' Puyol, Ricard Pruna and the
Barça medical team helped me through the injuries. It was a very hard
time for me.

The ball sat up so perfectly. All I could remember was the silence.
Soccer City, Johannesburg, World Cup final 2010.

'Dani Jarque: always with us.'

The special moments that live with you for a lifetime.

*Above:* Our wedding day, 8 July 2012. With you Anna, I know the best is always yet to come.

*Above:* My coach, confidante and best fan: Pep Guardiola. *De puta madre!*

*Right:* Mamá. All the things I enjoy now would not have been possible without you.

Valeria, my princess.

My little champion Paolo Andrea.

Victor and I came all the way from La Masia, where he looked after me, to the Barcelona first team.

Luis Enrique, from team-mate to coach.

The *tridente*. How could I possibly fail to supply these 'assassins'?

And they said we couldn't play together! My 'twin' Xavi and I with the La Liga trophy, May 2015.

*Above:* Sesi, Joel, Karlitos, Jordi and Juanmi, my *amigos*.

*Left:* Mamá, Papá and sister Maribel. Without you I would be nothing.

*Below:* My family. My life. Our vineyard Bodega Iniesta.

on tape, me and millions of Barça fans, as well as millions of football fans the world over. It was brutal, brutal, brutal. It is impossible to find the words to describe how I felt in that moment,' says Andrés as if he was back at Stamford Bridge once more.

'I wasn't really thinking about anything; not even whether or not Leo was going to shoot. Everything was lost. It seemed impossible that we could score so late when we hadn't managed a single shot on target all night. So many things had happened in that game. Essien, for example, scored a fantastic goal from outside the area with his weaker foot. We went down to ten men. Everything just seemed to be going against us. I was going forward because what else could I do? Throwing ourselves forward was the last option left open to us. I went up to the edge of the box but without any real expectation. I remember that we had attacked down the right-hand side and that Leo had got on the ball inside their penalty area. But the Chelsea defenders soon closed him down and that was when he saw me. Seeing that he could not take a shot himself, he passed. And then . . . ,' says Andrés, waiting for the big finale.

In the moment it takes for him to strike the ball, the majority, if they had had time to, would have thought: Iniesta will not shoot. Frank Lampard was in that majority. He watched the shot from three metres behind Andrés. He had made no effort to get back to defend it. Why? Because he must have believed, like the rest of his Chelsea team-mates, that the best option was to let him shoot. It was a mistake. He didn't just shoot, he scored. It was unstoppable.

'The ball ended up in the only place it could go to beat the goalkeeper,' says Andrés. 'Outside of the boot, swerving slightly outwards and away from Cech who is such a big keeper that he really fills the goal. It was destiny or whatever you want to call it. People ask me if there was time to think about how I was going to hit it. No way! I couldn't ponder the possible outcomes of hitting it with my instep or the outside of my boot or just with the laces. If you think about it for too long, the chance is gone. It was just pure instinct. The ball arrived a little bit on top of me, so I took a step back and hit it perfectly. There was no time to think of whether he Cech going to reach it or if it was going to go in. You just hit it and the next thing you see is the ball in the top corner.'

And then they were in paradise. Andrés takes off his shirt (first the right arm, then the left) as he runs to the corner flag. Lampard, knowing that he had not tracked back, bends down to adjust his white socks. It feels like a gesture of absolute surrender. Bojan runs after his friend but cannot catch him. Eto'o is the first to lay his hands on the hero. 'I had not seen anyone make a run like that in the entire game. This kind of thing could only have happened to Andrés. It was simply incredible,' he says. 'I can't remember what I wanted to say to him. But there were millions of things that I wanted to say, millions.'

Messi spread out his arms as if to the embrace the Barça fans congregated in that corner of the old stadium. Andrés slides on English turf, Bojan slips and so Messi arrives before because Eto'o has gone to celebrate with the supporters. Leo initiates the bundle of bodies that will now bury Iniesta beneath it. The last player to pile on top is Víctor Valdés, Andrés' soul-mate from their days together in La Masia; arriving last because he has had the furthest to travel. 'It was magical. All Barça fans know where they were when that goal went in. Some have told me that they broke things at home because they were jumping about so much,' says Andrés, hugged by everyone who could reach him, even by Emili Ricart.

'It was fantastic,' says Bojan. 'When he scored, I tried to run to embrace him but I couldn't catch him. I arrived and he was already buried, so I threw myself on that mountain of players. I think it was Leo who was on top of Andrés, but we couldn't see anyone's faces. Then suddenly Andrés looked up and shouted: "The tickets, Bojan! The tickets!" I couldn't believe it, there in the corner of Stamford Bridge having just scored one of the most important goals in the history of Barça and the first thing he does is remind me about the tickets. He could have told me in the dressing room, on the plane home, or back in Barcelona but no, he chose to tell me seconds after his goal, the goal that had made millions of people so happy.'

'Did you give them to him?'

'Of course! How could I not?'

Miles from that corner of London, there were also celebrations in Sant Feliu, a city close to Barcelona, where a certain José Antonio Iniesta had still not stopped shouting with joy after having seen the goal scored by his son.

'Essien's goal never bothered me,' says José Antonio. 'I always thought that those boys were going all the way to Rome. I said it when we all met up in our house at Sant Feliu de Llobregat to watch the game. They did it at the Bernabéu in that 6–2; how were they not going to do it at Stamford Bridge against Chelsea?

'But I have to admit that the commentators were making me nervous during the game. They kept repeating that we had not had a single shot on goal. Every time they said it I would shout back: "Well, the first shot we have *bang!* We are going score!" They would insist and I would shout back again: "We will only need one shot!" And thanks to Valdés, well, thanks to all of them, it was true.

'We only had one shot but what a shot it was! When I saw that Alves' cross had gone long, when I saw that Eto'o had miscontrolled the ball I thought: "Oh, to hell with it!" Then the ball reaches Messi and the magic begins. At first I thought he would lose it. He has three defenders closing him down but he protects it, he draws them to him, he even thinks about taking them on and then he sees Andrés and gives him the ball. And because he is brilliant he gives it to him with pace on the pass. There has to be pace on the pass, because Andrésito is right-footed. If the ball arrives to him from his right side, then there is no problem, he can strike it cleanly. But it comes to him from the other side, so if it does not come to him with pace it will be more difficult. It reaches him and *bang!* He hits it with the outside of his right foot and it picks up speed and height, and even though Cech dives well, I know he is not going to get to it. It goes faster and faster until it's past him.

'We shouted. We hugged. I threw myself on the ground face down. I started to cry, beating down on the ground with my hands and feet. A couple of my friends threw themselves down on top of me; one, two, three. Then I started to hear the car horns and the shouts. I opened the front door and I saw the Andrés official fan club were out in the street. And those who had been watching the game in the bar were celebrating. The whole town had gone crazy, my family, the Barcelona family. Then the mobile phone rang. And it's him! It's Andrés and I say to him: "Brilliant Andrés, brilliant!" and he says to me: "That's it, Dad, that's it." Too right that's it. Andrés has taken us to Rome.'

• • •

Andrés had put his heart and soul into it but also his body, which was already at breaking point after a long season full of injury problems, each worse than the last. From one leg to the other: from a torn thigh muscle in the right leg to a hamstring injury in the left. Every visit to the physios' room was pure torment and it wasn't just for the games that he couldn't play; rather, it was the return of old anxieties that he thought had been forgotten.

It was at that time when he played just as much as a false right-winger – against Chelsea on 6 May 2009 – as he did as a false left-winger – against Villarreal at the Camp Nou four days later. Every seat in the stadium was taken as the crowd welcomed Guardiola's Barcelona back from Stamford Bridge, and Iniesta's name was chanted every time he touched the ball. His fans applauded him, expectant for the champions to be crowned. They were just one win from the title, but the crowning was put on hold by Llorente's late goal and there was far worse news to come.

The game ended 3–3 against Villarreal. Andrés left the field feeling his right leg, the same right leg he had used so majestically at Stamford Bridge. He feared the worst. He knew he had injured himself again. It was the fourth muscle injury in seven months. The thigh in November, the hamstring in February, a groin muscle in the right leg in March, and now in May, magical May, another tear to the right thigh.

Things had come full circle in the worst possible way and just ahead of his 25th birthday. 'It's far worse news than not having won the league today.

It's very bad news, very bad,' said a disconsolate Guardiola. He assumed that he would now be without Iniesta for the Copa del Rey final (he did not play against Athletic nor did he even travel to the game at the Mestalla with his team-mates) and for the Champions League final against United two weeks later. 'I don't think he is injury prone, but every three days we have a very hard game at the moment,' said the coach, remembering the Bernabéu, Stamford Bridge, and Villarreal. 'In the end, the body says enough is enough. Andrés is very important. Andrés gives so much to us.'

Andrés was just as forlorn. 'What a shame! It happened to me in the last move of the game. I tried to chip a ball forward and due to all the accumulated tension of the end of the season this happened,' he said. Perhaps another player would have given up then. Perhaps. But he took this as another hurdle to get over. 'I will make the final even with both legs crocked,' he told himself. That was when Óscar Celada, one of the Spain team doctors, turned up to see how Andrés was coping. He met Barcelona doctors there, among them his good friend Dani Medina. 'Andrés is in a bad way,' Medina told him. Celada, ever attentive to the emotional as well as physical state of a player, had not imagined it any different, but even he was not aware of just how low Andrés was.

'They told me he was annoyed. It was, in effect, an injury to the shooting muscle in the right thigh. He knew it was a serious matter. He had been betrayed by the muscle he needed most and it would take time to heal,' says the Spain doctor who was concerned for Andrés and also for Vicente del Bosque because the Confederations Cup, his first major tournament in charge, was just around the corner.

Andrés spent his 25th birthday, on 11 May 2009, in hospital in Barcelona, alongside Barça team doctor Ricard Pruna. 'It is a very small tear; it's nothing like the one I suffered in November. And it's not in the same place,' said the player, a spokesman for his own latest injury woe. 'Luckily, it's a bit lower down and it's nothing; about two centimetres, no more.'

Two centimetres meant two weeks of recuperation – and the Champions League final was still 16 days away. The tears had all dried and there was no sign of the desperation he had showed in the dressing room when he had laid flat out on fitness coach Emili Ricart's treatment table nursing the third injury in his right leg of four he would suffer that season.

He had told Pruna as he left the field: 'Whatever happens I am going to Rome. Whatever happens I will be there.' He began work there and then. His recovery would become his obsession against the clock. Perhaps another player would have given up. But not him; obstinate as he is, he never doubted.

'It's a blow. If there is one player that deserves to play the final, then it is Andrés,' said Puyol recalling, without needing to actually mention it, the Paris final three years before. The game Andrés had to win coming off the bench.

'For games such as this one you have to take risks. I know I would. Andrés is a superstar, he makes a difference in these games, he never hides.' He already took it as read that nothing would stop Andrés from playing in the final. Andrés would make it. Celada, was concerned, but also knew he would get there. 'They have told me I will play the final,' said Andrés. Celada had told Pruna and he in turn had told Andrés.

But Pruna also told Andrés how difficult it would be; he told him what he really had in his right leg. 'No, it wasn't just a small tear. I told him:

"Andrés, you have a hole in the shooting muscle in the right thigh."'

What was certain was that he would miss the Copa del Rey final at the Mestalla against Athletic, the first final of Barcelona under Guardiola, the manager who was revolutionizing everything right down to the preparations for such games, deciding that the team would travel on the day of the match.

Guardiola was accused in some quarters of not having given enough protection to a player who had started 16 games straight since his last muscle injury. 'Iniesta? It could be that I got it wrong not taking him off,' admits Guardiola. 'But in London, I could have taken him off six minutes before and we would not be in the final.' Iniesta was not on the flight to Valencia. He had stayed behind in Barcelona, still on what he hoped would be the express road to recovery. He was making every minute count with time ticking down to the Rome deadline, and he could not waste a second. The entire squad went; everyone except him.

In his absence, Barcelona won the Copa del Ray. Iniesta was determined that he'd be there to help them to add the Champions League trophy. 'No problem, Dad. I will play in Rome,' he had announced to José Antonio, using almost exactly the same words that he had uttered to Ricard Pruna, the doctor, while they were still on the Camp Nou pitch as Barcelona supporters' hearts sank in unison at the sight of him touching that blessed and, at the same time, cursed right leg.

Ricard, Emili and Ramón would take care of everything. 'It is one of those occasions when a player and a doctor become one person,' says Pruna. The magic hands of Emili Ricart, something more than just a physio, and the science of Ramón Cugat, the doctor that every Barcelona player went to (even Guardiola when he was a player in need of rebuilding) in search of a route out of his problems. 'The shooting muscle is really a group of four connected muscles – it can be a very troublesome area,' remembers Emili of those tough spring days in 2009 when the dates of the calendar were being crossed off without the corresponding signs that the muscles would be cured in time.

'These injuries can be extremely deceptive,' says Cugat, the doctor explaining that the 'rectus femoris', to give it its correct name, has two tendons which makes it vital for any footballer. 'We were conservative with the treatment that we applied to Andrés' injury, while every three or four days Dr Marta Ruis would carry out a scan to follow with great precision the evolution of the injury.

'It was going well, or at least it appeared to be going well, but we all knew that time was not on our side,' admitted Cugat. He knew that Andrés was not completely right. 'We look for a common goal that will help the player in those delicate moments: "We think the injury will not prevent you from playing, Andrés. We are going to work towards that end,"' says Pruna.

Everyone had vowed to beat the clock and of course the shooting muscle – torn so frequently – had no choice in the matter, it would have to mend. Doctors, physiotherapists, manager and player fought the good fight every day. In the meantime, Spain's Vicente del Bosque waited nervously in Madrid.

'You play until you can't play any more. Last as long as you can, okay?' That was what Emili whispered every day to Andrés in the search for some positive stimulus that would help make the player better. As for Pruna, he had instructions: 'Look, Andrés, you can play as much as you want, but there is one thing I have to forbid you from doing: you can't shoot. Don't shoot!' Andrés was stunned at first, but the desire he had to play in a final as an important player was greater than his anxiety. In spite of the injury, he felt like an important player, not like in Paris where he had been a substitute, an afterthought from the coach.

●　●　●

'It went well from the start. The video, the opening goal from Samuel [Eto'o], everything,' Emili recalls the moment in the build-up to the 2009 Champions League final when Guardiola, unexpectedly, decided to cut short the pre-match warm-up and called the players back in early, leaving Sir Alex Ferguson's Manchester United, Cristiano Ronaldo included, still out on the pitch.

They all arrived together and the lights were turned out. Just like that. No one knew what was happening. Just a few minutes before his first Champions League final as a manager, Guardiola, Iniesta's childhood hero alongside Michael Laudrup, was about to break the routine with something out of the ordinary. In the dark of the Olympic Stadium dressing room in Rome, he played a video. It wasn't very long. It lasted barely eight minutes. But that was enough to penetrate the souls of his players.

'My name is Gladiator . . .' were the first words they heard as they watched a montage of the film of the same name and aerial shots of the stadium where they were about to play the final with the sound of helicopters shaking the Roman night sky in the background. They then watched images of Valdés' saving twice to deny Drogba in the semi-final at the

Camp Nou. Next came Pinto's penalty save in the Copa del Rey semi-final. 'I'm diving that way,' he had told the penalty-taker Martí pointing to his left. The Mallorca player put the ball to Pinto's left and Pinto saved it. Pinto had offered his hand to Martí before he took the kick, already feeling like the winner of the duel. And on it went with every single player, on Guardiola's strict instruction, appearing in the short film. Andrés featured of course but not, at first, in all his glory, scoring that goal at Stamford Bridge. Instead he was playing passes back and forth with Emili, as if they were together in the school playground, in one of his daily rehabilitation exercises. It came before a clip of him scoring with a precise right-footed shot from outside the area against Sevilla; skipping past an opponent on the touchline against Athletic; and pouring water over his head, all in about ten seconds' worth of footage.

One after the other, each player had his moment even if it was hard to find images of them playing, as was the case with Argentine defender Gabi Milito, massively respected and popular in the dressing room but injured for most of the season. Sometimes the leaders are not the most talented players or those that play all the time. It was also tough to find footage of reserve keeper Jorquera, who had also suffered a serious injury, but he was there too in the film. It became increasingly difficult for the players to remain in silence as they watched Guardiola's epic *Gladiator* unfold. 'We've got a better chance of survival if we fight together,' comes the battle cry from behind the helmet that covers his face; the voice of Russell Crowe resounding in the darkness of that dressing room in Rome.

In the stands of the Olympic Stadium, thousands of Barça fans, thousands of United supporters, and millions of football fans the world over were waiting for the start of a final that would usher in a new era. Meanwhile the players, on edge, watched the story of their season with the closing images of Messi scoring, of Xavi burying a free-kick, of Eto'o running clear from defenders, and then finally of Iniesta's goal. A goal as seen from the stands of Stamford Bridge with images taken from Barça supporters, everyone running with Andrés, buried first by Messi and Bojan in a human mountain of euphoria. 'There was once a dream that was Rome,' says Crowe, Ridley Scott's Gladiator, before he goes out to do battle in the Colosseum, just as Andrés appears on the screen, pressing the palm of his hand against Xavi's in the tunnel before a game and smiling a winning smile. The film ends with the heavenly sound of 'Nessun Dorma' from the opera *Turandot*. It seemed like a premonition.

Santi Padró, a journalist from Catalan television channel TV3, had put together this beautiful audio-visual call to arms, requested to do so by Pep and his brother Pere Guardiola who is also Iniesta's agent. He had no idea how it would turn out and you can imagine the pressure he felt when he received a text message from his friend the Barcelona coach: 'Do me a favour, Santi, help me win the European Cup.' He had to read it several times before it sunk in. 'My legs were shaking,' he admits. 'Whatever you say, Pep,' he replied.

'I need a video in which all the players appear. Do it however you want, but they all have to be in it,' specified the coach. Everyone did appear. Everyone except Pep. 'It was Pere who suggested that I use *Gladiator*,' Santi confesses.

'We were lucky Joan Buixeda and Ángel Muñoz, my colleagues at TV3, had prepared a special video about Barcelona's three Champions League finals in London, Paris and Rome, using the music from *Gladiator* and some Barça goals. On the Friday before the final, I bought a DVD director's cut of *Gladiator*. On the Sunday three days before the game, we locked ourselves away in a room with Jordi Gayà, another of our top producers, a man capable of taking whatever good idea you have and making it even better.

'We started at 11pm on the Sunday and finished at 8am on the Monday morning.' It took eight hours of work to create a film of seven minutes and ten seconds. 'Here Pep,' said Santi on the Monday, 48 hours before the final, in Barça's Sant Joan Despí training complex. In silence they watched the video in Guardiola's office. Then the coach called in his assistants. When Santi left the training ground, he heard the voice of the coach: 'Hey, Santi, If we win the Champions League, I will let you show the video on TV3.' Santi had not even thought about that possibility. When it did finally air, it got the day's biggest audience. No fewer than 1,375,000 people watched what the Barça players had watched before they played the final; an incredible 42.3% share of the audience.

That was the furthest thing from Santi Padró's mind when he was given the job by Pep and Pere. 'I was watching the final on the television and when the team came out on to the pitch "Nessun Dorma" was playing. "I don't believe it!" I had goosebumps watching the team line-up with the opera sang by Andrea Bocelli.' It was the same song as used on the inspirational video, and Andrés was smiling the same winning smile.

'I wanted something that would reach people; something that would really touch a nerve. The intention was good, but I'm not sure if it had the desired effect because in the first ten minutes we almost threw the game away,' remembers Guardiola. Barcelona had a terrible start against a powerful Manchester United side, boasting a young Cristiano Ronaldo who had won his first ever Champions League the season before against Chelsea in Moscow, plus Tevez, Rooney and Giggs.

In nine minutes there were three shots from Ronaldo, each more venomous than the last. Barcelona were forced to take refuge in their goalkeeper Valdés, but Andrés felt Barça would win the final and his mind had not been changed by the shaky start. He had already won his own personal battle, defying the natural laws that told him it would be impossible to recover from another muscle injury in just 16 days.

Ronaldo was beating on the door and Barça were suffering. Sir Alex chewed his gum ever more furiously, while Guardiola paced up and down, perturbed. But Andrés, still with the advice, 'play on for as long as you can' in his mind, picked up the ball in midfield on ten minutes and changed the course of the game. The video was no longer at the forefront of the players' minds as the football took over. Anderson and Carrick went in pursuit of Andrés, men with huge strides and imposing physiques compared to their opponent. They were there in that midfield checkpoint to make sure that Andrés could advance no further, but he got away from both, the ball seemingly sewn to his right boot. Carrick was the most persistent and felt he had caught him, but in the last instant, just as it seemed he might be dispossessed, Iniesta released Eto'o who eased away from Evra and homed in on goal.

'Only Andrés could play me that marvellous pass in Rome. The ball arrived to me so perfectly, helping me to get away from the first defender.

I actually get past him just by adjusting the shape of my body because the pass does the rest,' says Eto'o.

Once he had received the pass from Andrés – 'It practically left me in the clear,' he says – Eto'o did what Eto'o does best, sidestepping two challenges and tricking two battle-hardy central defenders such as Vidic and Ferdinand before flashing a shot inside Van der Sar's near post just as he was beginning to dive towards his far post. Ferguson began to understand that his team did not have the final under their control, for all that Ronaldo appealed for calm to both team-mates and United supporters immediately after the goal. On the Barcelona bench Emili was not watching the game; he was only watching Andrés Iniesta's right leg.

Iniesta was not thinking about any of that, however. At least not when he set off on that mazy run that silenced the United supporters, carrying the ball as if both he and it were floating. Andrés flies with the ball at his feet. And there is something about the way he takes care of it, as if it were the only treasure in his life. It's the same ball that he has taken from Fuentealbilla to Rome, via Paris.

'Take care of yourself. Those movements create muscular tension and you can tear something, Andrés,' said Emili. The game had started, the shock of seeing the video had passed, and everything was flowing as if he had never injured that right leg of his just a fortnight before the final.

'I couldn't even watch the game. I did not take my eyes off Andrés: his movement, his control, his passes, and the runs he was making,' says Cugat, who sat in the stand while Pruna and Emili were on the bench; they were all part of this other game that was taking place between Andrés and his injury. 'When Samuel scored, I was up the other end and I only realized because of people's reaction. I was watching Andrés' every move. I was looking to see if he was hobbling, or if he was starting his runs without any discomfort,' says Cugat. All he wanted was for the game to end as quickly as possible, and for it never to occur to Andrés that he should do something as crazy as shoot.

'I did not want him to shoot, because that is what works the rectus femoris muscle the hardest.' He was hunched in his seat in the stand, with his fingers crossed that nothing bad would happen. '"Play the ball, Andrés. Don't shoot." It helped that he was not a player who took a lot of shots anyway. And what is more, he was looking stronger and stronger until almost at the end, right in front of me, I saw him shoot towards goal. He came up with one of his unfathomable trademark dribbles to get away from three United players before taking a shot. I have the image etched onto my brain. I broke out in a cold sweat with that shot. "*Madre mía!* What have you done, Andrés! That's it! You've done it now. It's over; you've forced the muscle." But thankfully, he made it to the end of the game and leaving the stadium I bumped into his father, José Antonio. I congratulated him but I also said: "Did you see Andrés shoot at the end? He didn't have to do that. It frightened the life out of me!" But his father said to me: "What else could he do? The ball came to him nicely and he took a shot. He could do nothing else."'

With the final as good as won, Andrés had felt a great release from all those fears. 'He played the game and we all know how well it turned out. But the sacrifices he made were huge. We then went ten weeks concerned about the injury,' says Pruna.

What a year it was. It was the year of the three out of three with the league, cup and European Cup treble. And it would become the year of the six out of six with the Spanish Super Cup, European Super Cup and World Club Cup added – utopia conquered, and something that had never been done before or since.

'I love Andrés to pieces,' says the Cameroonian. 'I have always seen him as like my own son, my own flesh and blood. And he is just an amazingly good person. Sometimes they kick him and he is the one who says sorry. That kind of thing just doesn't exist in football. There are some footballers who are ten out of ten; he is a twenty out of ten. And as a person he is a two thousand. I adore him, I adore him,' says Eto'o, who celebrated his goal in Rome by tapping furiously on his left arm over and over again. It seemed as if he was whipping himself, while Andrés, who was the first to jump on his back, was able to hear Samuel shouting: 'Blood of my blood! Blood of my blood,' celebrating his African origins. Everyone jumped off the bench to celebrate the goal except Emili who sat still with his fingers crossed. 'The thing is, you never know how long your luck is going to hold out.' He managed to play the whole game as if by tricking his own muscles, drawing forced smiles from Emili who could not believe what was unfolding before his own eyes, grateful that he was still out there on the field.

United did not know that Andrés was playing with an injury. Nor were they aware of Thierry Henry's physical problems after a knock on his right knee in a clash with Sergio Ramos at the Bernabéu. It was a blow that could not take the shine off one of his greatest nights in a Barcelona shirt. He had scored two goals in that famous 6–2 away win, both on the counter-attack as Guardiola's Barcelona hit a new high. 'What a shame, that I arrived so late to his team,' Henry lamented afterwards. What he had really signed for was to win the European Cup, however, and erase that memory of being a beaten finalist in 2006 when an Iniesta-inspired Barcelona had mounted a second-half comeback to defeat Arsenal. Now he had done that.

Alex Ferguson could never have imagined that Barça's injury problems were such that Guardiola had wanted Keita to play at left-back, only for the impeccably-mannered midfielder to respond: 'It would be best if I didn't, boss. There are team-mates who are better prepared for that role.' That meant it was Sylvinho who played on the left of a completely untried and improvised back four. 'We had so many injuries, so many,' remembers Eto'o. Valdés' goal was protected by Puyol at right-back (playing where he used to operate back in his days in the Barça B team), Piqué (the only piece of the puzzle in its correct place), Yaya Touré (a central defender as of two weeks since the Copa del Rey final) and Sylvinho (a left-back all his life but one who had hardly been used by Guardiola). It was a defence made up of emergency solutions. At least in midfield it was the holy trinity of Busquets, Xavi and Iniesta and ahead of them was Barça's first *tridente* Eto'o, Messi and Henry (two world class centre-forwards playing wide to accommodate a false number 9).

With Padró's pre-match video locked into the players' thoughts, things began to turn in Barcelona's favour when Valdés saw off, with hands, feet and knees, the bombardment of shots from Ronaldo, and when Andrés floated forward with the ball at his feet to make that last ever date with Eto'o. Then Messi would hang from the Rome sky above Rio Ferdinand, as if suspended from the clouds, to score that slow-motion header. It seemed only Xavi, disguised as Barcelona's right winger, had spotted his diminutive figure giving him the chance to subtly glance the most precise of headers past the giant Van der Sar in the United goal. Messi lost his right boot in the act of scoring, such was the superhuman force used; a bright blue boot that he would pick up and kiss as the team celebrated. Andrés had almost completely forgotten his injury.

With a 2–0 lead and the triumph assured, and with a change that would be more symbolic than was appreciated at the time, Guardiola took off Andrés and put on Pedro. It was the 92nd minute of the final. At last Emili could breathe easy. Because of the third European Cup in Barça's history and because of the reassuring look he exchanged with Andrés, Pruna heaved a sigh of relief too. Padró, watching at home, had no idea of the emotional impact that his short film had had on the players and on Cugat, whose eyes now shone at the satisfaction of a job well done looking down from his seat at the Olympic Stadium. 'I really enjoyed that game. I suffered a lot for him [Andrés], knowing what might happen. There was a lot at stake. I enjoy watching it more afterwards safe in the knowledge that he played the game and that he won the final. I've seen it many times since,' he says.

Paco Seirulo, the physical trainer who oversaw the players' warm-up in Rome, also felt a sense of liberation when the game ended, in love with the football Andrés had been capable of producing even with his damaged thigh. 'People don't appreciate that great change of pace that he has. It can seem as though he is dragging his feet along the turf and then suddenly he's gone and nobody knows how. The opposition can be fooled into thinking that he is not in the game, but he is always in the game.'

That is what happened in Rome. 'He has a very specific idea of movement. He always watches the feet of his rivals. It's wonderful just seeing Andrés play,' adds Paco, student of the game and also of each of his players' muscles.

'He has greater resistance than strength. There is elasticity to his strength. He benefits from knowing how to do things at exactly the right time because he is great decision maker. Others force their way around the pitch, Iniesta floats.' In Rome Iniesta floated. And Messi floated too.

'Muscles are a lot like Andrés,' muses Paco. 'White tissue, compact, unpredictable like a field hare, you never knew what will happen with them. He is a genius.'

What no one was prepared for was the sudden and cruel disappearance after the Roma final. Andrés would need four months and two days to recover properly and start his next game. In between times, there were four failed attempts to come back and feel like a footballer again. He had started a journey into the unknown. Out of Rome and into chaos.

'It should have been the best summer of my life, but it ended up being the worst,' Andrés says. All the same, and with not a single doubt, he knows he did the right thing.

'I would do the same again. For my club, for myself, for my team-mates, for my friends and family, and for the supporters. The sportsman has something special inside of him that takes over in difficult situations. I was driven on by the desire, the passion, the feeling, and the pride of being a footballer. It was not easy. We were up against the clock, the final was so close. But I wouldn't have missed it for anything in the world. It was my prize for everything that had happened to me that year and for the last Champions League final in Paris. It was my duty to play in Rome. I owed it above all to myself. I just wanted to get out on that pitch and play that match. I could not allow myself to miss it. It meant too much, there were too many sporting and personal connotations; too many for me not to be in Rome.'

There was no choice. Andrés had to play that final. 'I remember when I finished the Villarreal game with that small tear in the muscle. I was furious but the truth is the fury lasted no more than the first night. The next day, on my way to the hospital, I had already turned things around inside my head. I was barely able to walk without a limp, but I had made my mind up that I was going to play in Rome. And I used every minute to meet that target. It was a challenge. I worked with Emili, every morning, afternoon and evening. Rome was waiting for us. What I did not know was the price I would have to pay. I had no idea. I could never have imagined. My career was not in danger, but I had taken my body to the absolute limit and that much was shown by all that happened in the months that followed those two weeks of such sacrifice. The toll was very high, but I would take exactly the same road if I had to choose again.

'It was worth the suffering.'

TOP OF THE WORLD

_'Hey Hugo, please . . .'_
_Andrés, one hour before the start of the World Cup final 2010_

Andrés waited until everyone else in Johannesburg was asleep. He has always been able to find a silent space to listen to his own body, and now finally off of Raúl's treatment table, that is exactly what he wanted to do. He carefully opened the door of his hotel room and he began to run. He began to run as if he was running for his life, from one end of the hallway of the team's South Africa hotel to the other. He was satisfying an irresistible urge to carry out his own personal fitness test, with no one watching, and even though there was no ball at his feet. He was a long way from the pitch, but this was enough to know that he was cured. It was enough to convince him. He wanted to shout: 'I'm ready, the torment is over.' At long last Iniesta could run, he could play, all the way to the World Cup final.

Those damned muscles injured months ago had finally been fixed as if by magic. After so many setbacks, they were once again synchronized like the hands of a Swiss watch. They had been made good again thanks to the precise care of Raúl Martínez and the advice of Emili Ricart – two men separated by thousands of kilometres but joined together by the common link of Iniesta.

'I was not there with Andrés,' confirms Raúl. 'Nor do I know when it was that he started running. He did not tell me. Sometimes certain injuries have no real scientific explanation. I never fully understood this one. After various tests we found a part of the muscle fibre, that we had previously ignored, which seemed to be provoking a sort of disorganization in the leg. I thought that could be the crux of the problem.'

Raúl unblocked the leg and Emili cleared the head with a video that Andrés watched every night before going to bed, as if he was reciting the 'Lord's Prayer' as a small boy in Fuentealbilla.

Pep Guardiola loved the subject of motivation and just as with the *Gladiator* video he showed his Barcelona players before the Champions League final in Rome in 2009, he also prepared, along with Emili and Santi Padró, a TV3 journalist, a video to inspire Barça to a second-leg comeback against José Mourinho's Inter in the Champions League semi-final of 2010.

That tape recounted various big defeats and then some very big victories; moments of huge frustration and of great euphoria experienced by sporting figures such as Roger Federer, Fernando Alonso, synchronized swimmer Gemma Mengual, the Spain basketball team and the Spanish handball team. It also included the 'Iniestazo' – as Iniesta's semi-final goal against Chelsea in 2009 had become known – and that Rome final with some opera from Bocelli to accompany Leo Messi's famous header and the image of him hanging from the sky of the Olympic Stadium as he scored the second goal of the 2–0 win that night.

The film started with the euphoria, the embraces, the high-fives, the unity in victory. But the glorious colour of the opening frames then gave way to the black and white images of defeat, of sportsmen free-falling towards failure. There were around 30 seconds of the suffering of finishing second – of Puyol and Estiarte lamenting Essien's brilliant goal from the main stand of Stamford Bridge in London in 2009 as Laporta nervously ran his hand over the top of his hair, imagining the worst. Then the colour returned as defeat was turned into victory once more, until the last image of Barça, together in a circle, celebrating the club's third European Cup in Rome. It was a great way to visualize beating Mourinho's team.

Guardiola, however, never let his players see that DVD in the Camp Nou dressing room before the game against Inter. The coach sensed a degree of over-excitement in the journey to the stadium, when the team bus came down from the hotel on the Tibidabo mountain through a sea of expectant Barcelona fans lining the streets. He decided he did not want to crank up his players' level of adrenaline any higher and so that video of four minutes and four seconds stayed in the hands of Emili. At least that was the case until he decided to give it to Iniesta at the 2010 World Cup.

Emili exchanged messages with Andrés every day, so he knew that it was working for him as soon as he found out about that solitary run down the hallway of Spain's team hotel. Raúl did not even need to speak to Andrés. The player gave the game away with that deliriously happy look of illumination on his face. Now used to playing with pain, he felt free at last, and anxious to reach the final in Johannesburg's Soccer City – the light that waited for him on the other side of those Soweto suburbs.

'You would struggle to find anyone as honest, dedicated and so willing to work as Emili,' Andrés says. 'I never knew him personally until Guardiola brought him with him to the first team. Since then we have become practically inseparable. I can identify with him, with his way of thinking and his way of working.

'He is very special to me,' says Andrés, who also feels much the same way about Raúl. 'I knew that Raúl was a phenomenon in his field. And he showed that during the World Cup. I can honestly say that, in sporting terms, he saved my life. He knows my body and how it works as if he had given birth to me. He has become indispensable.'

One is 'special' and the other 'indispensable'. Both are there to help Andrés. They understand the doubts and concerns of a player who needed to test his fitness in private; who needed to listen to his body and hear that everything was now in the right place. 'Yes!' resounded in the hotel hallway from the mouth of Iniesta, whose World Cup started at that very moment.

* * *

'On 13 April 2010, I injured my right hamstring training at Barcelona's Cuidad Deportiva,' remembers Andrés. 'It really felt that I had torn it and there was only a little over a month before Vicente would name the squad for the World Cup. Time was very tight and I really believed that I was not going to make it.'

That moment of pain is still remembered at Barcelona's training ground at Sant Joan Despí. Everyone was shocked to see Andrés abandon the session in tears accompanied by Emili, and eventually also by Carles Puyol as soon as he realized just how serious the injury was.

'Cheer up, Andrés, everything will be fine,' the defender whispered in his ear as they left the training pitch together. Andrés heard nothing as they took the long walk back to the dressing room. He was paralyzed by the fear that he was now back in the abyss, one that he was convinced he had left behind for good. All he could hear was his own sobbing.

'I told him: "Don't worry, Andrés. You are going to be the best player at the World Cup," but he was crying so much I don't think he heard me,' says Paco Seirulo, the fitness coach at Barcelona whose words had been almost lost in the sound of the falling water from the shower. 'Of course I heard Paco. But I could not bring myself to respond,' Iniesta says, remembering the scene inside the dressing room moments before Puyol, captain, friend and confidant, would open the door to the solution to his problem. 'You have to talk to Raúl, okay? Everything will be fine but you must speak to Raúl.'

'My heart and my morale were on the floor. I had suffered with injuries for a year, but it seemed I was in the clear and full of excitement for the World Cup. But now I was back on the brink of missing the tournament,' says Andrés. 'And yes I spoke to Raúl.' It may have appeared that Andrés had not been listening, but he was soon surrounded by the best specialists, and they were determined to put the boy from Fuentealbilla right once again.

'The first thing Raúl told me was: "Don't worry, you will make the World Cup! And once you are there, we will do everything we can to make sure you get back to normal."'

'Normal?' Such a low-key word for such a desperate situation – a footballer on the verge of missing a World Cup finals. 'It is one of the most difficult moments that I have had to go through. But life has shown me not to give up, ever,' Andrés wrote at the time. There were now less than two months before Spain's first game in Durban.

'Before the tournament began we had a month of spending every evening together. After dinner, it would be "time for Raúl" and I would lay down on the treatment table and put my body in his hands,' says Andrés.

'What did I do to him?' Raúl still takes a few seconds to answer the question he has set himself. How did he change Andrés' body? The video from Emili got him through the night but it was the magic hands of Raúl that helped him survive the day-to-day struggle to get his muscles right to play again. Both men knew that something was not right with Andrés. Something that not even the calm transmitted by Vicente del Bosque could remedy.

'Don't worry, I will wait for you right until the end,' Del Bosque had told him. The man from Salamanca, fair and sensitive as ever, a man of his word, was showing his usual common sense. The patience of the coach was as decisive as the work of the two physiotherapists and the work and attitude of Iniesta himself.

One week before his World Cup debut against Switzerland, Spain played their final friendly, in Murcia against Poland.

Andrés was back. The midfielder from La Mancha picked up the ball on the left wing, where as a right-footer he had always been so comfortable finding space and then bringing the ball inside. This particular move lasted 16 seconds and took him to the edge of Kuszczak's area. He had swapped passes with Xavi and Silva before receiving the ball again with his back to the Polish goal. He controlled with his left foot, stepped on it with his right and turned to face the five Polish defenders between him and the goal. With the Murcia public on the edge of their seats, he flicked the ball up and over the Polish wall and played in Xavi who squared for Silva to score. Now you see it, now you don't, and all in the blink of an eye.

'There we saw a magician inventing a pass, inventing a space, Xavi arriving from deep, the assist, the finish from David, real team play.' That was Andoni Zubizarreta's version of the goal. He was an analyst for TVE1 at the time and would later become sporting director for Barcelona. It was another expression of a long-held admiration and one that told him what would happen as soon as the ball left the right boot of Iniesta. The game was no more than 14 minutes old and Raúl and Emili, the former sat on the bench of the Nueva Condomina stadium and the latter preparing a holiday to the Dominican Republic, were smiling broadly, accomplices in the happiness of Andrés who after setting up Villa with that right-footed pass for the first goal, had now played in Xavi for the second.

There was euphoria in the stands and in the squad as everyone celebrated Iniesta's recovery. Until he came over to the bench and asked Del Bosque to take him off. 'I have to learn from my experiences,' argues the player, wise enough to know that if he feels even the slightest pain he should ask to be replaced as he did in Murcia. Del Bosque was concerned and the team doctors were worried because this was minute 39 of a game being played on 8 June, just one week before Spain's opening World Cup match.

'We took him off because he felt some discomfort in the back of his thigh,' Spain doctor Óscar Celada told journalists after the game. 'It is not a tear and it has not deteriorated since. It was at the start of the game and he felt the discomfort so we made the change. It is a minor injury. We will do some tests, but initially we can rule out anything serious. We just need to be cautious.' He was speaking for the press but also for Andrés who was now unsettled once more, trapped between the contrasting feelings of positivity for the way he had played and negativity because of the new setback.

The right thigh was broken . . . almost. According to tests carried out in Barcelona there was a slight hamstring strain and the inflammation would require patience if it was to heal. 'There is some small swelling in a muscle in the back of the right thigh. Initially the prognosis is good because there are no torn muscle fibres. We are not ruling him out for the Switzerland game,' said Juan Cota, another of the team doctors.

The initial prognosis was good. But that word 'initial' had been cruel on Andrés in the past. He had suffered other injuries that had an 'initially' favourable diagnosis and turned out to be much worse, none more so than the torn thigh and the groin problem that blighted his season at Barcelona. The World Cup was about to start and Del Bosque was even more worried because he knew the subtleties of Spain's best football came from Iniesta. The player himself felt suffocated, annoyed at himself for having suffered so many injuries – too many.

Iniesta did make it back for the game against the Swiss at the start of the World Cup but he injured himself again, this time after an hour of play, when he was brought down by the right-back Lichtsteiner. He took his time getting back to his feet. Obsessed with avoiding another major setback, he spent the next minute or so touching the back of his right thigh. That was the root of all his muscle problems. He was so worried he was unable to remember if, as nearly always, it had been Pedro who had gone on to replace him. The ritual repeated itself regardless of the opponent and even at a World Cup. Del Bosque would start with Iniesta, he would get injured, and Pedro would come on to replace him. And it seemed the better he was playing the more likely it seemed he would pick up an injury. Andrés had played two passes inside the Swiss central defenders that had left a team-mate alone in the area. One found Piqué who had become an auxiliary centre-forward as Spain searched for a goal. Then he played a magical back-heel in another of Spain's best moves. He was on good form as he showed with a curling shot from the edge of the area from almost the same spot on the pitch from where he found the back of the net at Stamford Bridge. Then came the foul from Lichtsteiner.

The injury appeared more serious this time. For a split second it seemed Andrés wanted to be swallowed up by the South African turf, something that did not pass without Canal+ commentator Michael Robinson noticing. 'I don't like the look on Iniesta's face,' the ex-Liverpool forward told co-commentator Carlos Martinez: it was going to be necessary to revive the routine of messages from Emili and massages from Raúl. The psychological and physical therapy would be needed again – and the blind faith that one day Iniesta would not have these relapses. 'I came on and saw him touching the back of his thigh and said: "It seems like a blow to the back of the leg, Andrés." "No, no doctor, it's cramp at the back of the muscle," he said, which sounded the alarm bells. "*Madre Mía!* Let's walk very carefully off the pitch without hurrying, Andrés, okay?" I said as we left the Durban pitch.'

The coaching staff assumed that he would not be fit to play Honduras in five days' time, but they trusted in him being ready for the last and potentially decisive group game against Chile. The Spain manager, a man of profound convictions, now had to face the criticism for the 1–0 defeat to Switzerland. 'We are not going to lose perspective, we will be true to our style,' said Del Bosque. 'It was a mishap that is difficult to explain,' said Xavi.

It was double frustration for Andrés with the defeat and the old injury now behaving slightly differently in South Africa from how it was in Barcelona. The situation was so delicate that they decided not to carry out tests on the injury and the doctors assured everyone that it was just a knock that would not become anything more. They didn't want to take it any further, convinced that if they showed Andrés one more image of the affected area, it could be the end of his World Cup. 'You can't treat a player by just showing him scans,' says Raúl. 'Sometimes you anticipate, or you take a risk, or you use your intuition with the aim of making sure he does not begin to obsess over his injury.'

'Between the Switzerland game and the Honduras match I had a very bad time of it,' remembers Andrés, immersed in a rehabilitation programme which naturally involved falling asleep at night to Emili's video and, of course, Raúl's treatment table. And it was there in that player's confessional, where a sportsman must lay himself bare and give up all his physical secrets to the perceptive hands of the physiotherapist, that he noticed the most subtle of changes, a change that would then need to be tested in the hallway of the Johannesburg hotel on the eve of the game against Honduras.

'Raúl had hit the right spot, I just knew it,' he remembers.

'It was not easy getting a handle on him; he's difficult to understand and sometimes I think I still don't,' says Raúl. 'But once you do, you see what an enigma he is. He lives in his own world, you never know what he is thinking, as if he is a little disconnected, and at first not overly-trusting. It's hard to get inside his head. And when he is injured, it's worse because he is anxious.'

Raúl did get through to him though; the pair did strike up an understanding: 'He is like a Swiss watch in as much as we both know how he works, what he responds to, and we have learned what makes him tick,' he says. 'He is as sensitive as he is mechanical. We had to harmonize his body again. And that is what we did.'

But if what was happening in South Africa pointed to him returning in time for the Honduras game, another message was coming to him from Barcelona. It was a phrase that he had heard so many times before that it echoed around his head. 'Andrés, you have to respect your body clock. You must always do that.' Emili never abandoned that one message – the timeframes had to be respected.

And so it was nine days later, on 25 June, when Andrés was able to celebrate a double victory after the defeat to Switzerland and his injury: Spain beat Chile and he scored the goal from a Villa assist – the world back to front, but who cared? He finished the game smiling like a schoolboy who had just got away with something, or at least one who had witnessed something turn out just as he had predicted.

● ● ●

Andrés loves nothing more than that feeling as he heads back up the tunnel of being completely exhausted but wholly fulfilled by a well-earned win, and even more so if one of his famous pre-match predictions has come true: 'Víctor, today I will score and I will dedicate it to you,' he had muttered to the team-mate on the seat next to him on the coach to Pretoria.

The best victories always make fertile ground for the more intimate of anecdotes. 'You could have cut the atmosphere with a knife,' remembers Del Bosque whose team were fully aware that they were playing for their very survival at the World Cup. There was a tense silence barely broken by the occasional whisper, such as Iniesta's murmured promise to Víctor Valdés, the boy who protected him in La Masia, the player who was justly given the opportunity to play for Spain precisely because of the influence of Barça on Del Bosque.

The goal was started and finished by Iniesta. He won possession and he combined with Torres and Villa before hitting the back of the Chilean net. A shot with his right foot, his good foot, now completely cured, unstoppable even for Claudio Bravo, one of the best goalkeepers around who would later become his club team-mate at the Camp Nou. It was not just any goal either, because he had only scored one other in 42 games for Barcelona in that dramatic 2009–10 season in which he finished up playing just five minutes of the last match, as Guardiola's team beat Valladolid to win the league at the Camp Nou.

Andrés had stopped touching the back of his leg and was now looking at his boots instead. He was no longer thinking about the games he had played, and was instead focused on the matches to come. There was no longer any trace of that tear in the right leg so well cared for by Raúl.

'A lot of the problems I have had with the hamstring derive from the injury I sustained playing the Rome Champions League final,' Andrés confesses. He might not be a doctor but he knows his own body as if he were a fusion of Raúl and Emili. 'There were so many months of difficulties, but when Raúl got to the root of the problem and liberated that area of the muscle everything started to work properly again,' says Andrés who always expresses himself best, not with words or gestures, but with his feet. When his body is right, stable and in perfect harmony, that's when he can let the ball do the talking.

'If I feel good, then everything else just flows.' There is no middle ground with Andrés, he is indestructible when he is fully fit, and fragile when he is injured; even slightly fatalistic. 'Why did this have to happen now, just at the moment when I was feeling so good?' he would ask after every setback, not differentiating between small or big injuries and demanding so much from his body.

But he felt good again now; good on that journey from the last group game in Pretoria to the final in Johannesburg. The muscle had healed, and so had the memory of it. In Cape Town in the last 16, the front pages had told of victory over Portugal and Ronaldo taking the defeat badly. In Johannesburg in the quarter-final against Paraguay, Casillas had saved a decisive penalty with a little help from reserve goalkeeper Pepe Reina who had previously faced spot-kicks from Óscar Cardozo and told him which way to dive. And the semi-final against Germany was a happy return to the scene of all the uncertainties from the first match of the finals. It had been in Durban on 16 June when he picked up the injury against Switzerland.

But it would also be in Durban, on 7 July, when he was able to enjoy the moment Puyol threw open the doors to the World Cup final.

'Please, Xavi. The next corner put it there for me, okay?' came the request from the Barcelona captain Puyol to his club team-mate.

'But why would I put it right in the centre for you? Can't you see how big the Germans are?' Xavi responded.

'For fuck sake, Pelopo! You just put it there on the penalty spot for me, can't you see they are like statues?' came back the response.

'Okay, okay! Like it's that easy!' said Xavi, or 'Pelopo', the nickname he has had since his days at La Masia (a body hair reference, explain his team-mates whenever asked).

'If you don't put it there, I'm not coming up for any more corners,' shouted back Puyol.

Television cameras captured this heated discussion at half-time as both players walked off with the score at 0–0, Xavi repeating the phrase to himself: 'Like it's that easy!'

It certainly was not easy, especially with the Jabulani, the glorified beach ball that despite having a life of its own had become the official World Cup match ball. Any doubt that Xavi could deliver lasted only until Spain won their first second-half corner. More convinced of his own ability than ever, he trotted across to the corner to the right of Neuer's goal. 'Right, now you are going to get it, Puyi.' Alongside him was Iniesta, no more than five or six metres away. Although Iniesta did not know it at the time, his job was one of distraction: Operation Xavi and Puyol needed a decoy. Xavi wanted the German defenders to think that Spain would play the kick short, as they were tending to do, trying to draw the German giants out of their area. The short corner was straight out of the Barça and Spain textbook, but the textbook was torn up in favour of the stubborn belief of Puyol and the complicity of Xavi.

The Jabulani obeyed the maestro's right foot and flew directly over the penalty spot where it was met by Puyol's head. The Catalan centre-back rose a split second before and jumped a centimetre higher than any of the eight German defenders marking the five Spain players in the area. It is no secret that the football of both Spain and Barcelona is precisely a question of time and space in which one centimetre and one second can make all the difference. Players have to think quickly and arrive before their opponents and even their team-mates – Puyol got to the ball ahead of Piqué. 'I was going to head it but right at that moment he got in front of me, I thought it was a plane,' joked Gerard afterwards. Puyol's header was as powerful as it was accurate and was only ever going to end up in one place. It took just two seconds to score such a historic goal – from Xavi's boot into the back of Neuer's net. It was a set-piece made in Barcelona and one which had already been successful against Real Madrid in the famous 6–2 Clásico win in 2009. Spain had not scored a goal from a set-piece before in a World Cup, and they have not done so since.

It had been the most important goal in Spain's history.

●   ●   ●

'What have you done to my country? Why? What have we ever done to you, eh?'

The question did not sound friendly or tongue-in-cheek. It was more rude and unpleasant; uttered by a disgruntled passer-by towards the table where Puyol, his brother Josep and friend Javi, Iniesta, and the players' agent Ramon Sostres, were sitting. The five of them lifted their gaze towards the arrogant-sounding German voice that had addressed the captain of Barcelona.

It was Lothar Matthäus, a proud Bavarian whose intimidating curriculum included no less than five World Cups and a winner's medal from Italia '90.

'I haven't done anything. Just a little header,' responded Puyol, smiling through that mop of curly hair. His reactions had been as quick as for the goal itself.

'Relax, relax! I hope you have a lot of luck in the final!' said the German.

Matthäus smiled and walked away. And everyone else smiled too, their conversation having been interrupted by what at first seemed like a provocation but had then turned into light-hearted congratulations . . . once the Latinos had decoded the German humour.

'Do you realize what you have done, Carles? You have scored the most important goal in the history of Spanish football and everyone knows it,' said his companions at the table.

'Let's hope only until Sunday,' said the goalscorer. 'Only until Sunday.'

'Relax, Carles, I will take care of that. Don't you worry.'

Suddenly all eyes were on Andrés. Everyone was surprised by the forcefulness of the statement he had just made, and filled with hope too, because whenever he made such bold predictions it was usually because he had seen what was about to happen. When everything seems straightforward, his is the voice that warns against complacency; and when everything seems difficult, his is the voice that announces the arrival of a better future.

'Do you believe in destiny, Andrés?' came the question from the table.

'Destiny is a very complex word . . . I was certainly in the right place at the right time.'

And if he was in South Africa it certainly was not by coincidence. The relief at being there after thinking his chance may have gone explained his relaxed mood leading up to the final; one that allowed him to intervene in these post-match discussions, to enjoy Emili's therapy video every night and to raise a glass to Raúl's treatment table.

●  ●  ●

Soccer City, 11 July 2010. The day of the World Cup final, and the minutes leading up to a game the whole planet would stop to watch. A planet intrigued by a Holland side who now played like one of the fierce Spain teams of old, up against a Spain team that now more than ever before resembled the classic Dutch masters whose Total Football may have lost the World Cup to Franz Beckenbauer's Germans in 1974 but won over the whole of football. Roles had been reversed since the arrival of Luis Aragonés and Del Bosque, who both encouraged teams that looked to control matches through possession, who were built around the talented ball-playing Spanish midfielder, and therefore, naturally, around Iniesta. With Aragonés, Spain won Euro 2008, their first title in 44 years; now two years later, they were 90 minutes away from a first-ever World Cup.

Andrés reached the dressing room and went deeper and deeper into his own world, only coming to the surface for a moment to speak with

Hugo Camarero. He had something to say to one of Spain's assistants, a member of the backroom physio team, one who has hands of silk that calm the most tired and pained of muscles. Hugo was in the dressing room when he heard Iniesta. 'Hey Hugo, please . . .'

Hugo, consumed by the usual pre-match hustle and bustle, and even more so because this was a World Cup final, stopped what he was doing to attend to Andrés.

'First, Jesús Navas sent for me to arrange to dedicate a shirt,' recalls Hugo. 'Then Andrés came to see me. He was working with Raúl at the time. I don't know if he had seen what I had done for Jésus. In the dressing room before a game so many things happen, so imagine before a World Cup final: treatments, bandages, massages.'

Andrés came over. 'Hey, Hugo, do me a shirt for Jarque, please.'

'What size do you want it? Big, small, short-sleeved, long-sleeved, a vest? Short-sleeved, okay don't worry, when you come back from the warm-up we will have it ready.'

'Please put: "Dani Jarque, always with us." And make sure it's written large on the front, eh!'

'Don't worry, when you come back in it will be there for you.'

Andrés went out to warm up. Hugo also had to go out on to the pitch at Soccer City to accompany and help the physical trainer Javi Miñano take the session. But before that he now had something to do.

'As fast as I could, I went to look for Joaquín who is one of the kit men with the Spain team,' recalls Hugo.

'Here you go, Hugo, the vest you wanted!'

But who gave him the marker pen? 'That was also Joaquín. They always have them for the corners and free-kick sheets that are given to the players before every match. But Joaquín, and don't ask me why, already suspected something. "Don't use too much ink. We are going to need that marker pen. You will see why," he said to me.'

With every letter he wrote, with a sort of accelerated patience, he could feel the stare of Joaquín on the back of his neck. Would there be enough ink?

'I am very meticulous and I was pressing down hard on each letter, using more ink than Joaquín wanted me to. Why? Because, I wanted people to be able to read the words. I wanted it to look perfect.'

Hugo was acting with an unshakeable faith that this shirt would be seen by the whole world.

Andrés was still out on the pitch warming up and Miñano was missing Hugo, but Hugo had still not finished.

'Come on, Hugo, come on!' Between the pressure he was being put under by Joaquín and the pressure he was under anyway, he finished as quickly as he could. 'Perhaps six or seven minutes. Not much more.'

When Andrés returned, the shirt was waiting for him. 'I don't think he said anything to me,' remembers Hugo. 'Maybe he raised his hand. You know what he's like. He says more with a gesture or a look than with words.'

Hugo returned to the quiet of the dressing room after the warm-up had finished. Andrés had withdrawn into his own silent space. It was the calm before the storm – a very delicate mix of subtle gestures, looks and whispers – ahead of the game they all knew was the biggest of their lives. Nobody saw him put on that second layer beneath his red and blue Spain shirt. Nor did anyone notice that Andrés, superstitious and never comfortable with long sleeves, had cut the sleeves on his shirt.

'I remember that the tunnel from the dressing room to the pitch was so long and steep,' Andrés says. 'When you saw the light at the end of it, it gave you the feeling of entering a Colosseum. You didn't see the stands until you were right in the mouth of the tunnel.'

In that tunnel, Andrés, with the sleeveless white tee shirt carrying Hugo's handiwork on the front of it, under his own Spain number 6, begins to feel something inside. It isn't fear or anxiety. Is it nerves? A little insecurity perhaps? He walks down that tunnel, on edge.

'When I see that photograph it still makes my hair stand on end,' says Hugo. 'So imagine what it was like for him! I see that message and my mind is swamped by a thousand flashbacks. And I think about all that he went through at that World Cup.'

Did he suffer? 'Yes, he did. He suffered a lot,' says Hugo. 'It was fifty-five days, including the preparation leading up to the tournament. Days and nights of treatment, sometimes until four in the morning. Look what happened in Murcia before the trip to South Africa. He was home free but the injury caught up with him. Look what happened against the Swiss. He was so nearly a hundred per cent right again, but he had to start all over again. Every morning the same routine, the same scene. Let's see now, the good morning greeting you get from Andrés . . . how does it go? We didn't really need words by the end. I think he ended up having more training sessions with me than with the rest of the team. If he gave you a smile, then that was enough. With a simple gesture, it was enough. There were nights when I spent more time praying than sleeping. Praying that the following morning, his good morning smile would be a reassuring one.'

The kit men for the Spain team worked with the utmost care to make sure Andrés wanted for nothing. Before going to South Africa, the Spanish Football Federation even set up a gymnasium at the team's training ground at Las Rozas with machines especially suited to his needs. 'We brought the same machines that Xavi and Iniesta used in Barcelona,' said Hugo. 'And then we pressured them to take similar machines to the World Cup, including the same running machine for Ramos.'

'Andrés is very superstitious,' says Hugo, 'but then many players are.' One day when Hugo was at training with Spain defender Raúl Albiol, the team doctor rushed on to the pitch shouting at Hugo: 'You need to be with Andrés so you can do the same exercises with him as always. Go now please and then you can come back to work with Albiol.' The patient was sure that with the same exercise routine every day, the body would end up synchronizing. That is why Hugo left everything he was doing and marched off for his meeting with Andrés Iniesta's legs. The routine could not be broken.

'We had to manage the process very well with Andrés,' says Hugo. 'The tests that we gave him, the information that we gave him, everything had to be really positive. I remember Raúl always repeating the same message to him so there were no doubts: "Relax, Andrés everything is going well. Relax."

'In fact, everything was not going well. It was going badly. But no matter how badly, we had to be positive.'

Hugo was thinking about so many of these tiny details experienced during those 55 days as he made the long walk down the Soccer City tunnel. He was happy because Andrés had found exactly what he had asked for when he got back to his locker in the dressing room. Everything was as it should be as he walked on to the pitch passing – without looking at it – the World Cup he hoped he would end up kissing that night.

'I've got no idea what happened to that marker pen. I was a little bit annoyed when I gave it back, that much I do remember,' says Hugo.

There was a message on Jesús Navas' shirt that night too. The same one, written instead for Antonio Puerta, who had died tragically on the pitch when playing for Sevilla. The shirts were different too. The one used by Jesús was short-sleeved and blue and the one used by Andrés, as the whole world saw, was white and sleeveless. Both were the handiwork of Hugo Camarero.

'Why did I never think of it before? I don't know. I don't think too much about things. Perhaps it was inspiration from somewhere,' says Andrés.

In the build-up to the final, Iniesta was occupied with more domestic affairs. He was making sure that his closest friends Jordi, Joel, Sesi and Alexis reached Johannesburg in time to see the final.

'I didn't need to think about the shirt when I scored the goal. It is something instinctive. You score and you immediately take off your shirt. If I had thought about it too much, then maybe it would not have worked out so well. It went perfectly, it never got caught up, I took it off cleanly, it never fell to the ground. I never fell to the ground. It was incredible.'

Hugo's handwritten message had ceased to be hidden beneath Andrés' Spain shirt. The message stirred millions of hearts, shaken by the unforgettable goal that had preceded it. 'Dani Jarque, always with us.'

'I saw the goal in a different way to everyone else,' Andrés says.

What is it like to score the goal that wins a World Cup and buries the footballing frustrations of an entire nation with one shot? 'When I received the ball, I couldn't hear a thing,' he says. 'It feels as though when I controlled the ball the whole world stopped. It is difficult to explain. I didn't feel anything in that moment, there was just silence. The ball, the goal, and me. It is true that just before the ball is passed to me I take a step back just to be sure I'm not offside. I knew that I wasn't, it was something instinctive. It's something your body does on autopilot. And then . . . then came the silence.'

The ball arrived and sat up sweetly for Iniesta to control it and strike it. 'You have to hold back for just a moment, just so that you catch it perfectly. You're in charge. You and only you. The ball was Newton's apple. And so that made me Newton. I just needed to wait for gravity to take its course. You control the situation. You decide the height the ball is at when you hit it, how hard you hit it, and where you send it. In that moment of silence, it's just you and the ball.

'My intention was to shoot as far into the corner as I could so that the goalkeeper could not get to it, but it ends up going in more centrally. But I hit it hard, that's for sure. The truth is I don't like to think too much about the process. When you think you lose a tenth of a second, and if you think too much you can miss.'

The ball, struck a little more centrally than planned, bent back the right hand of Stekelenburg. With the Dutch keeper now on his knees beaten by the shot, Andrés turned towards the linesman hoping he had not committed the monumental injustice of raising his flag, because he had been onside. He also looked back towards the centre of the pitch remembering something else: 'I participated in the entire move for the goal.'

He speaks with pride about the way he had helped knit together the move that went from Sergio Ramos' zone at right back, to the centre-forward position, formerly the home of Fernando Torres before he injured himself in that second period of extra time.

The back heel to Navas, the movement into space, the pause; all of it necessary for the move to go down in Spanish football history. Andrés is there in all those details – the player who says he doesn't like to think too much.

He did not suffer in those agonizing final minutes despite the nervous moments in the Spain area. 'When I saw Robben homing in on Casillas I was expectant. Nothing more than that. In the end you trust the goalkeeper, it's as simple as that. Now, after watching replays of the chance many times, I think Robben had enough pitch to dribble around Iker. But, luckily, he hit the shot and met with an immense Casillas. That save was so vital. What is more, the more minutes that were played the better I was feeling. I had the feeling we were going to win. The team was getting stronger, I was getting stronger. It is something you can feel. You can see it in the way you are receiving the ball. And I wanted to play an important part. I wanted to take responsibility and I had the energy levels to do so. I felt no fear. With the ball at my feet, I was empowered. And I'm not saying that just because of the goal because that was just one of the many moves we put together.

'Before the goal I remember one chance when I controlled the ball well but just could not finish. There was the move when Heitinga was sent off, and two or three other chances. I had the feeling I was going to have to dig even deeper than the rest for us to win that final. Don't ask me why, that is just the way I felt,' says Andrés.

What is more, it was not an easy final and not just for purely football reasons or because it had gone into extra time. Andrés knew right from the first kick that he was playing a thousand mini-matches in one massive game. This felt like something that had started four years earlier in 2006.

'Of course I remember the challenges from Van Bommel. How could I forget them! He stepped on me on purpose and then committed two fouls against me that could have both been straight reds. And to think I was almost the one sent off! Imagine if I had been shown the red card. That was when I stuck my hip out and he went down as if I had killed him. I was furious when he had deliberately stepped on me to hurt me. I know in that moment I could have been the one receiving the red card, so . . .'

He can't even bring himself to finish the sentence. But then the memories come flooding back of that moment when he became unrecognizable even to himself.

'They kicked us all over the place in the final: the foul from De Jong on Xabi Alonso, the ones on me. And it's true that I don't usually lose my cool.'

But he did lose his cool to the point where for a moment, caught up in that conflict with Van Bommel, Andrés was no longer himself.

Rather than talk about what almost happened, he prefers to talk about what did happen. The goal. 'It is not the goal the people see on the television,' he says. 'It resembles it but it was not quite like that. Through my eyes, the perspective changes. The feeling I had on the pitch is something I can't put into words. It was just very much my goal and I know I have never scored a goal like it. I don't know how to explain it. I don't know how to do it justice. Everything around me froze for a few seconds. I heard the silence. That sounds like a contradiction, but I can't think of a better way of describing it: an audible silence.' And then the ball hits the net, Andrés removes his Spain shirt and the world sees that message and remembers Dani Jarque.

That white sleeveless t-shirt, written on by Hugo, is in Daniel Jarque's spiritual home – Espanyol's Cornellà-El Prat stadium. There where the crowd applaud their former captain in minute 21 – his shirt number – of every single game. The game plays on but the supporters forget the football for a moment and give Dani, Andrés' friend, a minute's ovation, match after match, season after season.

The blue Spain shirt with the sleeves hurriedly cut in the Soccer City dressing room is another football artefact and that is not in Andrés' possession either. Who has it? 'That particular treasure is in very safe hands,' he says. Emili still can't believe the gift that Andrés gave him when he came back from South Africa. A blue Spain shirt with something very special written on it.

'Our secret worked, we became Champions! Thanks for being by my side! With affection, A. Iniesta 6.' This time it was the hand, not of Hugo but of Andrés, dedicating the shirt that still did not have the star above the badge reserved for teams who have won the World Cup, but would be here for ever more.

Everyone remembers the goal. No one will ever forget it. But few remember that Andrés played six of the seven games at the World Cup and in three of them was voted man of the match; including the final, of course.

RIVALS

13

*'It's Andrés! You can't kick him.'*

*Sergio Ramos, Real Madrid*

'God appeared to us when Robben went through one on one with Iker,' recalls Sergio Ramos. 'When I say God, I mean the toe of Iker's boot that prevents Holland scoring. And even with the touch that he gets on the ball, it still doesn't go that far past the post. If they had scored against us in that moment, then we definitely would not have won the game.

'When Andrés' goal finally comes, I was in the right-back position and I ran to the left corner flag at the opposite end of the pitch. I must have run the 100 metres in about nine seconds; I think I was going as fast as Usain Bolt. I went from one corner to the other like a man possessed. The efforts of an entire lifetime are in that goal.'

Those are the crystal-clear memories Sergio Ramos has of the two most decisive moments of the World Cup final in South Africa in 2010. The Real Madrid defender and Spain's right-back at the time lets out a laugh when he says that God disguised himself as Casillas.

Iniesta's memories of the moment are less dramatic. He insists that he was never worried Holland would score. Ramos continues: 'When he says: "I looked, I saw the goalkeeper, and I thought that nothing bad could happen," I always say: "Of course, it is easy for you to be relaxed. For you, it was something that was over in about three seconds. To me, it felt like an eternity."'

Casillas takes up the story: 'It was strange for us to make such a massive error in the World Cup final. Our defence was so solid. But it happened. Sneijder did really well and put Robben through on his own. We already knew that they were the most dangerous players in the Holland team. The problem was that the ball went between "Puyi" and "Geri" [Puyol and Piqué] and we reacted slowly. There was nothing we could do once he received the ball, nothing except have faith.'

There was a small advantage. Ramos and Casillas knew Robben from his time at Madrid and that experience was decisive as the forward homed in on goal. 'I tried to get one step ahead of what I was sure he was going to do,' says Casillas. 'I thought he would try to go around me by dragging the ball to his right, my left. If he went past me, he was all alone. That is why I dropped to that side. Then when he shoots and it hits my foot, I knew it was not going to be a goal. A keeper knows straight away. I was convinced it would miss the goal. And that is just how it happened: it hits my foot and it goes wide.'

Iniesta was calm because he could see Casillas. The keeper on the other hand was not so relaxed watching the midfielder before he scored the winner, because he could see time ticking down and Spain's energy draining. Casillas and Ramos shared the same anxiety.

'During extra time of a World Cup final, you are more worried about not committing mistakes than going on the attack,' says Ramos. 'That's why we all asked ourselves: "Is that really Andrés, so far forward he is almost offside?" The answer was yes. It was really him and he knew how to stay the right side of the last defender. He took the step back and then scored. If there is one player in the world who deserved to score that goal, it is Andrés. It made me so happy. And all this after I'd had three chances myself, above all the header which goes just over the bar. We were playing with the Jabulani ball and, as it tended to, it did something strange in the air before it reached me.'

Casillas was another surprised to see that Iniesta was now the furthest forward for Spain. 'Not many people could understand what Andrés was doing there. I have asked myself many times: "What was he doing on the edge of the six-yard box?" And when the ball reaches him I thought: "Oh my God, it's sat up perfectly for him." The problem is that then Stekelenburg gets a touch on it, and I thought he had done enough to save it. I was convinced he had. I couldn't relax until I saw the ball hit the back of the net.

'I have another natural reaction that kicks in during these situations: I look straight across to the linesman to see if he is running back to the halfway line. When I saw the goal later on television, I noticed that Andrés, at the other end of the pitch, does exactly the same thing. And when I saw that the linesman was running back for the restart, I think the last drop of energy I had went out of my body. I didn't even have the strength to celebrate the goal and certainly not to run to the far corner flag to join my team-mates. And that is despite the fact that I'm usually very expressive when it comes to celebrating goals and that this goal was about to win us the World Cup just four minutes from the end of extra time. But I just couldn't. I hugged Busquets who was the closest to me and that was it. Then the nerves kicked in. People don't realize the emotions you go through playing a final like this. We had various chances, but as time passes you inevitably start to think about penalties. And so many things go through your head. That is why when Andrés scored, I just started to think: "We could be world champions. It's incredible! Incredible!"'

Casillas couldn't move. Sergio Ramos couldn't stop moving. 'Look how Andrés takes the chance. He is so calm, frozen in time and space. Every time I see the goal, it never fails to move me,' says Ramos. 'I have the World Cup, the Champions League and the European Championship trophies at home and not a day goes by when I don't touch them. The World Cup is the trophy that all the great teams have; football owed us something like that. Spain have been world champions in many sports: basketball, tennis, motorsports. We were missing that in football, but now we have it.'

Just as happy, if not more so, was Fernando Torres, Iniesta's old friend from so many different Spain squads at so many different age groups. 'I couldn't believe that the ball had gone in; I just had the feeling that we were not going to be able to avoid penalties,' says the Atletico Madrid forward.

'I remember a lot of evenings spent confessing things and revealing secrets to each other in South Africa,' says Torres. 'Andrés told me many personal things that had happened to him that year. They were things that I did not know about – things that made my admiration for him even greater. And above all, I'm proud that my friend scored that goal. You could not find anyone better to be the scorer of the goal that wins us the final in Johannesburg.

'We both went through bad years in terms of injuries and other problems. Maybe we had not reached South Africa in completely the right state, physically and mentally. Andrés grew in the tournament, though. He got going in the group stage and he ended up scoring a goal for the history books. In contrast, I played sooner than I should have because of the opening defeat [1–0 to Switzerland] and my fitness went from bad to worse as the tournament went on until my knee could take no more.'

They both got what they wanted, however. And once they were back home, with the 'World Champions' star sewn into their shirts, Andrés approached Fernando.

'Do you remember the shirt that you signed for me after the World Cup in Trinidad and Tobago?' Iniesta asked him.

'Of course I do, Andrés. Of course I remember,' responded Torres recalling the scene that took place in 2001.

Up until that moment, Andrés had remained silent about the shirt as if it did not exist. He has always been the same brave and transparent, but at the same time, prudent and respectful boy that Fernando first met when they were both 14 years old.

'We first met each other in the Under-15 Spain team. We debuted in the same game in Villafranca de los Barros,' Torres remembers, 'and from that day on we went through all the age categories together. Our first big tournament was the Under-16 Euros in England. We lost Andrés to injury in the group stage before going on to win the final against France with a goal from me that I dedicated to him; we needed him and we missed him so much. Then we won the Under-19 Euros, beating Germany in the final with me scoring the goal again and Andrés was by my side once more.

'But in 2001, we went to Trinidad and Tobago for the Under-17 World Cup and it was an absolute disaster. We had big expectations that we could become world champions, but we were knocked out in the first stage.

'That tournament helped both me and Andrés grow up fast, because it showed us the flipside of this game: the pain of defeat. We were the main players in that squad and so we were singled out for blame when it all went wrong. That is what the coach told us, to our faces and in front of the rest of the squad. He said that we had let everyone down. We were accused of having changed too, and that also made us the ones to blame.'

That defeat would mark both Fernando and Andrés forever. One of the big favourites for that Under-17 World Cup had been knocked out in the first phase, in a group topped by an Argentina team that included Mascherano, Tévez and Zabaleta, and in which Burkina Faso pushed Spain into third place only above Oman, who came fourth. 'It was terrible being singled out that way, but it served to teach us how football can be sometimes. If we were going to go right to the top, we needed to be prepared for just how tough it could be,' says Torres.

'On the way back from Trinidad and Tobago, we wrote a letter telling of the hardships we had experienced. The awful training facilities, the completely unacceptable standard of hotels, the debatable quality of the food, the travelling . . . the truth is, if boys of that age notice all these things then it really must have been bad.'

They were two teenagers on the flight home expressing their frustration in a letter that would never see the light of day. 'Andrés kept it and I don't know if he still has it, or if he threw it away. It was more sarcastic than serious in tone and we had a laugh writing it. Then we exchanged shirts and each player signed the other's.'

It was on that shirt from Trinidad and Tobago that a prophetic dedication was written. 'One day, you and I will win the World Cup together. Fernando Torres.'

A shirt given to Iniesta and signed by a young player with an almost utopian dream. 'Who would have thought that the dream would come true!' says Torres. 'Deep down I felt that together we were invincible. I believed that destiny had something very special in store for us. That's the way I saw it and that's the way I wrote it. Our World Cup story was not going to end up being just about that Under-17 failure.'

The journey, however, was anything but easy for them, or for Spain. 'It all started at Euro 2008,' says the Atletico forward. Casillas confirms, 'Those of us who were in the team between 2006 and 2008 only ever received criticism, "verbal battering", as Luis Aragonés would say. They certainly made us grow up fast.'

'Luis taught us to be confident and to respect each other. He built a team and he created an idea,' says Torres.

Casillas adds: 'We received a lot of criticism. We were twenty-one, twenty-two, twenty-three years old, and we knew we had to mature quickly. Luis changed the mentality of the squad and then Del Bosque knew how to maintain the same course. It is not easy to win a European Championship, a World Cup, and then another Euros. No one else has ever done it. Luis's mantra was "Win, win and win again". We had grown up with a Spain that usually went out in the quarter-finals and that then looked for excuses. When it wasn't the referee, it was something else. There was always a reason why.'

Luis Aragonés, popularly known as the 'Wise Man of Hortaleza', was the revolutionary, the 'Che Guevara' of Spanish football. He changed the fire and the fury for the passing game, or tiki-taka as it became known first by the sceptics who wanted to make it sound frivolous, then by those who embraced it as a new successful approach.

He knew that Spain's strength was neither in defence, nor in attack, because in both penalty areas there would always be a German or an English player who was bigger than all the Spanish. Its strength was in the middle. The new essence of Spanish football was to be found at the feet of the midfielders; it was about talent, touch, the ball. Euro 2008 was the beginning of a special era, that took in the 2010 World Cup. For the first time ever, Spain were the best team on the planet.

'Luis stuck with the players he really believed in and he gave all the responsibility to the little guys: Andrés, Xavi, Silva . . . ,' says Torres. 'They now dictated the style of the team. It was great to watch, but it was also a lesson to those who believed these players could not lead a winning team. The criticism, the doubts, the slights and the insults, everything we had experienced up to that point had been totally unfair and really hard to take. But Luis always believed in us, and in our ability to achieve something. And everything that happened to us just made us more united in the pursuit of our dream. It was an amazing change of direction. I am convinced that without 2008 there would have been no 2010 and 2012.'

Torres and Iniesta felt vindicated. That shirt from the Trinidad and Tobago tournament which Fernando had signed for Andrés was beginning to make a lot more sense. Together they were starting to believe there was nothing they could not achieve.

'Andrés is a genius; he is someone who knows what is going to happen a second before it does. He is one step ahead of the rest,' says Torres.

There are others who feel the same way about Iniesta, even though their journeys together don't go quite as far back. 'I only coincided with Andrés in two Under-21 games; then we went up to the first team,' says Sergio Ramos. 'There are a lot of players who are totally different to how they were when they first appeared on the scene,' adds Iker Casillas. 'When I first saw Andrés he just seemed small, another Barça youngster. But when he needed to step up, when he needed to shine, he did.'

'Andrés is a magician. He is different to the rest. And he has marked an entire era both with Barcelona and with us,' says Ramos. 'I have been his team-mate for ten years, we are very fond of each other and there is a lot of trust there. From the very first meeting I always liked him. I prefer people who are simple and straightforward to those who try to force a friendship. I don't like pushy people who just want to show off, or those who look to make cliques. Andrés is one of those people who you have to help along at the beginning so that he integrates into the group. But once he is in, he becomes part of the group and then one of its most important members. Things happened that way with me and him even though we played for rival clubs. We clicked from day one.

'He is the boy any mother would want for her daughter because he does almost everything right and never causes any problems,' Ramos adds. 'He is not always very expressive but he transmits good energy, and although it can be difficult to make him smile sometimes, he still projects happiness. That's why I stay close to him, both on and off the pitch. And when it comes to football, he is someone I can learn from.'

Casillas agrees: 'When you see him on the pitch, he can seem cold because he very rarely loses his composure. It takes something really big to wind him up. He is someone that you respect just because of the way he is.'

'He has also suffered a lot too,' interrupts Ramos, 'There are two sides to football and people forget that we are not machines. We have been playing for many years and there are times when the body just can't take any more. The mind can become exhausted too and all this shows up in performances. There are some people who understand this, but there are others who don't. When you play at such a high standard for so many years, as Andrés has done, then people come to expect exactly the same level all of the time.'

Ramos is grateful for the fact that he gets to train with Iniesta. 'You have to give everything if you are up against him,' he says. 'You can pass the ball to him a little harder than normal, but with one touch he kills it dead. You can even give him a bad pass – we call them *fresas* (strawberries) or *sepias* (cuttlefish) – and he will still get it straight under control with one touch of the outside of his boot. There are not many players in the world on the same level.

And when you have to play against him, then you know you are going to suffer. He is very skilful and very direct. He will take you on and he just seems to make space so easily. And he has something else very special that forwards don't have – his generosity. He is one of those who will say to you: "Go on, you tap it in" when he is just about to score. When you play against him, you are always left doubting because you know that if you follow him you are leaving another player unmarked. He has an incredible sense of timing with the ball. He can play the ball long, put it between the lines, or in the top corner. When he is on your side it is a blessing, but if he's your rival it can be torture.'

'He is thirty-two now and every year he seems to get better,' says Casillas. 'There might be a season when he is not quite as good as in others, the year under Tata Martino for example. But then the next year he reinvents himself again. You only have to look at how he has been under Luis Enrique. A year ago he had an incredible season, fabulous, and he won everything. He is a player capable of having a couple of incredible years and then another one not quite as much so, and he has been that way throughout his career.'

Casillas elaborates on the way Iniesta's game has developed under Luis Enrique at the Camp Nou. 'He is an even more complete midfielder now. He gets into the box more, he is quicker, he shoots more. These are things that we didn't see as much before. He seems quicker to me now. I don't mean over a long distance but using his dribbling to get away from opponents. I remember a move from a game against PSG at the Camp Nou in the Champions League. That was when it really hit me how quick he has become; quick movements full of speed, strength and energy.'

Casillas and Ramos have faced Iniesta many times and it has not always been on the best of terms, above all when the context of their encounters had been poisoned by the difficult relationship between Barcelona and Madrid when the clubs were coached by Pep Guardiola and José Mourinho.

'Everyone defends their own,' says Ramos. 'We have gone through some very bad moments between the two teams, and there were even some brawls out on the pitch. In three weeks in 2011 we played a Copa del Rey final, a Champions League double-header and a league match. It was five matches in three weeks and there were some altercations.

'I was the first to put my foot in, the first to make a mistake. You are young, you are impulsive, and your pulse is racing. But after one Clasico in which I had slapped Puyol and got into some trouble with Xavi, the first thing I did the next day was to speak with both of them.

'It would not have been very intelligent to turn up for training with Spain having allowed a bad atmosphere to fester, especially with the great team that we had. But the truth is, there was never a falling out with Andrés. I never stopped having a great relationship with him, even during a period when there were sparks flying between me and Xavi, Geri [Piqué] and even Puyi [Puyol] who was the one that I got on with the worst during that time. But with Andrés there was never any problem. Not with Busi [Busquets] either. Between Andrés and myself, we made sure of that. What is more, I am convinced that when the football is over for the both of us, our friendship will continue.'

'It is impossible to not get on with, or to fight with, Andrés,' Ramos adds. 'It's also impossible to kick him. Sometimes you catch him without intending to. But there are other times when he gets away from you and you have to choose between kicking him and bringing him down, or letting him go. And in the end, you let him get away.

'It's Andrés! You can't kick him. Then another player gets away from you and this one yes, this one you can put in the stand if you want to. But you can't kick Andrés.

'There are so few like him; so few who behave the way he does. That is why I have so much affection for him. I love him as a team-mate. My only regret is that he doesn't play for my club. I would have loved to have had Iniesta alongside me at Madrid.'

DEL BOSQUE

*'I always want midfielders in my team, as many as possible.'*

*Vicente del Bosque*

Vicente Del Bosque, the former Spain manager who won the 2010 World Cup and 2012 European Championships, is a huge fan of Iniesta. 'He's a wonderful footballer, with a physical talent that you don't see often. He has special qualities. The way he uses his body is so elegant. That coordination and technique can't be taught. You can work to improve it, sure, but you're born with it. He's like a dancer, he does everything with grace, as if it was effortless. His game is natural, it flows. He plays in a relaxed manner, always comfortable, as if he is walking with the ball at his feet. It never escapes him. He never seems to be under pressure; it's all smooth, delicate.'

Del Bosque recognizes those same qualities in Andrés that Guardiola does. 'It's not obvious at first, but Andrés has evolved in the way he plays. He's a different player now. For example, both Pep and I envisaged Iniesta playing on the wing, running at people. I've said it to him lots of times: "I see you and I wouldn't want to be a full-back facing you." But there are other elements to his game now. Bit by bit he has come away from the wing and now he feels more important, more comfortable, in the middle of the field. He has earned the right to play that more varied, central role.

'We weren't wrong to put him wide before and we're not wrong to play him as more of a central midfielder now; it's the way he has evolved, the increasing responsibility and protagonism he has taken on. What I most like about Andrés is that he has become the complete midfielder, a total footballer. By "total" I mean a player who defends, constructs, reaches the opposition's area but also plays close to his own area and gives the final pass. The kind of footballer who doesn't look fast but always gets the ball before you do.

'I always want midfielders in my team, as many as possible,' Del Bosque says. It is the kind of phrase you'd expect from Guardiola. The two men see football in similar ways: a game created by and unfolding in the middle, built there and conducted by midfielders of vision and talent. The more players of that quality and understanding a team has, the better. Del Bosque and Guardiola were both midfielders themselves, at Real Madrid and Barcelona respectively. Del Bosque says, 'I'd love everyone to be a midfielder, but not just to come and receive the ball, to get a touch, to play, but also to know when to distance themselves from it, to understand the right moment for the right pass. Football is not just about being close together, constantly in possession, moving the ball between players; it's about knowing when to get out of there, when to stretch the game and seek a pass beyond the opposition.'

'Andrés has an uncommon intelligence and awareness,' Del Bosque says. 'Sometimes you think it's as if he was watching the game from up in the stands, not down on the pitch. When you're sitting up there you think: "He should play the pass now," And Andrés does. "I'd do this now." And Andrés does. He can't see what you can up there, where it's easy, but somehow he does the right thing anyway. He sees it.'

When it comes to the World Cup final, Del Bosque admits: 'I haven't watched the game back in full. I have, though, watched part of it, particularly extra-time. I remember that Andrés could even have been sent off, although in truth he didn't do anything; Van Bommel exaggerated the challenge. I don't like to talk ill of anyone, but Holland, which has always been a country that has produced great footballers, weren't Holland at that World Cup. They were worried about Spain, which you can see in the way they played, the tackles they put in, the *patadas* . . .' *Patadas* means kicks, fouls; hacks, even. It's a word that never normally comes out of Del Bosque's mouth. 'That wasn't the true Holland, the Holland we knew,' he adds.

It was, in the end, the Holland they defeated. 'I saw the goal,' Del Bosque says. 'But I didn't celebrate it much. I was contained. Why? Because I remember Bilic, the Croatian coach, and what happened to him in the quarter-final of Euro 2008. Croatia scored in the 119th minute and he came running out from his bench to celebrate it with everyone. Then Turkey took the kick-off and, suddenly, scored a belter that flew into the top corner. I've heard Bilic say lots of times that he expended too much energy celebrating that goal and in the end the Turks won on penalties. So when Andrés scored, I had that image of Bilic stuck in my mind. There were still four minutes left.'

The final whistle arrived and Spain celebrated their first World Cup; at last Del Bosque could celebrate Andrés' goal. 'Andrés has always felt important with the national team,' he says. 'He has won everyone over. He has everyone's respect. Some 100,000 people go to the Camp Nou every week and I'm sure you'd struggle to find three of them who don't like him. Maybe it's because he doesn't have tattoos, and because he's never involved in trouble. Everyone appreciates him as a person, not just as a player.'

Del Bosque draws a parallel. 'You get these politicians, for example, who talk a lot at rallies and so on, but aren't there at the hour of truth. There's nothing. None of what they say has any substance at all. Then there's the opposite: the person who barely says anything but who's credible, calm, and when it matters he is there. That's Andrés.

'We used to watch this video with the national team,' Del Bosque reveals. 'It was very short, barely twenty or thirty seconds. It was from a game played at Cornellà. Barcelona are winning 4–1, I think, against Espanyol and Andrés leaves the field. Espanyol's fans, Barcelona's rivals, get out of their seats to give him a standing ovation. It's a fantastic sight. It says so much about what Andrés is, who he is. As a person and a player. They're losing to their biggest rivals and they applaud him from the field. Cornellà defines him. The footage is incredible, wonderful. Really, really wonderful.

'That doesn't happen to anyone else.'

DANI

*'Seconds before the goal, I knew it was coming. I started to cry just before you scored.'*

Jessica, wife of Dani Jarque, to Andrés

'It's difficult for me to let go of this shirt, but I think this is the best place for it. I scored the goal, but Dani will also be remembered forever.' And so it was that Andrés, emotional with memories of his friend who had died before his time, delivered the historic white vest with the famous marker-pen message written on the front of Espanyol's stadium – the home of their former player Dani Jarque.

Andrés only ever scored that goal once. But everyone has seen it so many times since, that they feel as though they scored it themselves. There was someone that night who just knew it was coming. Someone who sensed what was about to happen, the moment Iniesta took a couple of steps back to make sure he was going to be onside when he received the ball.

Jessica, Dani Jarque's wife, had briefly got the better of her interminable grief (it had only been a year since the death of her husband, while he was in Italy training with Espanyol) and had sat down in front of the television to watch the game – the World Cup final between Spain and the Netherlands at Soccer City in Johannesburg. It had taken her 11 months to be able to watch a football match again. This was the first game she had seen since the passing of her husband. It was her first match, and also the first game for her daughter – their daughter – Martina.

'I didn't watch any football. I never even turned the television on. I just needed to be in silence; in silence with my grief. But that night I decided to watch the final. Don't ask me why. I was at home with my mother and with Martina. She had still not passed her first birthday. She was only ten months old. I remember I had just had a shower and I had my hair rolled up in a towel and I sat down nervously in front of the television. It was the World Cup final after all.

'It is something Dani would have loved to do, surrounded by his friends. Maybe that is why I said to myself: "Am I going to watch it? Yes, I'm going to watch the final." My mother was looking over at me with a worried expression on her face and she kept repeating: "Are you sure you want to watch it?" She knew it was the first game I had seen since Dani left us, and she knew it was going to be tough for me.

'Watching a match without him for the first time would be an acceptance of my new life; a life without him. "Yes, Mum, I want to watch it." And there I was on the sofa. It is also true that I don't know a lot about football. I remember many times Dani saying to me: "How did I play?" That is why if he was playing away from home I would have my own ritual. I would need to be alone, I would put the television on and I would light some candles. I love candles, they transmit so much peace and serenity, and at the same time it is as if the light keeps you company. I would say to him: "You were very good, Dani." And he would say: "But I got everything wrong today, nothing worked out for me." I would say: "Well, I saw you a lot on the television." Other times when he asked me: "How was I today?" I would say: "Terrible Dani, I hardly saw you!" And he would say: "But I was brilliant today, everything went right for me!"

'In all honesty, I only watched the games because it was something I could share with him – his nerves, his excitement, his perseverance, and, in a way, share in every game his boyhood dream of playing football. I also tried to transmit positive energy his way. For all those reasons, I had not watched a game since he died. There was no one to share it with any more. And yet suddenly I found myself watching the World Cup final with Martina and my mother, Maria – sat down together for football's most important match.

'I knew something was going to happen seconds before the goal. I started to cry before Andrés scored it. I remember the moment when he receives the pass and he is all alone in front of goal. He scores, but by then I'm not watching, my hands are already over my eyes.'

Jessica stops telling the story and falls silent. Her hands are covering her eyes again. She is so full of light, but she is back in darkness once more, just as in those final moments when the ball arrives at Andrés' feet in the final.

'I saw him shoot, but then my eyes were behind my hands. Then I saw nothing else. The goal, and even more so the celebration that followed, made my mother shout: "Look! Look! Look!" But I couldn't look because I knew that Dani was going to be there. I didn't know how exactly, but I just knew. I knew the goal was coming; I knew Andrés would score it; and I sensed Dani would be there too somehow. Andrés could have dedicated that goal to anyone of those dear to him, to his wife, to his children, to so many people. But he dedicated it to Dani.'

Jessica, Martina's mother, struggles to string together more than a sentence without breaking down. She speaks, and then she cries. She cries and then she speaks a little more.

'Why did he dedicate the goal to Dani? I think that says a lot about Andrés but also about Dani – about what he meant and what he will always mean to those who had the opportunity to share their lives with him. It says something about the values he taught us, and his unforgettable gift of being able to live life to the absolute full.

'When I finally looked up, I couldn't even see the shirt that Andrés was wearing. My mum kept saying to me: "Look, look . . ." But by the time I'd raised my head again, they were all on top of Andrés and I couldn't see anything else. It was only afterwards, when I watched the replays, that I saw the message he had written for Dani. I have thought about it many times since. Why was Dani with Andrés that day? Why was I with them both watching that goal after such a long time disconnected from football? We were all in a different place, but we were all there together in Johannesburg. Heaven and earth brought together in one goal.

'You know, Dani did not have a single one of Andrés' shirts. They used to swap them whenever they played together, but then they would disappear.

There is not a single one left at home. I imagine that he would have many of Dani's, but that is normal because they are not so easy to give away.

'A Barça shirt of Andrés is always going to be in high demand. Friends would come to our house and if they asked for an Andrés shirt or a Barça shirt then Dani would give them one. He was very generous and never put too much importance into those sorts of material things. They were just shirts to him and if he could make someone happy by giving them an Andrés shirt then that meant more to him. He was someone without emotional hang-ups. The shirts belonged to Andrés, but they were just shirts. In contrast, the affection and admiration that Dani felt for Andrés stayed with Dani no matter how many of his shirts he gave away; they were not tied up in a piece of material.'

Jessica smiles her contagious smile constantly. But she also cries as she talks. They say time heals all. But it's not true. It heals nothing.

'Andrés is somebody who transmits tenderness and admiration. Sometimes when I am out walking with Martina and she alerts me to some new advert or billboard that features Andrés, she says immediately: "Mama, look, Andrés!" And she always does so with a big smile on her face. I don't care who someone is; it is more important what they transmit. He is one of those people who makes you happy that he is happy in life because he deserves it. Emotionally he is very intelligent; he's just one of the good guys. He has a lot in common with Dani. In this world that can be cold and materialistic, he stands out because he is just a simple, humble guy.

'I don't want my part of the book about him to be sad. Please, that is the last thing I want. Everything that we live through makes us who we are. And all the hard times in life that we overcome serve to remind us that we can survive and that we can be happy. He was in Johannesburg and I was in Castelldefels, but I just knew he was going to score that goal. I just knew it. There are some things that you can't explain. It is like when you love someone completely, there is always a connection that goes deeper than the physical. I don't know what it is, but there is something more.'

Suddenly, and thanks to that final, Jessica rediscovered football before returning to the loneliness of her grief. She cried at home and Andrés cried too out on the pitch. They were connected, and they remain connected.

● ● ●

When the game ended and the tears were still flowing, players with clenched fists, flat out on the turf of Soccer City, Andrés was joined in an embrace by his friend Victor Valdés.

In the Champions League semi-final against Chelsea, Valdés had been the last man to throw himself onto the pile of bodies celebrating Iniesta's late goal. 'When he took that shot at Stamford Bridge, I was shooting too,' he says. In South Africa, with his substitute's tracksuit on, he was one of the first to arrive. 'I crashed down to the turf and I saw the tears, and I ended up crying next to him,' says the former Barcelona goalkeeper who still refers to Andrés as his little brother.

'I don't know how to explain so much happiness,' reflects Andrés. 'It is just a feeling of infinite pleasure to have something that you always thought was just out of reach and suddenly it is in your grasp, after so many setbacks that season had stood in my path. But in the end, football pays you back for everything. If you work hard and you believe, and if you feel this sport and live for it, then it rewards you.'

Football took his hand during that horrible summer of 2009 when Dani departed and then it connected him to his friend once more. 'I owed him that. I never had the chance to pay homage to him and he deserved it. I wanted to share all the happiness I was feeling with him and with his loved ones. That is why, before the game started, I put that vest on.'

That is why he went looking for Hugo and asked him to write the dedication, convinced that the World Cup trophy, kissed by so many legends of the game, would soon be his to embrace. He was perhaps not counting on getting the goal, for all that he had spoken of scoring it to Carles Puyol, now the scorer of the second most important goal in Spain's history. The goal that meant he could elegantly, slowly, peel off his blue Spain shirt and reveal the message: 'Dani Jarque, siempre con nosotros.' ('Dani Jarque, always with us.')

He owed that game to Dani, his 'amigo periquito' (Espanyol's nickname is the periquitos – the parakeets). And as if directly addressing his friend he says: 'I regret not having made sure we saw more of each other, or that we spoke more often to each other, but I never imagined that life would be so unjust as to leave me without a friend like you.'

They lived in the same city but they were very different. One was the symbol and captain of Espanyol, the other became captain of Barça. They met in the Spain youth team, sharing a dressing room together at both Under-15 and Under-17 level. They then won the Under-19 European Championship together and played alongside each other again for the Under-21s.

Dani's heart never allowed him to make it to the senior side, but he will always be present in its most important goal. On that road to the top of their profession, Dani and Andrés became close friends, away from the pitch too, sharing the journey back from Barcelona airport whenever they returned together from international duty. 'He was a year older than me and we always got on really well. What is more, he became my taxi driver. He had a car and I didn't,' remembers Andrés. Football brought them together and at no time more so than in Oslo in July 2002 in a game that, although they did not know it at the time, would have repercussions for the future.

It was the Under-19 European Championship final. Iñaki Sáez's Spain were up against the German side coached by former Real Madrid player Uli Stielike. The game ended 1–0 with a goal from Fernando Torres – the same result, with the same scoreline and the same scorer as six years later when Spain won Euro 2008 in Austria. 'I really enjoy watching Iniesta, he is so good on the ball,' said the German coach hours before the final – one of the ultimate highs that Dani and Andrés would share. They were always together on that trip to Norway in which Torres scored the goal that gave them the title.

Stielike was right to pick out Andrés before the game. In the 54th minute he received the ball inside his own half, still 60 metres from the German goal. After two delicate touches Andrés nudged the ball over the halfway line and with the third he played the perfect pass for Torres who was already galloping into space behind the high German defence. It was the kind of pass that Stielike had feared. Torres was now running on to it between two German defenders who thought they had the situation under control, but reckoned without the finishing of 'El Niño' and his right-foot shot won the game.

The connection between the number 8 Andrés, the same number he would debut with for the senior side three months later in Bruges, and the number 14 Torres, worked to perfection, just as the pass from another number 8 Xavi Hernandez would assist the number 9, Torres again, to seal the first of three extraordinary triumphs for Spain's senior team in 2008. Memories inevitably crystallize around the 2010 World Cup, for Andrés especially, but that was the moment it all began. And there had been a forerunner to it years before.

Spain Under-19 coach Iñaki Saéz recalls: 'I first saw Andrés when I went to coach Albacete in the 1995–96 season.' It was his newly appointed assistant Ginés Meléndez who, in the middle of concerns about impending relegation, approached him one day to say: 'Iñaki, we are going to look at a kid, okay? Let's see what you think of him.'

Sáez recalls his first impression: 'He was a dwarf, tiny, really really small. But you know something? He never lost the ball once, and he ran the game exactly the way he wanted to, always knowing who was in front of him and who was behind him. I said to Ginés: "He is a natural."'

Sáez lost track of Andrés for a couple of years. He says: 'I found out through Ginés that of course Barcelona had signed him and then I started seeing him in the Spain youth sides, until eventually I found myself coaching him in Oslo. I remember it all so well. What is more, a lot of people told me not to take that job because I had been offered the senior squad. But I had a lot of confidence in those kids. I believed in Fernando and Andrés, in Jarque, and in the goalkeeper Moyà. I said to myself: "I'm taking these to Norway whatever happens." And then we got Germany in the final, the toughest team you could face as they proved. It was a real test. But we had a fantastic side. It was faultless.' Sáez knows a thing or two about great youth teams. He also coached the Under-20 team that won the World Cup in Nigeria in 1999 with Iker Casillas and Xavi as emerging talents.

He did not know it then but Sáez had, within that group of players, the first shoots of a new Spain. A Spain that would change the natural order of things, initially under the inspired leadership of Luis Aragonés, who was the first to believe in the 'little men' in midfield, and then under the generous wisdom of Vicente del Bosque.

'They had a good keeper, a couple of nice centre-backs, the clarity of Andrés in midfield, and the goals of Fernando. They had everything,' says Sáez. 'The winning goal was a bit strange, a bit scrappy, but it went in which is all that matters. Half the goal was in the pass from Andrés.' Sáez thinks back to 'that calm centre-back who resolved everything without a fuss, always helping his team-mates. Dani was a phenomenal kid. The Espanyol boys were always nice lads.'

That victory was only the beginning for Fernando Torres and Andrés Iniesta, two anonymous boys from Spain, one from Fuenlabrada and the other from Fuentealbilla. It should have been just the beginning for Dani Jarque too. But he was there in South Africa. Thanks to Andrés.

● ● ●

'I was five years old when I played for my first team, Parque 84,' remembers Fernando Torres. 'I took part in a marathon of football organized in the Fuenlabrada Sports Centre. The games were crazy – about fifteen or twenty boys, all chasing after the ball.' And while Torres chased a ball in a marathon of football in Madrid, Iniesta was doing the same in another corner of Spain, dribbling around the tables and chairs of the family bar. Torres started out as a goalkeeper and ended up a goal-getter, honing his skills every day in his neighbourhood and every summer on holiday in Galicia. For Iniesta, summer meant football and more football, from the school playground to the streets around his house.

The boy from Madrid born in March 1984 and the boy from La Mancha, born two months later in May 1984, started their international journey together in the European Under-16 Championships in England in 2001 although it would prove tough for both of them.

Torres injured his knee in a friendly in April of that year just before the start of the youth league. He thought he would miss the opening matches of the Under-16 Euros that would be his first taste of international tournament football, but he did make it. And Iniesta had stopped crying at La Masia by then. Just four months earlier Serra Ferrer, the then-Barça coach, had invited him to train with the first team. In just under four years he had arrived and now the Under-16 finals was another prize for his rapid progress.

Fernando and Andrés arrived together at Durham in northern England and got ready to discover a new world together: the lanky freckled forward and the tiny midfielder whose Spain shirt looked several sizes too big for him on all sides.

Andrés made friends with another Espanyol defender at that tournament, the flawless Carlos García who had originally made rather too much of an impression on Andrés when they first clashed. 'I injured him,' Garcia says. 'He was playing for Barcelona and I was playing for a Fundación Ferran Martorell XI. I challenged him from behind and caught him. I think he twisted his knee. We were thirteen or fourteen years of age, and I felt embarrassed more than anything. The following week I was walking down Travessera de les Corts and I saw him. We were on opposite sides of the road. And both of us, being shy, just acknowledged the other.'

They started seeing more of each other playing on opposite sides in the derby matches and they began to connect, with Andrés even staying over at Carlos' house. They became friends and that first meeting had long since been forgotten. Now as young internationals, they were enjoying their first European tournament together.

Coached by Juan Santisteban, the team kicked off their tournament by beating Romania 3–0 and Belgium 5–0. Then they faced Germany, the same Germany who both Iniesta and Garcia would beat years later as adolescents and then as young men. The Germans were prepared to stop Andrés by fair means or foul. Fair means didn't get them very far, so they resorted more to foul, and with ten minutes left Iniesta was finally scythed down and had to go off injured.

'They set out to hurt him,' says Garcia. 'We could hear the German bench make it clear how they wanted to stop Andrés: "Kick him, kick him." And they kicked him so much that in the end they kicked him off the pitch. It was a big blow because of what he meant to us in football terms and in terms of our own morale.

'Andrés was someone who generated a lot of affection from his team-mates. When you have a player who is clearly a level above those around him, but does not show that in the way he behaves, it makes him popular,' admits Garcia.

Spain were beaten 2–0, but they made it to the quarter-finals on goal difference. The problem was that they had lost Iniesta in the process. He would not play again in that championship. Torres was left all alone, Garcia too.

Iniesta returned to Barcelona disconsolate and with a badly sprained and swollen right knee. He was frustrated and worried for a Spain team that were now also without the injured Gorka Larrea who picked up a knock against Italy in the quarter-finals. But with the talented Diego León in the team, they still made it to the final and won with a penalty from Torres. Iniesta wanted to be in that game to support his team-mates who had dedicated their victories to him, but Barça would not allow it.

'Larrea was going to San Sebastián and Andrés to Barcelona. The Federation wanted them both to return so they could be with us in the final. La Real allowed Gorka; but Barça said no,' recalls Garcia.

Barcelona was an erupting volcano at the time. Joan Gaspart was the president, Rexach was the coach having replaced Serra Ferrer, and Pep Guardiola had announced his departure from the Camp Nou. There was more concern about the signing of the Argentinian Riquelme than the future of Andrés.

'You cannot go. The doctors will not let you.' That was the somewhat cold argument served up by the club. Andrés was heartbroken. 'I felt a sense of helplessness. I was excited about being a European champion and I wanted to be with my team-mates.' His team-mates did their best to make sure he had some sort of presence at the final. After scoring his penalty, Fernando Torres lifted up his Spain shirt to reveal a very special message.

'Fernando had written something for Andrés and for Gorka. Something similar to what Andrés would do for Dani at the World Cup in 2010,' reveals Garcia, remembering how both players suffered for not being able to play in that final. Gorka was in the stands; Andrés was at home.

'When the final ended in England, the team delegate kept Andrés' medal. But everyone knew what had to be done with it. Nobody had to say anything.'

So on arrival at Barcelona airport, Garcia completed his last mission of the tournament by delivering the medal to Iniesta. 'This is yours,' he said as he hung it around his neck as if they were both still on the winners' podium.

'Everyone knows that I have huge admiration for Carlos García,' says the Barcelona midfielder of his old Espanyol pal. 'We are very good friends and we don't have to hide it, despite the local rivalry.'

Just like the friendship he had with his Perico pal, Dani Jarque. The friendship he revealed to the world on that July evening in 2010. 'Dani was always easy-going and even-tempered. He had a personality very much like mine. Off the field he would joke around; on the field he was a player who always did the right thing without making a fuss. He was a future centre-back of the Spain team, but . . .'

It's a sentence he can't bring himself to finish, but theirs is a footballing friendship that survived all the way to Johannesburg where it was Andrés the midfielder, and Dani the centre-back. They played that final together. With Jessica watching in tears.

NUMBER 8

# 16

'That's enough. You can stop now, please. We're dead; you've won.'

*United player to Eric Abidal, Champions League final 2011*

There is still some way to go in the Champions League final at Wembley. The ball makes its way across the grass with the ease of a game in somebody's back garden. Andrés to Xavi, Xavi to Messi, Busquets comes to get it, again and again. Round and round it goes, Barcelona's most treasured possession. Alex Ferguson, the man who has done it all in football, can't find a way of stopping them. It is not for want of trying. He couldn't in Rome 2009 and he hasn't been able to since; two years later, United are set to fall in London too. Barcelona are about to become European champions again.

'The thing I most remember about that final is the last half an hour,' says Barça's Eric Abidal. 'The English players were angry, really furious, because we had turned Wembley into a huge *rondo* and there was nothing they could do about it. They kept swearing, shouting everything under the sun. It was incredible. Some of my team-mates couldn't understand them, but I could. "That's enough, stop fucking about. We're dead. And there are still twenty-five minutes left!" Xavi, Iniesta, Messi, Busquets, Alvés, who was practically a midfielder that day, kept going: *pim-pam, pim-pam, pim-pam.*'

Abidal doesn't so much talk about that game as commentate on it. Like the moment, the image, is burnt into his mind. It was, after all, one of the best games he played for Barcelona. 'Almost the perfect game,' he calls it. 'Not just because of the atmosphere at Wembley, not even because Puyol and Xavi did the most wonderful thing and handed me the honour of lifting the trophy. No. Those are mental images that will be with me forever, of course. But what I remember most of all is the football.

'For the first goal, Andrés plays the ball to Xavi. Xavi looks towards the stands but, with the outside of his boot, finds the run from Pedro. As Pedro shoots, Van der Sar goes down early, to his right, and the ball goes past him to the left. The second Barça goal is much the same: Andrés, Xavi, Leo, the three little guys combining to put us back in the lead after Wayne Rooney's equalizer. I don't really remember the goal from Leo, but I do remember him kicking the microphone.'

When it comes to Andrés, Abidal feels a special affection. 'He played just in front of me and he was forever getting me out of trouble. You'd give him the worst possible pass, an "English pass", and you knew he would still control it. You couldn't explain how but he would bring the ball under control and go past players, one, two, three, four or five of them, as if it was no problem at all. I was endlessly amazed by the way he seemed to be able to get the ball to do whatever he wanted, and then his ability to see everything that was happening on the pitch. He was always looking forward and yet he saw it all, every detail around him.'

At Wembley in 2011, Andrés reached his peak. He had often been decisive, but that day he was untouchable. It was the first final he had played pain-free. No stress, no concerns, no discomfort, this was a game he could actually enjoy as if he had been transported back to the playgrounds of Fuentealbilla. This time he could just play. Rijkaard had left him on the bench in Paris in 2006; three years later in Rome he was playing on one leg because of injury; in London in 2011, at last, he was in perfect condition. 'Andrés never says anything on the pitch,' Abidal explains. 'He just plays football. His quality talks for him. He never moans, even if he has more reason to moan than anyone else. The more they kick him, the more they try to wind him up, the better. For him and for his team.'

United's players never really got the chance to kick Iniesta, or Xavi or Messi. The ball moved too quickly for that; they were overwhelmed by the team in red and blue. When Barcelona are at their best, their play can be measured by a split second, by a single centimetre. The precision is such; the speed too. No one controls space and time like they do, Iniesta especially. United only committed 16 fouls in 90 minutes; they weren't able to commit more even if they wanted to. Once David Villa's goal went in, curling towards the top corner from the edge of the area on 69 minutes, United's fate was sealed. Ferguson's players had been chasing shadows, always arriving too late, never quite getting there. They didn't so much play, as follow the play. They were at the mercy of a Barcelona side that committed just five fouls, took 16 shots, 12 of them on target, and scored three times. And that in a Champions League final.

It finished 3–1 to Barcelona. There could have been no better homage to Johan Cruyff's philosophy, the one that changed Barça forever. 'If I have the ball, my opponent doesn't,' Cruyff said; Wembley expressed that perfectly. The English are said to have invented the game, but in their national stadium the biggest club in England only managed three shots, two of them off target. '*Pim-pam, pim-pam, pim-pam* . . . it was never ending,' Abidal says.

No one expected Abidal to start the game that night. Two months before, a statement from Barcelona revealed that he had been diagnosed with cancer. Doctors had found a tumour in his liver. That was 15 March 2011. The next day, he went down to the dressing room to see his team-mates, where he encouraged them, not the other way round. He was the positive one, the optimistic one. 'I'm a lucky guy,' he told them. 'They found it in time.' As he went into the operating theatre two days later, he joked to a team-mate: 'Hey, give me your liver. I could do with it.' After all that, there he was at Wembley on 28 May, as if nothing had happened.

'I never imagined that I would play in the final,' Abidal says. 'Not in my wildest dreams. The only thing I said to the manager was: "I'm available if you want me." But I didn't think that I would even be on the bench. In fact, I was happy just to have the chance to go to Wembley and support my team-mates from the stands.' But then in his last team-talk in the Wembley dressing room, Pep Guardiola changed everything. 'It was an hour before the game when he told me I was going to play,' Abidal remembers. 'He told me at the same time as he told everyone else. I couldn't believe it. What a surprise! I would have liked him to have warned me earlier, but those are the kind of surprises you like. And maybe it was good to only find out at the last minute, when you think about everything I went through between that moment and the start of the game.

'The only thought that crossed my mind was: bloody hell, don't be the player that lets them down; they'll kill you if you do. Imagine that, ten players in peak condition and you're the one that's not. I can't let that happen.' It didn't happen. 'I was lucky that we had such a great team,' Abidal says. 'Very lucky.'

'Abi's right,' Xavi recalls. 'Rooney came up to me before the end of the game. It must have been around the eighty minute mark, something like that. And he said to me: "That's enough. You've won. You can stop playing the ball around now."'

It was around then, too, that Carles Puyol (a substitute) came on, ready to collect the European Cup at Wembley, just as José Ramón Alexanko had done in 1992. It was a gesture from Guardiola that would end up not being fulfilled because Puyol was about to make a gesture of his own. He handed the captain's armband to Abidal, recently recovered from liver cancer, and sent him up to lift the fourth European Cup of Barcelona's history.

United's players stood and watched enviously, dressed in white. All bar one. Paul Scholes stood wearing a red-and-blue shirt with a number 8 on the back. The opponent that Barcelona's players admired more than anyone else, and whose shirt they had argued over, had been so overwhelmed by what he saw, so enamoured of that player who floated around the field at Wembley, that he had approached him before the end and asked for his shirt.

'Well, of course!' Abidal says. 'How could he *not* want Andrés' shirt? That's no surprise; it strikes me as the most normal thing on earth. I have one of Andrés' shirts too. One day, in thirty years' time, I'll open my wardrobe, look at that and think: "I played with Andrés Iniesta." There are shirts you don't show off, but that one . . .

'I'm convinced that if you asked the United players whether they knew that Iniesta was injured in 2009, none of them would have had the slightest idea. It's better if he's a hundred per cent, but with the vision, technique, experience and talent that Andrés has, even sixty or seventy per cent is enough,' Abidal says.

'Sometimes it is better to suffer some pain, because it shows you where your limits are. It's when everything is going perfectly that *bam!* something happens. I don't know why but injuries, muscle tears, always seem to happen when you're flying, when you least expect it.'

Andrés played through the pain in Rome, but when it came to that footballing cathedral in London two years later, he won the European Cup . . . and the admiration of Paul Scholes. At his home in Fuentealbilla is a wine cellar, and on the wall hangs a framed Paul Scholes shirt from that night at Wembley.

## TWELVE YARDS

*'Míster, I want to take a penalty . . .'*

*Andrés to Del Bosque, semi-final, European*
*Championships 2012*

Most coaches suffer during extra time at football tournaments. It's not easy to give orders from the touchline, and out on the field things happen, good and bad, that you can do nothing about. Time soon runs out, and then a piece of paper gets passed about. On it, the names of potential penalty-takers get written down, ready for the shoot-out.

It's easy enough to write them down; the problem comes when the final whistle goes and the manager can't find the five men on his list. Some refuse. Others offer to take one when they shouldn't and no one really dares to tell them not to, or to wait until the next round of penalties if it's still level after five each. It's not easy to stay calm in situations like that. Unless you are Vicente del Bosque.

It was the semi-final of Euro 2012 and Spain had finished level with Portugal. The coach had worked it out. He knew who he wanted to approach to take the penalties, when he found Iniesta standing there. '*Míster*, I want to take a penalty . . .' Del Bosque couldn't believe it. Neither he, nor any of the players, nor anyone else, could ever remember seeing Andrés standing over the penalty spot. Penalties are usually reserved for those who hit the ball particularly hard, or the cool-headed players out there, the ones who never get nervous. Cold-blooded characters, like snipers, and not angelical figures like Andrés: quiet, shy, rarely seen at set-plays, not expected to stand up and say: *I'll take one*. Not at times of tension and risk like that night in Donetsk, Ukraine.

'What I said to the manager wasn't the worst thing,' recalls Iniesta. 'Worse was that behind me was Sergio Ramos and he said the same: "*Míster*, I want to take one."'

Del Bosque froze; he knew that Ramos took penalties a little differently. His last one had come just a few weeks before in the Champions League semi-final against Bayern Munich and he had sent it sailing miles over the bar. Spain's European title was on the line in a penalty shoot-out, and here were Andrés and Sergio, two men Del Bosque didn't expect to step up and ask to take one.

'Okay, take one,' he said.

'In truth, everyone who took a penalty was doing so because he had offered,' says Del Bosque. There's little sense saying no to a player who is prepared to stand up and take a penalty at a difficult moment, who feels confident. Still less when it's a player like Iniesta: serious, selfless, not given to moments of madness or the tug of protagonism. Even if no one could ever remember him taking one for Spain or for Barcelona.

'The last penalty I can remember Andrés taking was when he was in *juveniles*, aged about seventeen,' jokes Jordi Mesalles, one of Iniesta's former team-mates at La Masia. Mesalles went from shock to fear as he watched Iniesta walk up in Donetsk. What's he doing there? Since when does he take penalties? And he, like everyone else, had forgotten something, something that made Iniesta stepping up now even more strange: he took a penalty on his Barcelona debut, in the Copa Catalunya against Terrassa when he was just eighteen . . . and he missed.

Well, not missed exactly. The Terrassa goalkeeper José Morales saved it that rainy night in May 2002. Barcelona, a club in reconstruction after the Joan Gaspart presidency, lost that final on penalties. And Iniesta was one of those who failed to score from 12 yards.

Xavi, a veteran and a leader already, always ready to intervene in bad moments, consoled him. 'Don't worry, Andrés. Anyone can miss a penalty . . . except the player who is not prepared to take one.' Iniesta barely heard Xavi, or the coach Charly Rexach, a man with a willingness to put football into perspective, quick to reduce the pressure and determined not to make a drama of the game. Instead, he went home and cried, alone. His father José Antonio couldn't comfort him and nor could his mother Mari. He still remembers it now. He also remembers how he overcame that moment.

A decade later, in 2012, Iniesta was confident enough to approach Del Bosque and ask him to let him take a penalty. Mesalles, watching on the television at home in Barcelona, put his head in his hands. 'Look, Dad,' he said. 'Look who is going to take it.' Neither of them could believe it.

In Donetsk were his mum Mari, his sister Maribel and her boyfriend Juanmi. But when that European Championships semi-final against Cristiano Ronaldo's Portugal went into extra time with the score still 0–0, Mari and Maribel left the stadium. They couldn't take the tension any more. How does that phrase go? *The heart doesn't feel what the eyes don't see.* Here was a chance to put that to the test. It turned out that it's not true.

Juanmi was nervous too, but he didn't move from where he was sitting. 'I suffer a lot but I can't stop watching, even if we're losing,' he says. 'I'm a masochist.' So he stayed to watch the shoot-out. 'You're going? I'm staying,' he said to Mari and Maribel. 'We might not see a shoot-out like this again in our lives,' he told himself.

And what of José Antonio? Iniesta's father hates planes. He doesn't usually travel to games. The Ukraine was too far away for him, so he decided to stay behind in Fuentealbilla, suffering alone, the way he prefers it. That way no one knows what he goes through but himself. He couldn't take the pressure either. As extra time came towards its end and penalties were inevitable, José Antonio turned off the television, left the house, locked the door and went for a walk around the town. Without his phone, of course. Isolated from it all. He had no idea what was happening across the other side of Europe. The hope and expectation, the fear of the Spain fan, overcame him. Whether you're in the stadium or walking alone in Fuentealbilla, the tension is the same.

Andrés took the second penalty. The first was Xabi Alonso, a specialist.

The first and the last tend to be your best takers, a guarantee when you need it most. Andrés watched Alonso from the middle of the pitch, along-side his team-mates, their arms round each other's shoulders. He had Jesús Navas to his right and Sergio Busquets, 'Busi', to his left. Alonso went left and Rui Patricio saved it. Even the best can miss.

Portugal's first taker, Moutinho, didn't score either. Casillas made the save to his right, feline as ever.

So then came Andrés' moment. Stubble on his face, a serious look, focused, all his thoughts on the penalty. He passed by Moutinho on his way to the penalty spot but didn't even see him, as if the Portuguese player was invisible. He picked up the ball, which had been left 15 metres or so outside the area, lifting it gently and carrying it to the spot in his right hand. Six seconds, give or take.

Casillas looked down. He couldn't watch. In the stands, Juanmi did. 'It was the first penalty I had ever seen Andrés take and I thought: "*Madre mía*, the responsibility! If he misses . . ."'

Back in Fuentealbilla, José Antonio didn't even know that his son was going to take one, which was a good thing for his health. Mari didn't either, nor Maribel. No one in the Iniesta family had the slightest idea. Only Juanmi. His sister and mother had left their seats, caught in the tension, waiting for news to come through from a friend of Maribel's. Arian told them that Andrés was going to take a penalty. 'Yes, really, a penalty.'

Mesalles watched on television, surprised. None of the commentators could explain it either. No one could remember him taking one before.

Andrés put the ball down on the spot slowly, carefully, softly, but without emotion. Routine. He lifted his head, looked at Rui Patricio, and took a few steps backwards. He went back so far that he was outside the area when he began his run-up, almost as if he wanted to distance himself from it all. In two and a half seconds, he travelled back to his childhood.

'Yes, that's true, I took it the same way as I had in Brunete, didn't I?' says Iniesta. 'I hadn't realised that. I didn't think of it.'

They were identical: the same movements, the same gestures, the same run-up, as if 16 years had never passed. There was just one difference. At the modest Los Arcos de Brunete stadium with its AstroTurf pitch, Andrés wore white, a number 5 on his back, with his name, Andrés. In the huge, state-of-the-art Donbass Arena in Donetsk, with its perfect grass pitch, he wore the red shirt of Spain with a number 6 on the back, 'Iniesta' too, and a star stitched on the chest: world champion. Otherwise, it was the same. Calm, focused, and precise with his shot, to the goal-keeper's left. Not too close to the post, but away from the keeper. Even the celebration was very similar. In Brunete, engulfed by a giant shirt on such a small frame, he lifted his left arm before his team-mates leapt on top of him and you couldn't see him any more. And in the Ukraine, he clenched his left fist repeatedly. Rui Patricio had gone the other way. Spain were 1–0 up.

Juanmi says, 'When Andrés scored, I turned to the Portuguese fans to celebrate the goal, but then I thought: "Careful, this isn't over yet. There were three penalties left still and if they win, they'll eat you alive."'

Despite the emotions flowing through him, Juanmi resisted the urge to cheer. 'But I wasn't scared and I didn't back down. I was alone, but I watched all the penalties. I didn't cover my eyes.'

Juanmi saw the goal that José Antonio didn't, the one that Mari and

Maribel missed too. Sara Carbonero didn't see it either. Sara was the touchline reporter for Tele5, the channel broadcasting the game back in Spain. She is also Iker Casillas' partner.

'Did you never think that you might like to take a penalty? Or is it the manager who decides? Would you have liked to have taken one tonight?' she asked Andrés after the game, Spain's passage to the final secure. The national team were on their way to a third final in a row, and their second European Championships final, from Vienna to Kiev via Johannesburg. Andrés, patient as ever, looked at Sara, bemused. He lowered his head a little shyly and replied: 'Yes. In fact, I took the second. At the end of the game we decided who was going to take them and fortunately it all turned out well.'

The gentleness of the response didn't make the question any less surprising. Realizing what she had done, Sara knew what was coming next. 'Thanks, Andrés,' she said. 'And Andrés' penalty will be all over Twitter tomorrow. I was so nervous that I have no idea what I was thinking . . .'

She was nervous, but Andrés wasn't. Not before, not during, not after. Only he knew he was going to take it, and he probably thought that his dad, his mum and his sister weren't even watching. He might even have thought to himself, a little mischievously, that Mesalles and his other mates would get quite a surprise when they saw him there standing over the spot.

'There are moments in your life when you have to take responsibility and I like to do so, more than ever before,' Andrés says, happy that he surprised Rui Patricio . . . and the people who know him best. No one expected Andrés to take a penalty, or to score one.

Since that night, he hasn't taken another penalty.

LUIS ENRIQUE

'I have bad news for you, Andrés.'

*Luis Enrique*

'Again boss?'

*Andrés*

Luis Enrique may be his current coach at Barcelona, but there was a chance meeting between him and Andrés way back in February 2001 when Andrés was still at La Masia.

'Remember it? No, I have no recollection at all,' says Luis Enrique. 'I don't remember that it was me who picked up Andrés at the Camp Nou barrier when he was only 16 years old. A couple of years later he told me himself. There were several boys from La Masia and they were not allowed to pass the gate. It was Antonio Calderón, the security guard at the stadium entrance, who asked me to give them a lift in my car. But the lucky one was not Andrés, it was me who got to take Andrés down to the Camp Nou dressing room,' says Iniesta's improvised chauffeur on that winter's morning.

He would become a team-mate of Andrés, and then his coach. 'When the kids came up from the youth system, the only thing we wanted to do was to make their lives easier,' Enrique says. 'If you see a guy like Andrés Iniesta, your only thought is to help him. You put yourself in his place and you don't even need to look at him to know he is scared witless. It's normal. Arriving in that dressing room is a big thing. You look at him and you say: "Take it easy, we are going to look after you." We were only doing what we would have wanted done to us when we were in that position.' Enrique remembers only too well how certain 'charming' senior players had dished out less than favourable treatment. Something that is all too common in many clubs.

He had no idea who Andrés was. 'I know that some of my team-mates knew him. They told me that he was one of the best players in the youth team, a real gem. But I didn't know anything about him,' confesses Enrique, whose foggy memory is now starting to clear. 'At the beginning they all came together to training: Xavi, Puyi, Gabri, Andrés. What stood out to all of us was how small they were,' says the Barça coach. 'The smallest players in Cruyff's dream team were Chapi (Ferrer), Sergi or Juan Carlos but they were all full-backs.'

Suddenly these small players were beginning to pop-up everywhere at Barça. In spite of their size they would become beacons at the club. 'They may have been small but they were great players. Even if it did take them a while to get the opportunity to show it as first-team regulars. When I left the club aged 34 in 2004, Xavi was being heavily criticized. They wanted to get rid of him. Now everyone that criticized him back then only has nice things to say about him – that he is the soul of Barça – but they wanted shot of him back then. Right up until 2008,' says Enrique in reference to the year when Xavi helped Luis Aragones' Spain team win the Euros.

'They have not always realized the extraordinary player that Xavi was; an incredible talent. They have changed their tune now and are lifelong Xavi fans. Something similar happened with Andrés Iniesta,' he says recalling those difficult early days for Iniesta.

'Andrés has that same ability as Xavi to keep the ball, but he also has the ability to go past people. He can dribble; he has a change of pace. Xavi will spin on the spot, make others play, and he has such great vision. What is more, Xavi could arrive in the penalty area, he was such a great player. Andrés adds that ability to go past people to all that he shares with Xavi. He maybe could score more goals; maybe shoot more, but then you think about the really important goals he *has* scored. They are both incredible. But Andrés is pure magic. We call him Harry Potter. He casts his spells on the pitch. I have never seen anyone do what he does.'

Suddenly, Luis Enrique wants to clarify his glowing assessment. 'Well, I have seen one other player do the things that Andrés does. Leo Messi of course. But those elastic controls that Andrés does are just things of beauty. It still happens to me in the training sessions. He does things that I have never seen before nor believe I will see anyone else do. Sometimes he controls the ball without even looking at it. *Bang!* He kills it dead without so much as a glance. And that is just in training. He is at another level, there is no doubt about it. There is no one like him and there never will be another like him. Now that I'm a coach, I get to see him every day. *Madre mía! Madre mía!* It's a privilege, a real privilege to be able to experience it,' he says.

'And then if you add the professionalism, which is exceptional, when you consider that because of who he is, he could be the most high maintenance player there is, his human qualities just complete the whole package.'

To think that there were some who said that the silky skills of Andrés would be out of place with the dynamic aggressive football that tends to be played by Luis Enrique's teams. 'The people who said that did so with bad intentions; people that don't know me,' says the Barça coach, who is far closer to the football philosophy of Guardiola and Del Bosque than it seems. 'All coaches like players with quality. For me, it is an absolute pleasure being able to train Andrés. What is more, I want to emphasize the importance he has to a team, as much through his performances as through the titles won. I remember after one of the games at the Euros in France, I sent him a message: "Andrés, they are praising you for something that you do every day for Barcelona. It's incredible. You do it in the games and in the training sessions. It's because they don't see you for Barcelona. You have done all these things you are doing now, during the last two seasons."

'It is also true that Andrés has been intelligent and this is something I would like to thank him for, because it is something I have put a lot of emphasis on. I know that Andrés wants to play all matches, but he is a player who needs to be looked after so that he is just right when the key games come around. It's only normal that a player wants to play all the time. Sometimes I tell him: "I have bad news, Andrés." He responds: "Again, boss?" And I tell him, "Yes, yes, yes!' But with the data at our disposal, thanks to the GPS vests after every training session, we have the information to guide us. "You should play the key games and the matches when we really need you. But I am not going to risk Andrés Iniesta," the coach says to the captain, who has, as Del Bosque argues, been capable of reinventing himself over the last few years.

'It's true that in some games the easiest thing for me to do is to just play him,' says Enrique. 'Let him play! But then I think: "No, I'm going to take care of him! Even if there is a greater risk that without him we could lose this game." But I do not want to risk Andrés. He has understood that and accepted it. He has made my life easy. And in the end he looks in better shape than ever, without any doubt. He is so important to us, scoring goals, being key in everything. And when I say everything, I mean it. Working hard, winning the ball back, setting the example that only great players can.'

That is why Luis Enrique treats him like a rare diamond. 'There will come a day when his brain tells him that it's over. But until that moment, we have to lengthen his career for as long as possible. If we were to do a comparison with another sport, Roger Federer will play tennis at the age of sixty just as well as he does right now, because it's no effort for him to play those rallies, he doesn't run or sweat. It's a bit like Andrés Iniesta. The football pitch is a bit bigger than the tennis court and you have to run a lot. But if you look at the numbers of Andrés, they are spectacular.

'For me, the moment that defines Andrés is not even a goal. It's against PSG here at the Camp Nou in the Champions League. Anyone else would not even dare to think about it, but he does it (the almost 180 degree turn in the penalty while he dribbles at full speed) as if it's the most natural thing in the world. He does it like changing the TV channel with the remote control. It's all second nature to him. That is Andrés Iniesta. I also remember in the Bernabeu, we were winning 3–0 and we were playing without the best, without Messi. So Andrés drops out wide on our side of the pitch, right in front of the technical areas. And he has his back to the ball as it comes to him and he flicks it with the back of his heel. I said: "I've seen everything now, everything. Unbelievable!" But again it's that impression that he gives that it all comes so naturally to him. It's football in its purest sense.

'It makes me so happy that this guy has gone as far as he has, and that he remains such a great example to kids. We have to look after him, we have to enjoy him, and we have to make his career last as long as possible, until he says that he can play no more. He still has plenty of time left. He will be playing, and what is more captaining Barça, for many years to come.'

## GUARDIAN ANGEL

*'There were two days to go until the final and I said to Luis Enrique: "This guy doesn't even need to train. Relax, Luis, he'll be fine in Berlin."'*

Xavi, before the Champions League final 2015

'We can't lose this final. Please, no. I couldn't say goodbye to Barcelona with a defeat in the Champions League final. But I felt like the stars were aligning. We'd won the league at the Camp Nou, the Copa del Rey at the Camp Nou, and now we were going to Berlin. There was no way we were going to lose this.'

Xavi Hernández played more games for Barcelona than anyone else in history, and his time was finally coming to an end, with three matches to win three titles. He had been the architect of arguably the best club side and the best international side ever, but, at 35, his final season was different, his role reduced. He was now decisive off the pitch, where once he had been decisive on it. His opportunities to play were fewer now and he knew it. It was hard getting used to his new status as a substitute, handed down to him by Luis Enrique: a friend, a team-mate, and now his manager. But even from the bench, he led. Even from there, he saw things that others did not. He understood the game better than anyone.

That understanding of the game encapsulated his team-mates as well. 'Andrés was in a bad way as the Champions League final approached,' recalls Xavi. 'It wasn't like in Rome where he was injured, but he had these constant niggles and discomfort that just wouldn't go away.' He took it upon himself to support Andrés, to encourage him. He'd handed his captain's armband to Iniesta, and in the build-up to the final he spoke to him constantly.

His were not empty words. 'Don't forget,' Xavi says, 'if Andrés had not been fit to start the final, I would have played. It was my final season and Luis Enrique was using me as the replacement for Andrés, to the left of the middle three, rather than to the right where he wanted Ivan Rakitic to provide cover for Leo Messi and for Dani Alves.'

A central midfielder at La Masia, Xavi had found his natural place further forward on the right of a three thanks to Frank Rijkaard, or as a midfield all-rounder under Luis Aragonés, the Spain manager who led the country to the title at Euro 2008, when Xavi was named player of the tournament. Now, in his final season, he found himself on the bench, back-up for Iniesta.

'There were two days to go until the final and I caught up with Andrés just as Luis came over to us. "How are you, Andrés?" the manager asked him. Andrés was barely going at 2 mph in training sessions, which was logical enough as he was worried that something would happen if he pushed it. That's when I said to Luis: "This guy doesn't even need to train; this guy has to play the final, and that's that." I looked at Andrés and said: "Don't push it. Relax, you'll make it." His head was spinning. That happens to any player in the build-up to a Champions League final, but Andrés is even more susceptible. That head of his . . . round and round it goes. "Don't worry, Andrés, you don't even have to train . . . and Luis, leave him be. He'll be fine, you'll see. He's going to be in great shape for the final."

If he was going at 2 mph at Barcelona's training ground, by the time he reached Berlin, Iniesta was flying. 'Just look at the very first move . . . *madre mía!*' Xavi says, as he looks back on that moment when Iniesta went past Juventus – tough, experienced, talented, *defensive* Juventus – and provided the opening goal for Rakitic, the man who had replaced Xavi in the team.

One-nil up with four minutes gone and Iniesta had already made his mark. Neymar's precise pass inside to Iniesta and from him to Rakitic. Two swift touches, that's all it took to unlock their opponents, even if Xavi did wonder why Andrés didn't shoot. In truth, they all wondered that, even Juventus' players. He was on the edge of the six-yard box after all, close to Gigi Buffon's goal. But then, at the last moment, with a subtle flick of the ankle, he had tricked them all. Rakitic scored.

'After they equalized, the Italians really grew,' Xavi admits. 'We should have reached half-time with a bigger lead. And after they scored, there were moments when we were nervous. They had Tevez, Pirlo, Marchisio, Morata up front, moving well. But I was still sure that we were going to win. If you had asked me in November, I would have said: "We're not going to win anything." But if you asked me in February or March, it would have been different. By then, I was thinking: "We're flying." It was an incredible way to end my career there. My last league game at the Camp Nou ended with us as champions. Then, a week later, we won the Cup there too, against Athletic. I wanted to share that moment with Andrés.

"Come with me, Andriu!"

"Where?"

"Up there, to get the cup. I want you to lift it with me."

"What are you talking about, *maqui*?"

"Come on. Both of us together."

And he came in the end. It was the way I wanted it; he deserved it.'

There they were together, Andrés and Xavi. It turned out that they did work pretty well together. So many people had said they wouldn't. Fans, journalists, analysts . . . there was no shortage of people who said that Xavi and Iniesta couldn't play together, as if their individual talent would cancel each other out somehow, as if they were incompatible.

'We can't play together . . .' Xavi laughs. 'When you look back on that debate now, you think: "My God!" That must have been hard for Andrés, but I'd heard it before. They had said the same about me and Pep Guardiola when I first came through. Then when Andrés came through, they said it about him and me. They said that there was only room for one of us: him or me, fine, but not both. They said we didn't defend, we didn't fit in the same midfield . . . blah blah blah . . . All that did was to make us mature that bit quicker; it made us stronger. And we're stronger than people think we are.

'We proved them wrong. In the end, the more talent you can bring together the better. Later on, people even tried to say that Busquets couldn't fit in that midfield. They said he couldn't defend! Some didn't want him to go to the World Cup either. But Andrés, Leo Messi and Busquets are the best players I have played with in my career. I enjoyed playing with them more than with anyone else.'

There was a moment when Xavi was on the verge of leaving Barcelona, though. In fact, there wasn't *a* moment, there were a few of them. And every time. Maria Mercé Creus, Xavi's mum, intervened. Andrés could have gone too, but he stayed as well.

So Xavi and Andrés played together as one. 'We didn't even need to say anything to each other,' Xavi insists. 'At most, I might say: "Andriu, come a little closer", or something like that. No more. Andrés isn't the kind of player who likes to spend the whole game talking either and we understood each other perfectly, almost just with a look. He always offers you a way out, he always gives you options, someone to pass to. He has a lot of character, even if it might not look like it. He looks small, feeble, but he's not . . . no, no, no. Not at all. On the pitch, he is a natural leader, even if he is a quiet one. He never hides. He knows exactly what to do at every moment: when to accelerate, when to slow, when to run, when to pass. He uses space in a way that makes it impossible to get the ball off him and impossible for the opposition to occupy the spaces they want.

'He comes towards you in a straight line and then at the perfect moment *pam!* he's off to the right or the left. Before you can react, he's gone. You're broken, beaten. Andrés isn't dribbling at you as much as bullfighting you. That change of pace breaks through lines on the pitch, eliminating opponents from the play, it panics them, scares them . . . and then he sees that final pass like no one else. He knows better than anyone whether the right ball is inside or outside. Those of us who have played at Barcelona, who have learnt there, read the game in a very particular way, but with Andrés it's natural. It's intuitive. Right now, he and Busquets represent that Barcelona DNA. Then there's Messi, who's a different case. But Andrés and Busquets carry the weight of responsibility for Barcelona and Spain.'

Once Xavi starts talking, there is no stopping him. He's a passionate defender of a particular vision of football. He calls it 'romantic', but in a sense it is the most pragmatic of all; he is convinced that this is the way to get results, too. Barcelona and Spain never won so much as when they played his way. Andrés' way. The idea was non-negotiable.

'That style is not easy to defend, to champion,' he says. 'You have to win over coaches, fans, the press, everyone. It wasn't easy for us, both for Andrés and for me.'

There is no doubt in Xavi's voice. 'He's a force of nature, a phenomenon. There's no other Iniesta and nor will there be. What other player is there out there with a style like his, still less the same? No one plays like him; no one can be compared to him. And as a person, he's the perfect role model: noble, honest, generous, altruistic.'

Xavi departed but he left Iniesta. One day, Iniesta will have to go too, but he will leave Busquets. More than just a generational shift, it's the passing down of a footballing philosophy, an idea that has changed the club and the Spanish national team.

'Andrés is still competing, he will keep winning things with Barcelona.

He is going to break every record there is. When you leave the Camp Nou, you realize the magnitude of what you have done. That's when you understand the significance of everything you do there. You appreciate the affection they have for you there. Everywhere I go, people talk to me about Andrés. Wherever you are: "Iniesta, wow . . ." People say to me: "That midfield with you and Iniesta. My God, what a midfield!" I'm proud that everyone associates me with him. I like the fact that people always say to me: "Xavi-Iniesta, Xavi-Iniesta, Xavi-Iniesta." There was a TV programme that did a report on us together. It's as if we were one, a single entity. Actually, we are. I'm proud of that. We've gone from people saying that we couldn't play together to being the same person. People even get us mixed up sometimes. "Eh, Iniesta . . ." and I say: "No, Iniesta is the other one. The one who can dribble, the one with the change of pace." They see us as a couple, two players as one.

'Sometimes I get the feeling that Andrés doesn't realize how important he is. One day, when he retires, he'll see the magnitude of what he has done. I remember the Copa del Rey final against Sevilla in 2016 after I had gone, I sent him a message to congratulate him, because he had produced a brilliant performance. "What was that?! That was unbelievable!" There was the 4–0 at the Bernabéu against Real Madrid too, earlier in the same season. My God, that was incredible. "What is happening to you?" the message said. He was a machine. I almost felt jealous not being there when I saw that. What a performance! What a way to play! How I would have loved to have been out there with him, playing the ball around. That was one of the best displays I can remember from Andrés and from Barcelona. I didn't really see Guardiola's Barcelona play, because I was out there on the pitch myself and it's not the same from there, but that 4–0 was the best. It could have been 7–0. I was practically drooling watching it.'

They have experienced a lot together, even the winning goal in a World Cup final. 'Sometimes I can be sitting at home, alone, and suddenly that goal will come to mind. We owe Andrés so much; we should be saying thank you to him every day. If it had gone to penalties . . . who knows what would have happened. Do you know what it is like to lose a World Cup final on penalties? Seriously. During extra time, those thoughts started going through my head. "Where should I put the penalty? That Stekelenburg, how big is he?! He must be two metres tall. What can I do against that? Right? Left? Through the middle?" And all that with the game still going on; you're trying to play, still struggling, but you can't get the penalties out of your mind. I kept reminding myself that with Barcelona we hadn't been through a shoot-out in a final yet; we'd won them all before getting to that point, apart from the Copa del Rey final against Madrid that we lost. So I felt like I didn't really know what awaited, what to do. "*Madre mía*," I thought. "We won all our finals . . ." And that was when Andrés scored. I won't ever forget that moment. I think about Andrés' goal all the time.

'I still get goosebumps about it. I remember the moat that surrounds the pitch at Soccer City. If you look at the celebration, you'll see that we were all down in the corner, right next to the moat. And I almost ended up in there. I was crying, overwhelmed. It's impossible to describe the sense of happiness I felt. I was in the middle of the pitch when it happened, but it was like I had a front-row seat. I know Andrés has said it before, but I had that same feeling: that sense that when the ball sat up in front of him, time stopped. Everything froze. The ball went up . . . and down . . . it wasn't easy to control but Andrés did, even though it moved oddly as it dropped towards him. His control was good, even if the ball made it look bad. Up it went and then as it came down again I was thinking: "Yes, yes, yes . . . Andriu . . . yes, yes . . . this is it, the goal!' And it was. The goal, *the* fucking goal. Andrés was decisive at Stamford Bridge, in the Champions League final, in the World Cup final. Incredible.

'Andrés has a gift. He has a guardian angel . . . *is* a guardian angel,' Xavi says. 'He appears when it matters. There are people who have that. Iker Casillas, for one. Andrés, too. When you need him, there he is. And me? I'm proud to be associated with him, and you must not forget Busi. People refer to that midfield as Xavi-Iniesta-Busquets. That midfield will be eternal, remembered for ever, for the way it played, and what it won.'

SECOND HALF

From the Touchline

## THE OTHER INIESTAS

*'When I see him play, it is as if I am watching myself still playing.'*
*Michael Laudrup, on Andrés*

'If you could choose one player from this Barcelona team, who would it be?' Juan Riquelme was asked in March 2013 in an interview given to the newspaper *Olé*.

There was a long pause and then he answered: 'It is difficult just to take out one . . . But if you are only going to let me pick one, then I would go with Messi. But if I can pick more than one, I take Messi and Iniesta.'

'Is Iniesta the most "Riquelmista" of the Spanish players, or is it more that you are the most "Iniestista"?'

'No, Iniesta is special and somebody that I have a lot of time for. I speak with him from time to time. I was annoyed because I could not go to his wedding, but that night I was playing the final of the Libertadores with Corinthians. Thank God he is there to ensure that Messi can just relax. Messi can play the ninety minutes so close to the rival's goal, because Iniesta takes on the job of getting the ball to him. He is the perfect team-mate for Messi, because he allows him to have ten or fifteen minutes without touching the ball and yet always knowing that it will arrive.

'He [Iniesta] is the one who takes care of making the team play. He is the one who you watch and think: "Look at the way Iniesta plays! No one can get the ball off him!" And eventually Messi takes the ball and finds a way through the rival's defence. If Messi goes ten minutes without touching the ball for Argentina, they say that he doesn't want to play for his country. But it's because we don't have an Iniesta. At Barcelona, if Messi goes ten minutes without seeing the ball, Iniesta takes care of entertaining everybody in the meantime.'

Riquelme, an exquisite player in his brief time at Barcelona, is now infatuated with Iniesta. 'He is still the best,' he repeated in another interview this time given to DeporTV. 'He shows us how the ball should be played. Ronaldo and Messi are different to the rest because they are so quick. But Iniesta sees the game from the thick of the action, as if he was looking down on it from high in the stand. He does everything well. Every time he plays, I feel obliged to watch him. When he does not play, Barcelona cannot play either.'

Riquelme offers up an even more graphic illustration of Iniesta's magic in an interview with ESPN: 'It is as if you are driving on the motorway. If there is a crash ahead of you, what do you do? Do you keep going or do you look for the alternative route. You turn around, don't you? You don't head into the congestion. Iniesta does the same. If there are a lot of people here, then he goes there. The only player who heads into the congestion is Messi. He goes in at one end and comes out with the ball at the other end, scoring a goal that even he doesn't know how he scored. He goes home and watches it on the television to get a better idea.'

The former number 10 for Boca clinches his argument when he says: 'I can't misplace a pass, I play the ball first time, I see things very simply, If I control the ball badly, then I get annoyed. Football is control and pass, control and pass. It's about the ball. Iniesta teaches us how to use the ball. You can see it when he plays. If he sees the number 4 is unmarked, he gives him the ball. He makes things simple.'

● ● ●

David Silva says of Iniesta: 'We are similar.' His Spain team-mate from Manchester City adds, 'We are both introverted; we don't like to talk too much. Perhaps that is why we get on so well together.'

Just like Riquelme, Silva loves watching Iniesta play. 'When I see him train, I say to myself: "This is something else. This is just on another level." It's spectacular watching him out on the pitch. Some of the things he does, you just can't believe.

'And he never loses his calm; that is what really astounds me. It doesn't matter if it's a training session or a game. It's no coincidence that he scored in the World Cup final. That goal reflects perfectly the essence of Spanish football. I was not lucky enough to play in that final, but I experienced that moment of huge relief from my place on the bench, and as a substitute it is always worse. I never thought we could win the World Cup but we did; and two European Championships too.

'The tranquillity that Andrés has, I have never seen in anyone else. I think he was just born that relaxed. It's in his nature. I have never seen him lose his calm. Just maybe once, in the World Cup final, when he was kicked two or three times from behind by Van Bommel. But we were lucky and he stayed on the pitch.'

Silva loves to talk football with Iniesta. 'When we finish training we stay a while to talk about life and football. You always learn something.'

On the pitch they have a very special understanding. 'Whatever state the game is in, even if the team is really struggling, you can always give the ball to Andrés. Then you stop worrying. You know it's in safe care. That is why I identify so much with him and with Xavi and Santi Cazorla. We are just the little guys who love to have the ball at our feet.'

There is one thing that Silva especially likes about Iniesta. 'It's the way he turns. I think that is what makes him really unique. It's incredible, because he turns and in a space of no more than two or three metres he's gone. The defender tries to stop him, but there is no way they can. It's crazy what he is able to do with that turn. He knows how to read every stage of a game and he can interpret each situation with intelligence. He does it perfectly.

'He has been able to overcome a lot of obstacles, and that is something that people and especially young kids coming through should be aware of. I can identify a great deal with Andrés and the way he is.'

● ● ●

Admiration and respect are also something that Santi Cazorla feels for his Spain team-mate. 'He is always the player I have looked up to since we met at Brunete when he was playing for Albacete and I was there with Oviedo. Then we were together in the Under-21s and we really got to know each other properly at the 2008 European Championships.

'I went straight into the squad of twenty-three without having played a single game before with the senior side. Luis Aragonés picked people such as myself, De la Red, Sergio García and Fernando Navarro. And Andrés always helped me; he is always there for you even though sometimes you don't realize it. When you are injured, he is the one who asks you how you are. He is a player but very much a person too. I consider him, alongside Xavi, as the greatest player in Spain's history. I adore him as a player and even more so as a person, because he is just a simple, humble guy.

'As Guardiola said: "He has no tattoos, he doesn't have any special look." He is the perfect player, but he doesn't consider himself to be any sort of football or social icon. But he is. He doesn't realize the magnitude of his football or what he means to Spain and to its young people.'

Cazorla adds: 'If you are on the bench and you see him, you think: "This guy never ever gets nervous." He plays at walking speed sometimes. The pressure never gets the better of him. "What pressure?" he says to us in the dressing room. He has this air of not being at all worried about anything. He's completely relaxed.

'He sees things that the rest of us don't see. When there seems no way out of a certain situation, he will end up finding the way out. You have to value him for his play, for his goals and for what he brings to Barcelona and to the Spain team. We have to enjoy every moment with him. Even Messi knows that he is the best in the world because he has Andrés close by.'

Finally Cazorla sums up: 'But over all that, I'll take Andrés the friend, the simple guy who has never let success change him. He is the perfect example for young people. I always tell my son: "You look at Andrés. Look at how he is as a person, how he handles the fame, how humble he is." It is a pleasure to share time with him. I'm grateful that he has always been by my side in good times and bad. He is a true friend.'

● ● ●

What about Andrés? Who inspires him? There is no question that one of the players he was most influenced by when growing up was the Danish maestro Michael Laudrup.

'Many times I have been asked: "Michael, does it bother you that they call Andrés the new Laudrup? And I have responded: "Completely the opposite. If they are talking about a new version of someone, then that means there was first an old version who did things well. It's not up to me to say who is like me. Everyone is the way they are." But what I would say is that sometimes you see a player and he does things and you see yourself in the way he plays. Iniesta is an example of that.

'The truth is, when I see him play it is as if I am watching myself still playing. I say that because of the way he moves. The way he dribbles, dragging the ball from one foot to the other, away from an opponent, "La Croqueta" as it was called when I did it. These are the little things that evoke memories of the way I played. At first I didn't know too much about him. People started to tell me there was a kid who based his game on mine when I was at Barça, and that he was even trying some of the things I did as a player. But I didn't really know what they meant until I saw him play.'

Laudrup emphasizes 'La Croqueta', something very few footballers have been able to do so well. 'I remember Onésimo, who played for a while with us at Barcelona, used to do it, but he did it a little bit differently. As Andrés has said, "La Croqueta" is a piece of skill that exists not because it looks nice but because it serves the purpose of setting you up for the next pass.

'It's a movement of the ball from one foot to the other. For example, you take the ball with your right foot and you knock it against your left foot, which acts as a wall, and then you play your pass. With just one touch you set yourself up for another pass, or another dribble or whatever you want. It is not difficult; at least it does not seem difficult. The difficulty comes when you have to do it quickly, surrounded by opponents. You might have someone pressing you from the front, another one from behind, and then a third player to one side. Unmarked and with time, anyone can do "La Croqueta" but to do it quickly when you are surrounded is the hard part. And if you look ahead of you without looking down to see where the ball is, it is even more difficult. I'm surprised that there are not more players who use it, because it works. Andrés says much the same thing – that he does it because it is effective.'

The quality that Laudrup most admires in Iniesta is his football intelligence. He explains this in a very visual way. 'How do players see a pass? There is the player who sees the pass that everyone can see, even those watching the game in the stands; another thing is whether or not it comes off but the player sees it. Then there is the player who plays the unexpected pass: everyone thinks that the ball is going in one direction and he sends it in the other. And then last of all, there is the third and most difficult pass: the one that goes through an almost non-existent gap or into a space that nobody has even seen. Andrés can play all three types of pass.

'Lots of players are capable of playing the first one, and the second one. But very few are able to play the third pass too. It's the most difficult. It is not just down to you; it's your team-mate too. And there we enter into another world, one in which one has to see not just the pass but also the player who will receive it. Everything is easier if the other player is as intelligent as the one playing the pass. It happened to me in my era with Txiki Begiristain. I would drop deep quite a way from the area and then I would put the ball in the space for Txiki. He was the smartest of players and he would move just at the right time to arrive as the ball reached him. Then he would provide the cross for José Mari Bakero. We scored so many goals that way; so many that we ended up saying: "We have scored more than 40 identical goals and we never get found out."

'It happens now with Andrés and his team-mates, whether it's Messi, Neymar, Suárez or previously Villa and Eto'o. It's because they have played together for so long and the connection works. That is why for these strokes of genius you always need at least two players: the giver and the receiver, the one who sees the pass and plays it, and the one who receives it and finishes the move.

'The two have to speak the same language. One intelligent player on his own cannot do it, he needs an intelligent team-mate. Then if you ask them how they have done it, they will not know how to answer you. There are many things that you can coach, almost everything in fact, but this . . . either you have it or you don't. And another thing: sometimes there are footballers who are intelligent in life but not on the pitch and vice versa. One type of intelligence has nothing to do with the other.'

Iniesta and Laudrup have spoken many times about genius and intuition. The Dane recalls: 'Andrés says: "The more I think, the more likely I am to make the wrong decision." I understand him because it happened to me too. One game in Albacete, I picked up the ball and played a pass through three defenders for Romário, that he then failed to finish.

'One of the Albacete players approached me and said: "Did you really mean to do that? Tell me the truth." I just stood there looking at him, I didn't really know how to answer him. And the funny thing is, as the game carried on he didn't stop asking me the same thing until finally I answered him. "Well, of course I wanted to put it there, what do you want me to say? If I have to start explaining how I did it, I can't." It's the same for Andrés and for all these players that have this special gift.

'We are talking about Iniesta when he has won everything, but he was already playing this way when he was ten years old. Now he plays like a central midfielder, he plays differently. He has some of the same traits, but he has others that are different. But for me it is a source of a lot of pride that a player like him has gone as far as he has, after starting out where he did.

'And when I see him play the ball off of one foot on to the other I am reminded of myself. It is just so rare that you see that. There is another move that it is now more common: to look in one direction and pass the ball in the other. I remember when I first did it, people would ask me: "What are you doing?" And I would answer: "Tricking my opponent." It's a trick that works in football and in life too. You improvise. There is no book on it. There is no recipe to warn players of a pass played in one direction when the passer is looking the other way. As Johan Cruyff always said: "The simple things are the most complicated. The first-time pass is the easiest, but you have do it at high speed which makes it the most difficult."

'Andrés' game reminds me again of Cruyff when he said that you play football with your head; with your brain. We also need players with courage and legs, but the ones that go the furthest in this game are the ones that think. Physique is important but not as important as touch. Forty years ago Iniesta, Messi, Guardiola, Amor and Milla would have had problems playing because of their physique, but today it is different. There are coaches who will tell you: "What is the point of a player who wins the ball 40 times if he is going to give it away 41 times?"

'I remember the day of the [World Cup] final we were in pre-season with Mallorca in Sweden. The team bus was going no faster than 90 kph and the players were following the game on their computers and iPads. I asked the driver if he could step on it a bit, but he said no way. We got to the hotel when the game was already at half-time, so we were able to see it properly from the second half onwards and we all saw the goal. Andrés takes a step back before he receives the pass. Any other player's natural instinct would be to attack the space so as not to arrive late or have a rival take the ball away, especially as the goalkeeper is coming off his line and the defenders are trying to cover. But he takes a step back from goal.

'It seems like the ball is never going to arrive before the covering defenders. And what is more the goalkeeper is coming off his line. The normal thing is to have an overwhelming desire to attack the space and make sure you get there first; to not be able to wait any longer. But Andrés waits for the ball to travel its course.

'The ball seems to hang in the air and the World Cup final is going to depend on what decision he takes. The problem is you have time to think about it when the best thing would be to improvise. Arjen Robben, for example, had too much time to think when he was running with the ball towards Casillas. Two or maybe three orders came into his brain: "Shoot to the right" or "shoot to the left" or "hit it straight down the middle." You are dead when that happens to you; there are too many options. Iniesta, however, was still able to take the correct decision. Right there in that hanging ball was victory itself.'

## BLUE AND CLARET

*'Come closer, I want you by my side.'*

Lionel Messi

He speaks slowly, in no hurry. If it is to talk about his friend Andrés, he has all the time in the world. Training is over and Leo Messi appears showered and relaxed. 'I heard people talking about Andrés virtually from the moment that I arrived at Barcelona. I didn't meet him at La Masia. I would go there to eat but we rarely crossed paths because I was preparing for my *Bachillerato* exams at the time. There are three years between us. Then I saw him more in training sessions than in games. But he has always been the same, as a person and a player,' he says.

There's something about Andrés that Messi admires, something that makes him seem almost ageless. 'I always picture him with the ball at his feet. That's the way I have got used to seeing him. He does everything well, with simplicity. At times, it may look like he's not doing anything, but in fact he's doing it all. Everything is different with Andrés. The hardest thing to do in football is to make it look like everything is easy, effortless, and that's Andrés.

'He has more contact with the ball than me; he's the person who starts moves, who gets things going. I know how difficult it is to do what he does. His play is different, it comes from when he was very little, even though he has clearly improved over time and with different coaches. Maybe you could say that both of us have something of the street in the way we play.

'When you're a kid playing on the streets you take on board things that are very useful to you later. You get used to playing with older players and not changing your game because of that; you play your way. Andrés and I are similar in that we both use our bodies a lot, to avoid opponents. But he has something that always amazes me: there's always a moment when you think you're going to catch him, when you think you're going to get the ball off him, but you can't. He's not especially quick, but he has that ability to always get away from you, which comes from his technique.

'We're more similar in the fact that we don't talk much. He sits in one corner, I sit in another. But we cross paths, we connect; with just a look we understand each other. We don't need more than that. On the pitch, I like him to be near me, especially when the game takes a turn for the worse, when things are difficult. That's when I say to him: "Come closer, I want you by my side." He takes control and responsibility; he leads the team. In the finals, Andrés, Xavi, Busquets and I have always liked to come together to give us a numerical advantage, to control the ball and the game. We've experienced very happy moments together and I particularly remember an emotional embrace at the Bernabéu after a goal. That was a lovely gesture from him.'

Messi is talking about the moment when Iniesta scored the third to put Barcelona 3–0 up against Madrid in the 54th minute of their meeting early in the 2015–16 season. As the ball hit the net, he turned and ran towards the bench to embrace Messi, who had started as a sub because of injury. Now, they are the club's two captains. 'That's lovely after so many years growing up together,' Messi says. 'We understand each other very well; we don't need to shout, we know. When Andrés talks, it's to crack a joke or to say something very specific at a particular moment. And then you listen. We have come to trust in each other a lot, we have gained in confidence over the years and we speak out more than we did, we let loose more. He's an admirable person, very humble despite being a magical footballer. Everything he does with the ball is incredible, and he seems to do it all as if it was nothing. Everything's natural to him.'

*'Slow motion.'*

*Neymar*

'I wanted to go to Barcelona since I was young to play with Messi, Xavi and Iniesta,' Neymar says. 'I watched them play and thought to myself: "One day I'd like to be out there with them."'

Neymar loves to talk about Iniesta. 'Of course!' he says. 'He's a phenomenon, a genius, a *craque* as we say in Brazil. A superstar. Football should be happy to have someone like him; we're lucky he wanted to play this game.' Neymar is a beach footballer, while Messi and Iniesta's influence comes more from the streets and the playgrounds of their childhood, then from La Masia. Yet there is something that is the same. 'I was happy with a ball, an improvised goal and that's it,' he says. 'I didn't need more.

'When the ball reaches Iniesta's feet, I feel at ease. I think we all share that sensation, that sense of security. Sometimes friends from Brazil call me and they say: "This guy must have ice in his veins! He's never nervous. Ney, get a syringe and stick it in his arm to see." He never seems overwhelmed or under pressure. He always has the right solution and he has the technique to ensure that when the ball reaches him it does so in the right conditions.

'He always guides me; he tells me what I have to do, he helps me take the right decisions,' Neymar says.

The Brazilian also says much the same as Messi: 'When the game turns difficult, I say to him: "Andrés, come closer to me please. More, more . . . closer . . . as close as you can get." The way he plays, that kind of happiness he conveys, the expressiveness of his game, his talent, makes him look like a Brazilian player. An old-fashioned footballer, like there used to be, among the best there has been.

'You watch him play and it looks easy. The way he dribbles, it's like it happens in slow motion. It looks slow, but it's happening fast. Fast, but slow . . . does that make sense? Slow motion football, but quick, that's Andrés. He loves to play right on the line; some players get nervous when they find themselves there with no space and then they're hasty and make mistakes. Not Andrés. He's running out of pitch, the ball is going out of play and there he is, happy as anything, dribbling with such ease and naturalness that he leaves you open mouthed.'

Andrés the player impresses; Andrés the person does too, all the more so now that he is the captain. 'You can feel his presence when you need him. He doesn't have to do the things others do to get themselves noticed. It wasn't easy for me to share a dressing room with players I admired. When I saw myself in the dressing room with them, I felt as if I was stuck inside a computer game. But Andrés has helped me a lot since I arrived. I admire him as a player and a man.'

> 'One day he said to me: "What's going on? You don't get on the end of any of my passes."'
>
> Luis Suárez

Luis Suárez wanted to play for Barcelona, just like Neymar. As soon as he knew that Luis Enrique was interested in him, he asked his agent Pere Guardiola to stop talking to other clubs and to negotiate only with Barcelona. Pere Guardiola's Mediabase company also looks after Andrés, which helped to bring them together even when they were at clubs as far apart as Liverpool and Barcelona. They shared a lot, even when they hadn't actually met.

'I still remember how surprised my [Uruguay] team-mates were when I celebrated Iniesta's winning goal in the World Cup final,' Suárez says. 'I was shouting so much that they asked me why. I told them that my daughter was going to be born in Spain.' Suárez's wife, Sofia, was eight months pregnant at the time and was staying at her parents' house in Castelldefels, just outside Barcelona.

Luis contacted Joel, who looks after the players represented by Mediabase, and asked him for Andrés' number so that he could send him a message to congratulate him. 'We exchanged messages. We'd never met but through those messages we built a relationship of trust. Even my wife asked me once how come I followed his career so closely when we hadn't even met. We didn't actually meet until a Spain–Uruguay game in Qatar. And from there we were even closer, until I finally joined Barcelona.'

Andrés was the first person Luis spoke to when he arrived in Barcelona. 'He even told me to take the locker next to his in the dressing room; he was the first to contact me, the first to put me at ease. He's like me in many ways: we're both family people and because we're similar we quickly got on. I'll never forget the message of support he sent me when I was accused of racism while at Liverpool. It surprised me that he took the time to send it. One of the most important people in football contacted me: that message meant more to me than the praise you get when you score.'

When Suárez turned up for his first training session at Barcelona, there were two *rondos* going on, piggy-in-the-middle exercises. Andrés asked him which one he wanted to join: the Spaniards' group or the foreigners' one. Or, to put it another way: the fun one, or the other one. 'So I went with him, to the fun one. He welcomed me with open arms. He looked after me throughout that session. There are similarities with Steven Gerrard at Liverpool: they're role models, important figures in the game, people who have a particular way of understanding football and life, people to learn from. Andrés is admirable, someone I will always be grateful to.'

Time has brought them together; Suárez has found that beneath the serious exterior, there's a joker inside Andrés. 'You have to get to know him and he has to get to know you. And it's not easy to be in sync on the pitch when you're talking about a midfielder of short passes like him and a forward like me who looks for balls behind the defence, who stretches the game more. You need to give it time. One day he said to me: "What's going on? You don't get on the end of any of my passes. I can't do more for you! What do you want from me?!" I froze. I didn't know what to say. And then he burst out: "I'm joking!" I didn't expect it; his sense of humour is very much his own, dry, and it can take a little bit of tuning in to; you don't always realize he's joking.

'I remember another time I sent him a joke by SMS and I ended up getting a bit worried because he didn't reply. I thought that maybe I'd upset him. It wasn't until later that he replied. There are times when you're sitting having lunch and Andrés throws one of his jokes into the mix and just carries on eating as if he hasn't said a word. He's the same in the *rondo*: if he plays a poor pass that you can't control, which he doesn't do often, he doesn't look at you. Instead he acts as if it's your fault. Nothing to do with his pass, of course.'

For Suárez, it's easier to decipher Iniesta on the pitch than off it. 'He expresses himself with the ball. You think you're going to get it off him but you never do; you watch as, at the last second, he pulls it away from you. He's done you, yet again. It doesn't matter if you go at him from the side or from behind. You can sneak up on him silently, thinking you're going to nick the ball off him, but he always escapes: suddenly, he's off in the other direction, going the opposite way to what you expected. And you're left chasing shadows. When he gets the ball, I leave him to get on with it. I'm out of there.

'And he does it all so effortlessly, there's something so natural about it. It's an honour to play with Leo and Andrés and they have something in common too. It's a dream come true for me. I really enjoy it.

'In part, I see a bit of me in Andrés in terms of the effort. It hasn't been easy for either of us to make it. We have had to persevere and we've both had to rely on our families. He's a great father, too. I'm quieter off the pitch than people think: I might look like a madman at times, but I'm a different person away from the game. Much calmer. Andrés has treated me so well and I really appreciate that.'

> 'Andrés and I know that we're not going to let each other down. That's our code.'
>
> *Sergio Busquets*

Serious in character, lovers of home life, sons of long-suffering mothers. Captains of Barcelona, too. Iniesta and Sergio Busquets have many things in common. 'We have had similar experiences,' Busquets says. 'There is a certain similarity between the way our parents have lived our careers too. We're footballers who don't feel overwhelmed or under pressure on the pitch or off it; neither of us want to be famous, nor will we turn our backs on our families or the simplicity of our lives away from the game. We admire each other and understand each other just with a look. We're not talkers, we don't shout, we hardly open our mouths, we just watch in silence. Maybe that's a Barcelona thing: we're a bit quieter, more reserved, shy even. We're not interested in making a scene; we prefer just to get on with it. Andrés and I know that we're not going to let each other down. That's our code. It's not easy to reach that level of complicity. It depends on the way you play but also on your personality.

'You need to know how to struggle, how to wait, how to remain strong, to work and have patience to reach the top. Then, to stay there, you need concentration, focus, to avoid distractions and always place collective goals ahead of personal ones. Don't cause problems. One day when we were with Spain in Armenia we came across each other in the dining room. We'd been given the day off by the coach, but both of us had decided to stay in the hotel anyway. We thought it better to recover, eat well, rest as much as we could. We weren't there on holiday; we just had a few hours to ourselves to forget that we were footballers for a bit. If I'm not playing, I take a siesta, try to switch off.' Busquets says. 'You need to be mentally strong and you have to be a perfectionist, improving the things you do badly. Of course, doing all that at a club that really feels like it is *your* club is doubly difficult. It's more likely that you will take your problems home with you. Andrés and I always try to be positive.'

An example: 'Last season [February 2015 at the Etihad] when we beat City 2–1 we got into the dressing room disappointed at the penalty that Messi had missed right at the end that might have settled the tie. Everyone looked down, as if we had lost. But then we had to turn that round, change the attitude and the atmosphere. That's part of being a winning team too.'

It's not just Barcelona that Andrés and Sergio talk about; other teams are on the agenda too. Other sports, in fact. And, more importantly, life away from sport. 'When we see each other away from the club, we never talk about football. And when we're "on duty" we don't really need to talk about it; we know what's required.'

When Andrés suffers, so does Busquets. 'When he gets injured, he's a different person. When he can't help out, he struggles; he has a bad time of it. And that's when you are closest to him.'

*'He's a silent killer.'*
*Dani Alvés*

Dani Alves could hardly be any more different from Iniesta . . . but that's the way the extrovert Brazilian likes it. 'We're night and day, different worlds, but a nice mix is important for any team. You need a balanced squad. And you also need a madman. Barcelona educate their players, but I'm not a gentleman; I'm a competitor,' Dani says.

'It's impossible to have a bad word to say about Andrés. He teaches you daily, with humility. I have so much respect for him. Maybe people don't appreciate how important he is because he has been there for so long, because we have followed him all the way through, but the day he retires people will realize that he is one of the greats. We don't celebrate his performances as much as we should, because we know that the next game he'll be just as good.'

Alvés likes nothing more than playing against Andrés in training because he sees that as the best way to prepare for a game. 'He makes you work really hard: stop, start, turn, always alert. He completes your preparation: if you play against him in training, you're more than ready for the game,' he says.

'Andrés is one of the hardest players to mark. I can compete in a foot race when I have to, when I'm up against a winger who's really quick. But Andrés can dribble past the fastest defender. He's skilful, agile and he can change direction superbly well. He has a rearview mirror and he always knows where you're going to pressure him and how to avoid that. Even if you tip-toed up behind him he would know. He'll spot you and before you know it he's gone off in the other direction.

'In some of his movement he reminds me of Thierry Henry. He would look at me and attack when he saw me relax. Andrés is the same. They always turn away from you, taking the ball to the other side, and then the shift between gears and acceleration is phenomenal.'

For Alvés, Iniesta is the prototype Barcelona player. It's not enough just to be good at football, to have talent, you also have to understand the game. And that is what makes Andrés different and what makes Barcelona different too. You know that when you have a problem you can pass the ball to Andrés and he'll find a solution; the same happens with Leo. His role is as an *interior*, rather than an actual wide midfielder doing a lot of running for the full-back, but he could play in any position except goalkeeper. He's a silent killer; when he does take a shot on, you know the ball's going in. And then there's that dribble on the byline or touchline which is impossible to work out. It looks like he's going off the pitch when in fact he's going past his marker. That's the magician Andrésinho.

'Andrés is a great captain too; he doesn't need to shout at anyone to gain their respect. I turn a deaf ear to those who scream and shout. He's the opposite. He's quiet but that doesn't mean he just accepts things. He understands everything and he approaches football and life his way, everything flows around him. Even when he gets angry, he's quiet, although you can tell: he speaks that little faster and his voice resonates a little more.'

*'He has that ability to move in the tiniest space . . . like playing on a single tile.'*

*Javier Mascherano*

'I remember facing Andrés at the Under-20 World Cup. As he was playing just behind the forwards and I was playing as a defensive midfielder, we crossed paths a lot that day. And back then, even though we were only little, Andrés already stood out. He was the player who made the difference.

'Iniesta is different to the rest, an attacking midfielder who can get moves going, break through defences, tilt the balance in a game and help out defensively. It's hard to find a player like him. There are lots of footballers who play in the same position as him, but none of them are the same.'

Mascherano thinks Iniesta has a gift. 'When I arrived at Barcelona in that first season, I talked to Guardiola about it a lot. I talked to him about

Andrés' ability to trick you with his body. He carries the ball to one side, calmly, with his head up and you don't know what's coming. He doesn't really dribble at you with the ball; he does it with his body. He can keep going in a straight line but he pulls you away from his path with the way he moves. The ball doesn't even need to change direction. It's special.

'Everything he does is so lovely to see, so aesthetic, that it lights up the game. Everything he does looks good. Every technical detail. There are very few players who give you that pleasure when you watch them. Maybe Zidane, although his elegance was of a different kind. The other day I heard Xavi say: "I'd love to have had that change of pace that Andrés has, one on one. When I have the ball, I can turn away from people and not lose it, but Andrés kills you when he accelerates away." Andrés hypnotizes you, he pulls you in, attracting you with the ball at his feet and then, when you draw closer, you suddenly lose sight of him. As a defender, I struggle with that. He looks slow but he's not. He looks weak, but he's not. There was a player in Argentina, Ricardo Bochini, who was similar. On a different level to Andrés of course, but similar in style. Physically, he looked weak, but you just couldn't get the ball off him. Andrés keeps the ball glued to his foot; there's never more than ten centimetres between him and the ball, it never escapes him. He's like Leo. It's almost as if the ball was part of their body, attached.'

Players can't help but pick up on that same quality. 'Andrés plays in the middle of the pitch where you have little space and a lot of opponents on top of you,' Mascherano says. 'And above all you see it when he gets to the byline or out on the touchline. There are so many of his moves where there is no space between the opponents and the line but where somehow Andrés finds a way through. I don't know how he does it, but he does. He has that ability to move in the tiniest space, doing it all in a twenty centimetre by twenty centimetre square – playing on a single tile, as we say here. You see him do it and think: "How did he get out of there?!"

'The problem with seeing Andrés every day is that you get used to it and you start taking it for granted; you don't value him as highly as you should. When you share every moment with him you're not conscious of what he is. It's like life; you get used to a good thing. But then you see other players and you think: "Pass it to me the way that Andrés does, please." They're not the same. That's the problem with being at Barcelona and surrounded by players like this. When I go to another club I know I'm going to struggle because it won't be the same; I'm never going to be given passes as good as I get here. And when I pass the ball to others, they won't control it and use it like my team-mates here do. Here, the ball travels at the right speed and at the right time and reaches you in the right position. A little further forward or a little further back makes all the difference; it conditions everything. Maybe the average fan doesn't notice that, but we do. We notice if a player delivers the ball well, helping you out, or if he causes you problems. That matters, especially at the élite level.

'I'm the kind of person who opens up easily, from the start. And Andrés is a big football fan, he loves the game, just like I do. So when you share something like that, when you can see that in someone else, it's easy to get along. We talk about football, although not only that. We're the same age, we have been through a lot of similar experiences, the same difficulties to get where we are. People remember the last seven or eight years of Andrés' career, but he had to earn those the hard way. In my own way, I had to fight too before I got here to Barcelona. It's been a long journey and so has his been, even if he was always here. It would have been easier to not keep going, to give up. But he's been chosen by football; he has something special. Not just the talent, not just technique or tactics, but temperament too. It's about your head as well as your legs. To be at a club like this for so long, you have to be very strong mentally, much more so than people realize.

'Beyond all those titles, beyond the fact that he scored the most important goal in his country's history, beyond all that, what defines Andrés is that he has always kept his feet on the ground. He has never changed. If you can take that all on board and do it so naturally, that makes you a great. Any other player and it might have slipped from his hands or gone to his head, because we're humans with egos and vanity and weakness. But he has somehow avoided that, managing to continue on the same line as ever. At difficult times and at the best of times, he has been the same Andrés. That's laudable, a model to follow. We should seek to emulate people like him.'

Mascherano and Iniesta are like a throwback, players from the past. 'Yes, we are,' he agrees. 'We've got no tattoos, no earrings, nothing like that. And I'm not saying that is a bad thing. Who am I to tell people how they should dress or look?! But it is true that in that sense it can feel like Andrés and I are from a different age. We love football, we love what we do and that's it. We'd rather avoid all the stuff that comes with football and just play. Every time we talk about football, Iniesta and I seem to find that we have more in common with each other.

'Real leadership doesn't come from words, it comes from the ball. You earn it on the pitch. That's where your team-mates come to respect you. If you offer nothing on the pitch, however much you talk, however much you fight, however much you gesticulate, you won't earn that respect. Andrés is a leader. He's like Leo. They earn respect.

'On the pitch we talk more than people think,' Mascherano insists. 'He's one of the players I most talk to on the pitch; we depend on each other, on the passes we play. I have him just in front of me, so the communication is there. When I have the ball I need a way out, someone to play it to, and Andrés always offers me that.'

Mascherano didn't come through La Masia like Iniesta, but he has become a determined defender of Barcelona's footballing faith, their philosophy. It started with long conversations with Guardiola. 'Andrés was one of Pep's weaknesses, a player he loves. He used to say to me that it wasn't just the talent; he loves players who play with passion, who really love football. He doesn't like those who take advantage of their profession, but those who give everything to it. Guardiola is a football romantic. He loves that amateur element of the game, its original spirit, more than the way the modern game is set up. He talked so highly of Andrés because he was prepared to do what the game asked of him. He wasn't there to show off, or be flash, or to pose, or to promote himself; he was there to play. Pep used to always hold up Xavi and Iniesta as an example for that very reason.'

*'He knows he is important within the dressing room, and that gives you a certain power.'*

*Gerard Piqué*

'Andres is different to all the rest,' Gerard Piqué says. 'If you judge him by statistics using the *Moneyball* logic, no one would sign him because he doesn't score many goals or provide a lot of assists for someone who plays in an attacking position. But can you imagine Barcelona without him?

'The team changes hugely depending on whether or not he is playing; the way we play, the way we bring the ball out from the back to the forwards, is very different. When he is on the pitch, everything flows; when you see that you realize that he's irreplaceable, so important that Barcelona don't play well without him. The statistics are cold, impersonal, lacking empathy or understanding; they don't reflect what Andrés means to us. It's not about numbers; he projects feelings that can't be measured or quantified. That's the play, the football, the feeling that Andrés always gives you.

'We've always got on very well. Obviously, we're radically different, but we're entirely compatible. Puyol was an introvert too, like Andrés, and we were brothers. You need to find a balance, and at Barcelona we have done that. We have a brilliant group, we get on very well and I think that shows on the pitch. There's always been chemistry with Andrés. The relationship with him hasn't changed since he became captain. He has always been a player who has a lot of influence over the squad and he handles that naturally, the same as he always did. He doesn't try to impose any more than he ever did before. If he was chosen to be captain in the players' vote, it's because we saw something in him that we liked and we want him to go on being the same person. One thing is true, though: he has improved when it comes to talking to the media. He is more comfortable now, and has more to say.'

And if Iniesta had not been a footballer? 'He'd be anonymous,' Piqué says.

'Maybe he'd been running a newsagent's or working at a bakery. He is very humble, a small-town guy, but he's different to the Catalan version of that, to people like Puyol who are strong, powerful characters, more than capable of shouting "fucking hell" at you. No, Andrés isn't like that. But that's one of his great virtues. He's happy just being with his wife and children; if it wasn't for the fact that he's a footballer, you wouldn't notice him. Over time, I think he has come to realize who he is and what he represents, I think he's perhaps not as naive as he was when he joined the first team. He knows that he is important within the dressing room and that gives you a certain power. The question is how you use that power. Andrés always uses it for good.

'The thing that most stands out for me about the way he plays is the way he sets off, that first movement with the ball; his acceleration from an almost standing start, that sudden shift in gears,' Piqué says. 'Those first ten metres are incredible. When he moves, it looks like the defender is slow. He's not, but it looks that way. I've seen him take on extremely quick defenders over the years and none have reacted quickly enough to prevent that sudden surge. It's magical the way he suddenly pulls away; I don't think I have seen anyone else do it like him. One second he's standing there, or jogging and then . . . *whoosh!* he's gone. There are other players, some of the best wingers around, who produce tricks, who do four step-overs, but don't actually go anywhere; they don't leave the place they started. Andrés is the opposite: with one touch, or no touch at all, he's escaped and left you looking daft. So simple, so impossible to stop.

'I've seen Andrés' goal in South Africa so many times on the television that I've almost forgotten what it was like to actually live the moment in the stadium. It's as if I am watching a different move. We were scared of the game going to penalties. We had to make the most of them being a man down, we didn't want that opportunity to pass us by, and in the end Andrés was the chosen one. It's not about luck. It happened at the World Cup, at Stamford Bridge, at the Bernabéu. He has that charm, that ability to generate key chances and finish them well when it matters most. That's the way he is. I'm sure that he'd send the ball flying into the stands if the same chance that fell to him in the World Cup final fell to him in a smaller game.

'Andrés' range of passing is incredible. He can switch the play with his right foot and his left, he moves the game. When he's at his best, everything revolves around him. He's a very safe player, even though he plays in a position in which the typical footballer loses the ball fifteen or twenty times a game. With him, it's different: he barely loses it at all. That's the kind of thing that people don't see but his team-mates appreciate. He sees things the rest of us don't and, like Xavi, he's always turning as the ball comes towards him, looking around to ensure that he knows where everything is. When I played in midfield at Zaragoza, I tried to do that but I was never really able to. I'd turn to look and they'd take the ball off me. That never happens to Andrés. In training I try all sorts of things to try to catch him out; I sneak up behind him, I try to hide from him then surprise him, nicking the ball away. But that bastard always escapes. He always sees me somehow. I don't think I've caught him yet.'

> *'Andriu makes everything easier.'*
> *Jordi Alba*

For Jordi Alba, it's not Andrés, it's Andriu. Andrew, in other words.

They met with the national team in 2011, just after Spain had won the World Cup. 'On the day of my debut for Spain they gave me number 6,' Alba remembers. 'Andrés' number. That day he was injured and when he came back, I gave it up again. Of course.

'Playing alongside Andrés is fantastic. It's very easy to understand him and he gives you a lot of confidence. Andrés makes everything easier.

'A couple of years ago I suffered a lot of injuries, for the first time in my career; I'd never, ever been injured before. And Andrés was one of the few that really helped me out, along with Xavi. Every day they asked after me. I'd be on my way to a scan or to do some tests, and they would be messaging me to wish me luck. Imagine how important that was for me, a new arrival at Barcelona suffering an injury for the first time. That tells you that they're good, generous people. They know that when you're injured, your mind matters as much as your body.

'At Euro 2012, Andrés and I combined very well on the left for Spain. Andrés trusted me and gave me the ball whenever he could. That filled me with confidence. He understood the way I am too: we're totally different characters. Thinking about it, Busquets has a touch of both of us. One thing we all have in common is that we've not really changed. We still do the same things we always did. When I left Barcelona's youth system and went to Cornellà, the temptation to leave it all behind was very real. But I wanted to keep going. Andrés does too.'

*'You could chuck a melon at him and he'd control it perfectly and play.'*

*Marc Bartra*

'I met him at seventeen. I remember seeing him in the dressing room with Carles Puyol. It felt like a different world; they felt untouchable. But now I can proudly say that he is a friend of mine. Sometimes you need to force the words out of him he's so quiet, but once he is comfortable with someone it's different; he'd surprise you. When that happens, he's fun, with a great sense of humour, and he plays on that impression people have of him. His sense of humour can be dry, and sometimes quite dark. You don't know if he's messing with you or not. That's how he catches you out.

'One day, during the first half of a game at Vallecas against Rayo, back when Tata Martino was the coach, we were sitting on the bench together just behind the linesman and we kept on at him, giving him an earful. When the half-time whistle went, Andrés approached him and said: "Don't take any notice of them. They're a bit over-excited, pretty nervous. There's a lot riding on this." I could hardly believe it because if anyone was moaning about the refereeing, it was Andrés. When I said that to Andrés, he said: "Don't worry, I've seduced him. You'll see how much better they are in the second half now." Andrés isn't daft; he knows how to use the respect that people have for him.

'I also remember a time just after I came up to the first team,' Bartra continues. 'He made sure that he looked after me a bit. Slowly, we were getting to know each other, the trust was growing. It wasn't easy for me, I was having quite a hard time of it. I was playing very little. And one day

I got a message from him: "It's Andrés. Chin up, things will get better, for sure. You're training well. Keep going. All the best!" I didn't have his mobile number so I assumed it was a joke, someone winding me up. So the next day I asked him if it was him who'd sent me the WhatsApp message. "What's WhatsApp?" he said. It was only a couple of days later that I found out for sure that, yes, it was him. I really appreciated the fact that he sent it, that he put himself in my shoes, even if he didn't admit it.

'Andrés has his little tics, too. In the morning, they sometimes lay out fruit for us, or smoothies, and he's the only one that eats coconut. If you see a weird-looking sandwich lying there, you know it's his. He's quiet, but there's a spark there. You can't help thinking that he's silently plotting something.

'I asked him once: "When did you finally become a regular starter?" He said at twenty-three or twenty-four. I told him that I'd played a few games at twenty-one already, so I should be satisfied. And he said: "I'd played a few at your age too, Marc. Don't let them pull the wool over your eyes; don't let them keep selling you that line." That made me think: "Next time someone tells me to be patient, that it took a long time for Andrés to make it in the first team, I'll tell them that he was playing at twenty-one."

'When Andrés is not on the pitch, you miss him,' Bartra continues. 'You can chuck a melon at him, an impossible pass, and he'll bring it down, control it, and play.

'He's also very sensitive. It can't be easy to come to Barcelona at the age of twelve from Fuentealbilla. I came daily by taxi; it wasn't the same. Just an hour and a half each day. And I moaned. There are some people who wish you ill because they're struggling. Andrés is the opposite. He has been through the bad days and wants the best for you because he knows how hard it can be. Maybe he thinks: "If only someone had helped me back then . . . well, I'm going to help them now." That's Andrés.'

> *'He took it upon himself to call the president . . . and persuade him to let me go.'*
>
> Pedro Rodríguez

The tridente arrived and Pedro left, his opportunities limited. He'd been a scorer of unforgettable goals, like those against Shakhtar and Estudiantes de la Plata which helped Barcelona to end 2009 with six titles out of six, but Messi, Neymar and Suárez left him with fewer minutes than ever before and seeking a way out. Pedro just wanted to play. The problem was that Barcelona would not let him go. Not until one of his best friends picked up the phone and rang Josep Maria Bartomeu, the president.

'Andrés means so much to me,' Pedro says. 'Everyone knew that I wanted to leave, that I was struggling. The days passed but nothing happened, there was a stalemate. Andrés knew how I felt; he knew what I was going through. And so he took it upon himself to call the president and see if he could sort things out, persuade him to let me go. He helped me a lot.'

Two days later, Pedro was a Chelsea player. 'No other player would have done what he did for me. There's something about him; it's like he knows what's going to happen. He's wise. I remember a game against Inter Milan, for example. I was in and out of the team. I wasn't getting any continuity, I was always the man who stood in for someone else. And he came into the dressing room and said to me: "You're *you*, you're not here as anyone's sub, okay? You go out there and you play like Pedro Rodríguez. That's your name, that's how you play." I was young and that made me feel so good; he filled me with confidence. When someone like Andrés Iniesta says that, it matters.'

Pedro started, Barcelona won 2–0. And Pedro scored.

'I'll never forget the way he helped me in the semi-final of the 2010 World Cup either,' Pedro says. 'Vicente del Bosque named the team and I was starting. When I heard my name, I felt the tension. No one expected it. "Relax, Pedro," he said. "Play the way you always do." There's something about him that means he always knows how to ease your mind. He's always positive and calm. On the pitch too: that coolness, that patience and timing. He waits until just the right moment to give the pass. He's unique.'

*'Andrés is life insurance, he always makes you look good.'*

*Carles Puyol*

When Andrés arrived at La Masia, Carles Puyol was already there. When he reached the Camp Nou, Puyol was already there. Now it's Andrés who remains, with Puyol having departed – too many injuries having taken their toll on knees ruined by jumping so many times to defend the goal and the badge of Barcelona.

Andrés still remembers the special gift Puyol left him when he departed the academy all those years ago. 'Here, take my mattress,' was the message as the defender, given his chance by Louis van Gaal, the same coach who would later give Andrés his opportunity, went up to the first team. Andrés was still sleeping on an old and well-used mattress, and it was another gesture from a friend who had always tried to look out for the younger apprentice. Football would later reunite the pair of them when they became established senior players and symbols of a glorious era at the club.

Puyol came to La Masia from deepest Catalunya and Andrés from deepest Spain: it was one boy from La Pobla de Segur and the other from Fuentealbilla joining forces at the Camp Nou under the strong powerful figure of Van Gaal. 'He has a great gift for anticipating the play, he knows where he needs to put the ball, placing it in the least visible of the available gaps,' said the Dutch coach who would give Andrés his debut. Frank Rijkaard's praise would follow along the same lines. 'When Andrés plays all those passes, it is like watching someone sharing out sweets with their friends,' he said. And then finally Pep Guardiola, who once told his assistant Tito Vilanova on the subject of the temptation to rest Andrés: 'The next time that I leave Andrés out, and there is nothing wrong with him, hit me on the head until I come back to my senses and put him in the team, even if it's at left-back.'

Puyol would also be prisoner to that magic aura, reduced to helpless spectator some days in training as Andrés – as Rijkaard would say – sprayed the ball around to team-mates as if he was sharing out candy. Journalists would also be in awe, with no other option but to praise the elegance of Iniesta, the lightness of touch, the serenity, the lack of unnecessary over-elaboration, that ability to move quickly as all around him time seemed to stand still.

'I always tried never to dive into a challenge against Andrés. I don't know the reason why. But if I had even the slightest doubt, I would not put my foot in because he could just swerve away from you so easily and you couldn't catch him,' admits Puyol, an honest player who would never hold back on the pitch even when up against a great friend, but who with Andrés could not shake off that urge to protect. The feeling that showed itself so regularly at La Masia, as on that day when he left and gave Andrés a parting gift. It was the same instinct that would put him in contact with Raúl, the Spain physio, who would be so decisive for Iniesta during the 2010 World Cup.

As strong as the Barcelona central defender has always been, he believes Andrés' physique deceives many. 'He seems weak but he is not: he looks like you would be able to push him over but you can't; he looks like he would be easy to dispossess but he is not. Andrés deceives you in that way,' Puyol says. 'For us defenders, we are lucky to have him in front of us as a team-mate and not a rival. When you are in a difficult situation, you just give him the ball and you know that Andrés is life insurance, he always makes you look good.'

Both used to having their own space, Carles and Andrés built a solid friendship. 'He doesn't say a lot. Everyone knows that. But when he talks people listen,' says Puyol, who does remember four or five deeper conversations with Andrés about life beyond football. He is capable of disappearing for a while if he has a certain problem to face before resurfacing, stronger than ever, having found a solution. And no one is better at bringing people together and ensuring that they all, according to Puyol, end up asking: 'What do you want from us?'

He needs to feel loved but without it sounding needy or demanding.

He is stubborn like his father and enigmatic like his mother; always elegant, this is the Andrés that exists beyond Iniesta the footballer.

> *'He has stayed close to his roots.'*
> *'Andrés knew how to be patient.'*
> *'He does not overdo it, he flows in perfect harmony.'*
> *'He is only interested in the game, he is pure football.'*
> *'He is a man of honour, like the players of old.'*
>
> *The Barça 'family'*

Ángel Mur was a masseur at the club for decades. He says: 'Andrés is a distinguished member of a very select group, from the school of touch and talent and style, taught to appreciate the game in a very specific way. Education is vital for the person but also for the player. You have to know how to live, to be patient, you have to know what your team is trying to achieve, you have to be able to read the game, but you also have to know why you should know the lyrics of the hymn and why you should sing it, you should know what the club means. And I always had the feeling with Andrés that he was someone who would listen and absorb, who would take on board, who would interpret and who, at the end of his career, would really have left his mark. And he never had it easy. His life changed completely when he was still very young: new school, new friends, new city. But in spite of all that he remains true to his roots – sometimes it seems that he is still just a boy from the village, although at the same time he is a proud citizen of Barcelona and a fine exponent of the football the club is famous for. He has known how to respect the institution just as the players of old – and there are not many of them left – used to.'

Carlos Naval, who is still a Barcelona club official, echoes those sentiments. 'Just like Guillermo Amor or Sergi Roberto now, Andrés knew how to be patient. I remember something Sergi Roberto's father said to me: "We spent the weekends waiting for one of three possibilities. He was either not in the squad; or he was in the squad but was not going to play; or he was in the squad and got to play." The player needs to learn how to be a footballer, to always be at the coach's disposal, and to not get ahead of himself making statements in the press that go against team spirit. You have to be part of the group. Andrés always knew how to do that.'

Naval first heard about Andrés from Oriol Tort, who told him that the new boy arriving at the club was special. He has not been disappointed. 'Iniesta only speaks when he feels he should, but he understands everything, because he observes; he knows how to read situations and if the situation is a difficult one he does not hide. When it was down to him to appear in the press conference the day after Edmilson had said that there was a 'black sheep' at the club, he did it.' And Naval adds: 'One day before the 2010 Balon d'Or presentation, the club prepared a special report with the three mothers of the three Barça finalists Messi, Iniesta and Xavi. We did everything we could so that he did not get wind of it. But just as his mother was crossing the road her telephone rang and it was Andrés asking: "Where are you going, Mamá?"' Iniesta felt bad about not winning the Balón d'Or but he was happy that if he couldn't win it, Messi could. 'Andrés knows how highly Leo regards him and that is why he took the result so well.' And finishing up, Naval says: 'He always obeyed the rules, he was always respectful. If, for example, every player has four complimentary tickets for a game, and he needed a fifth ticket then he would happily pay for it. Because he likes to be ordered, a perfectionist even, on the pitch, in the gym, in life; he likes these routines and guidelines.'

Emili Ricart shares Naval's opinion: 'He brings stability to the team, he dictates the pace of a game, he unsettles rivals. I never get nervous sat on the bench watching Barça if Iniesta is playing. He is a Rolls Royce player and if he is in good shape physically then nothing stops him. His musculature is very good,' says the physio who best knows Andrés' body. 'He knows how to look after himself. He does not overdo it, he flows in perfect harmony. He is football, pure football. And he does everything well. He is a 9.95. Only Nadia Comaneci is a perfect 10; if we give him a 10 it will go to his head,' jokes Ricart.

'It is not easy to decode Iniesta,' says Raúl Martínez. 'He is an enigma, you never know what he is thinking; He is Mr. X. Or he could just as well be the boy who sat behind you in school, who went all the way to the top. He was never the leader and you ask yourself: "Why did he make it and I did not?" He always makes the right choices. He picks the right people in life the way he picks the right passes on the pitch. And what is more,' continues Martínez, one of Andrés' most trusted physios, 'he is a man of habit and of honour. He is old-school both as a person and a player. And in the same way that musicians have a very special relationship with their instruments that is how Andrés is with the ball. More than an exhibitionist, he is an artist,' says Raúl.

'He is as good a person as he is a player,' says Paco Seirulo, a member of the methodology department at Barça, a former first-team fitness coach, and one of the most respected men at the club. 'Everything he does is for a reason; he never does something on the pitch just for the sake of it. He gives no advantage to the opposition and the team flows as a consequence. Even though it sometimes seems he is trying to go unnoticed on the pitch, he is always where he knows the team needs him to be.'

Seirulo picks out Iniesta's change of pace and ability to carry the ball, but also never tries to hide how biased he is when it comes to Andrés. 'It's as if he were my son. I remember when he was studying at college, he never wanted to stand out. Some people say he doesn't like to be too jolly, because it might upset those who are not feeling so good about things. He acted very naturally and never tended to talk too much about hairstyles, brands of football boots, films. He is only interested in the game and everything connected with it. As far as I'm concerned, when he is good physically, he is the best.'

## GUIDING HANDS

*'Andrés is very loyal. He never lets his loved-ones down. He needs them and likes to have them around him.'*

*Joel Borrás*

There are four people who look after Andrés professionally: Pere Guardiola, Joel Borràs, Ramón Sostres and Dani Marín. But their relationship is not just professional; it is personal. They're close, virtually a family. The trust has built up over the years, sometimes with the involvement of his father José Antonio as well, and now it is complete.

Pere Guardiola worked for Nike discovering new players when he found Andrés. 'The first time I saw him he was playing in Barcelona's Cadete B team,' says Guardiola. 'I had a very good relationship with Albert Benaiges, who was one of the directors of youth football at La Masia and I asked him: "Who's the best out there?" There were three or four who stood out, but Andrés was the best. "Watch Andrés, Pere," he said. And although we knew that he was so young still, fourteen or fifteen at the time, that you can never be sure what will happen, and that you should never force a player through but let them find their space and do things in their own time, we knew we wanted to sign him up. We also knew that he already had an offer from Adidas. But he agreed to join us just before the Nike Cup, an Under-15 tournament that's held at the Camp Nou.'

That was when Pere Guardiola, who was looking after marketing issues at the time, discovered what others who had met Andrés had seen too. 'Some days I would go to La Masia and ask permission to take him out to eat at a restaurant near the Mini Estadi. He always ordered spaghetti carbonara. I would start talking and keep talking; he barely said a word: "Yes, no, well, okay . . ." and that was pretty much it. We'd be there for three quarters of an hour and that was all he'd say. And yet I felt like there was something there; I felt like we got on, like I was becoming close to him, his father José Antonio, his family, everyone. Bit by bit we got to know each other. Andrés was, and is, very likeable; he was the kind of person you warmed to, that you felt like you wanted to help. You almost wanted to take him home with you, as if he was your little brother. And it wasn't just me who felt like that; you asked anyone at La Masia and they all said the same thing. He was the kind of person who just made you like him.'

The Nike Cup was the first real stage on which Andrés shone. 'Barcelona won the competition and we knew that he was the kid we had to go for. He played as a central midfielder and he gave the team such security. He was never out of position, but if things were going badly he knew it was up to him to step up and sort it out, and he did just that. In the final against Rosario Central, he scored the golden goal with the score at 1–1.

'That was a glimpse of how he would play his whole career, maybe because of how he made his way alone most of the time. He doesn't show off or puff out his chest, but he steps up when he's needed. I don't know what goes on inside his head, but he always seems to take the right decisions. He might not be the player who usually scores, he might not be the player rising to head it in, but if you look he is always at the heart of the decisive moments, the move that wins the game.'

By then, Pere had already told his brother Pep about Iniesta. 'There's a kid coming through who is the best of them all in the youth system. He's easy enough to spot: he's the skinniest, the smallest, and the most pale. His name is Iniesta.

'That first year with Pep as coach was very important for Andrés,' Pere says. 'I'm sure he thought: "My idol's coming, my teacher, the coach that's going to make us better; he'll back me, promote me, make me more important." I say he "thought" that because he never actually said it: he very rarely tells you what he is thinking. I'm convinced he told himself: "I have to show him I can be the best; I have to give him back everything he gave me."'

A lot of things came together for Andrés back then: the excitement of a new manager, but the pressure too. There were injuries and tension. Emotionally it was quite a ride, the demands and the extraordinary success, then the sad death of Dani Jarque. The first season under Pep ended with a treble, but things had built up over the year and it ended up giving way to Andrés' most difficult period, those dark days when it felt like everything was slipping away, when he no longer felt in control.

'He wasn't sleeping well, he kept getting injuries that were tearing him apart and he was feeling depressed,' Pere says. 'I remember his dad telling me they had gone so far as to go and see some kind of mystic down in the south of Spain who cut his hair and told him that he had some kind of curse hanging over him, that someone somewhere loved him so much, or hated him too much, that it wasn't letting him live free and that was what had created this crisis. There was no way out of it. Andrés said there was something in his stomach, he couldn't train, he couldn't do anything, he didn't understand what was happening to him when he should have been so happy. Pep gave him space because he knew Andrés needed time, he needed to be able to dedicate twenty-four hours a day to how he was feeling. It was very *heavy*, very hard. In the end, he came out of it, and stronger too. But it hasn't been easy.

'No one has gifted Andrés anything. He has worked so hard to be where he is,' Pere says. 'He's done it all on his own. It's easy enough to say: "This kid is the best" but that kid has to prove it and not many of them do. To start with, he was always a sub or the first player to get substituted. He never complained, never moaned. He had to fill in where others couldn't, play in lots of different positions, perform well time after time. Until, at last, people saw the truth: the team had to be Andrés and ten others.

'Even now, with everything that has happened and everything that has changed, you can still see that there are two Andréses. The shy one you see off the pitch and the other one you see on it, the real Andrés, the one that lets himself go, that really lives. That's his natural surroundings, his habitat: grass and a ball. I think he's unique. Yes, his football fits with Barcelona's identity, but he is so good that wherever you put him, whatever system he had to play, whatever tactics, he would have kept progressing. If he played at an English club, there would be a statue of him at the main gate by now.

'Andrés has been a winner his whole life. But he never says so, never speaks out. Only when you need him, then he steps forward. At bad times, he says: "I'm here." He lives for football, he's an example to us all.

'I would compare him to Scholes or Xavi, club men, consistent performers who never hide, who always want the ball and who have a special talent with it, men who improve the players around them. He's a blessing for any coach. That's why he ends up playing: not because anyone has ever gifted him anything, but because he is the best. He's the easiest person to take off because he never complains, never makes a fuss, and then trains brilliantly the next day. If they put him at right-back one day, he'd play well. He'd play well anywhere. And his coaches know that. So do his team-mates.'

● ● ●

'One day his father came to see me,' Ramón Sostres says. 'I can still picture him walking in. He wanted to ask about a tax issue that was worrying him. A law firm had made a mistake with Andrés' tax returns, but it was something that we were able to sort out quite easily. From that very first moment, we got on well.

'José Antonio doesn't like all the paperwork, he has too many other things to deal with, but he is sharp and organized. He has a clear sense of what's going on, what is best for Andrés, and he is honest and open, easy to deal with. I remember that first time, after we sorted it out for Andrés, he said: "What do I owe you?" I said: "Nothing, it was just a couple of calls, and a letter to the tax man. Don't worry." And from that moment on, there was trust. He started to explain things to me, ask my advice on various issues, not just tax. He wanted us to help Andrés out with playing contracts, sponsors, image rights and, particularly, his relationship with Nike, who did his boots. Later came his relationship with Barcelona itself, and eventually he asked us to represent him. It was a responsibility for us, a challenge too. And we ended up looking after him in a wide range of questions: legal, tax, footballing, finance, commercial, professional and personal. His father is the central figure in everything when it comes to the Iniesta family's financial questions, the lynchpin. He runs the "Iniesta Bodega", their growing wine label – his real treasure – and all the family business and affairs. He keeps Andrés in the loop with everything of course, but he is the one that runs it. The aim really is not to weigh Andrés down with those kinds of things, to keep his head clear so that he can focus on his football, the thing that really matters.

'When he was looking for someone to help, someone he could trust, José Antonio asked advice from a lot of people in football. But I don't think he made any decisions without consulting with Andrés first. And I am sure that Andrés would have followed things carefully himself. He doesn't ask many questions, Andrés, but when he does, it's always the right question: he gets straight to the point. He makes sure that he understands that key point and then he gets on with his routine. If you change things, or break that routine, he's not comfortable. He don't change cars or houses just for the sake of it. In fact, I think he might even have his first car still: like a lot of players, it serves as a kind of symbol of how hard he worked to get here and how far he has come.

'He's not capricious, he doesn't spoil himself, he doesn't do things on a whim. Far from it. He's very stable. He sticks to the same routines: he eats in restaurants where he has eaten well before – and where they stock his wine! – or where he has felt comfortable with family and friends; he goes on holiday to the same places; he does the same things. Then there's Fuentealbilla, where he escapes more often than people think. When it comes to organizing his life, Andrés is straightforward; when it comes to overcoming problems, it's the same. It hasn't always been a bed of roses, but he's pragmatic about things and he approaches them almost as if he was playing: facing them, going straight at them and taking them on.'

Sostres says that Andrés' attitude and behaviour don't change, however complex the problem before him, however important. 'Andrés is discreet and rational, taking it all in his stride,' he says. 'He just wants to ensure that he knows what is going on. "All okay, Ramón?" he'll ask. And that's pretty much it. He asks for a brief, clear outline of everything that's being offered. He weighs up the pros and cons mentally and then he speaks to his dad. José Antonio doesn't normally attend the meetings, although occasionally he needs to be there. Andrés isn't the kind of player who gets obsessed with what offers there are out there or new contracts. He's not one of those players who plays well and wants to use that to get a new deal. Quite the opposite in fact: he doesn't like the idea that performances can be better or worse based on some desire to chase a bigger salary. He appreciates what he has, in every sense. It's not just about the contract for him. It's everything that goes on around him.

'He's quite placid, passive. Actually, "patient" is a better word. He knows that in the end, things will fall into place and common sense will prevail. As if he's in control of time, not in a hurry. A bit like how he plays, in fact. I don't recall any time when he has been affected by contract negotiations or any off-field issue, even those moments when the situation has been complicated and potentially problematic. And there have always been solutions, anyway, and usually quick ones.'

Andrés' future at Barcelona has never really been in question, even if there have been times when it wasn't always secure. There have been moments of doubt, despite the fact that his friends and advisers know that it would be very hard for him to go anywhere else. 'There have been times when he has got angry, just like anyone,' Sostres says. 'And he prefers to have things written down. He tends to communicate with you via text messages; it's rare that he actually calls. We do see each other, of course: after games, at his home, in the office, at the club. When there's an incoming call and his name appears on my phone, I always think: "What's happened?" It has to be something important for him to call. And if he's calling, it's best to answer; the chances are he is worried about something.

'He called me the day of the Champions League final in Paris,' recalls Sostres. 'I was on the bus with his family. He was angry, *very* angry, because he wasn't starting. He didn't say that he wanted to leave Barcelona, but he did say to me: "Ramón, I think I deserve to play." That wasn't a nice moment.'

It hasn't always been easy to negotiate on behalf of Andrés, especially when it came to devising a strategy, like the time when contract talks with Txiki Begiristáin, the sporting director, seemed to have reached stalemate in 2006. 'I told Andrés what was happening and what I thought would happen,' says Sostres. 'His reply was: "Do what you want to do, Ramón, but I'm not leaving here, okay?" Well, okay. But I did ask one thing from him: "Don't say you don't want to leave." If you say that, then Txiki's work is done.'

Sostres has a spreadsheet with every game Andrés has played on it, detailing every minute he has been on the pitch. That detail is a key part of any negotiation and has an influence on the bonuses due or the length of a future deal. 'That year when I was battling it out with Txiki, Andrés had played in more games than anyone else, but not more minutes,' he explains. 'He came on for Guily around the sixtieth minute of almost every game. The last league game was in Seville, and that just left Paris and the final. He was right on the edge. If he didn't play in the final, or if he missed out in Seville, he wouldn't reach the figure he needed for a bonus that made up a key part of his deal. It would have cost him a lot of money. I rang Txiki and told him that it wouldn't be fair to "rest" him in Seville, because the Champions League final was coming up, and for that to mean he missed out on the bonus. The club agreed, so I was able to tell Andrés and that was one less thing to worry about.

'Andrés is a good person; he and his family are very grateful and they don't forget those who have helped them out. If someone treats him well, he remembers. It doesn't matter if it is a fan, a team-mate, a physio, a journalist or an agent, he doesn't forget. He has a good memory. He has to have: plenty of people have crossed his path since he became a footballer, after all. Footballers have a lot going on around them; the fact that he remembers people, even anonymous people, not just the big names, tells you something about him. You see it when people go and say hello to him; they don't think he'll remember them but he does and you can see that it really makes their day. When he goes back to Fuentealbilla he remembers them all: he can name every coach he's ever had.

'Andrés is happy in Barcelona and in Fuentealbilla; they're his home. And you can see the difference that off-field happiness makes. His home life is a big part of his success. Anna, his wife, is one of those people who likes to spread the happiness around and the first by his side when the bad times come. She is very positive, very happy and optimistic, strong and a great mother. She showed that when they so sadly lost the baby that would have been their second son.'

●　●　●

Joel Borràs first met him one night in Mataró, near Barcelona – the same night Andrés met Anna in a bar called El Teatre. Andrés has shared 'thousands of things' with Joel. Few people spot Joel but he's always there, looking after every detail. 'Andrés must have written me a thousand emails; he loves to write,' Joel says. 'I really got to know him properly one day when I went to his parents' house. He wasn't interested in the PlayStation or going out for the night; he just sat there reading the messages people had left him on his new website and replying to them. He likes to talk to people anonymously and he's a perfectionist. I remember one day we went to help him move house; myself, Guille Pérez, a colleague from Mediabase, and three friends. At the end of the day, he gave us all some trainers and boxes of wine to say thanks. Not many players would do something like that and it tells you what kind of person he is: generous, appreciative. That's Andrés. When I was ill he came to the hospital every day to see me. He demands a lot, but he gives a lot too.

'One day I made the "mistake" of telling him how many emails were coming in to his website asking for shirts, photos, videos, autographs and so on, for fans or charities, or whatever . . . he insisted on replying to them all and asked me to send out everything they asked for. We reached the point where I had to take him a printout of every email that had arrived for him over the course of the week. It didn't matter if there were a hundred of them or more, he wanted to read them. I don't know how he found the time to read them all, but by the Monday he would be back in touch. "Joel, can you go and get a shirt of mine from the training ground and send it to this address . . . ? Joel, don't forget those photos . . . Joel, they asked for a video. I'm going to record it and send it to you, okay? Can you send it on? . . . Ah, and can you get a shirt for a school raffle in Galicia? They're raising money . . ." And on it went. He was like that from the very first day. I've never seen him say no in his life. The other day he asked me to take some toys to the Raval neighbourhood in Barcelona. Valeria, his daughter, didn't play with them any more, but he didn't want to throw them away. "They're still practically new, Joel," he told me.'

Andrés admits that Joel is the person he talks to most in the world. 'I don't know if we talk a lot, or if we actually talk very little,' Joel jokes. 'What we really do is share a lot. If he wants something, he can be on top of you all day long. I'm here to help him, day to day, whatever he needs. That can be sorting out his diary, arranging an event, or helping him find something he needs. I wake up with him and go to sleep with him; in the morning there's usually a message from him and the last thing I see at night tends to be an email from Andrés too. So I don't know if I'm the person he speaks to the most, but I am the person he writes to the most, that's for sure.

'He loves to sit in front of a screen, take his time, read things carefully, and think about what he is going to write: whether that's football, politics or life. Sometimes I think that must be what relaxes him. The odd thing is we have very different opinions on a lot of things and we argue quite a lot. Maybe it would be harder to have those kinds of debates face to face; it's easy to be daring by text. Andrés loves to read and write, to send messages. "How you doing?", "Everything okay?" It's constant. And yet, actual calls? Hardly any. Three or four a year, maybe.

'Andrés is a man of habit, methodical, punctual to a fault, the complete opposite of me. I'm chaotic and disorganized. But our relationship has evolved over time. It used to be very professional; now there is more to it than that. We spent our last holidays together, for example. He involves you in everything he does; he wants you by his side. All that's left for me now is to run onto the pitch with him!

'He's changed a bit with the arrival of his children, Valeria and Paolo Andrea. He's a dad now. But in most things he's the same as always. He's still the same person: generous, quiet, someone who doesn't want to stand out, happy just to spend time with his people. Andrés makes an impression on you because he is who he is, there's no pretence. Everything happens naturally with him. With Andrés, what you see is really him.'

● ● ●

'I met him a little later, in 2011 when I joined Nike,' says Dani Marín, a former Catalan footballer with a sweet left foot. He connected with Andrés from the start. 'I had that advantage of having played the game; I knew his world, up to a point.' Dani played in the Under-19 team at Damm before joining Mallorca, his first professional club. He played for a number of clubs in Spain before he ended his career aged thirty-six.

'Andrés never ceases to surprise you. You see him do things and you think: "What a perfectionist." He's on top of every little detail. He's aware of everything and always appreciative, quick to thank you and to show his gratitude. There are kids in this sport who don't say anything to you, they take it all for granted. You send them things and you don't even know if they have received them, but not Andrés: it's like he's more excited about a new boot, say, than a youth teamer is. It's like he's still a kid and this is his first pair of proper boots. Some kid? Sure. But Andrés, a player who has won it all? That enthusiasm never dims.'

Andrés never forgets what it meant for José Antonio and Mari to spend what little money they had on his first boots. They cost a fortune, more than they could really afford. And there's something of that gratitude in him still, every time a new pair of boots arrive. 'Andrés loves to ensure that everyone around him is happy,' Dani says. He's used to getting an email at the start of every season, in which Andrés asks him to arrange for a new Barcelona shirt to be sent out for his kids (Valeria, Paolo Andrea), his sister, his cousins, uncles, aunts, friends . . . the whole family. 'He does it himself, always wanting his family to be looked after. He's very likeable; he makes an effort for everyone.'

ANNA

# 23

'With his children, Andrés looks at life another way. They have changed everything for him.'

*Anna, Andrés' wife*

'That night our paths crossed. Perhaps it was destiny; the coincidences of life. I don't really know why, but on the evening of 23 June 2007 it all happened. I don't know how it all came about; what I do know is that from that moment on, without having searched for it or expected it, I had found the love of my life, my journey's companion, my confidant, and the father of my children. A marvellous father and a man prepared to fight for them, who dedicates his time to Valeria and Paolo Andrea and who will do anything for them. And they have also given something to him – a different way of looking at life.'

That is Anna, the wife of Andrés, an interior decorator and image consultant, someone who loves to feel the water of the sea or the swimming pool around her. There is nothing unusual about that for a young girl from Maresme. Now she swims for fun, but she was once a competitive swimmer in Mataró's swimming club. She was very young when she started and she had retired by the time she turned 18, having been a fine exponent of the front crawl and the back-stroke. Competitive swimming has left her with some wonderful memories. Some of her best friendships come from her time spent travelling around Catalonia and Spain in competition. 'They were healthy and genuine friendships,' Anna says. 'Because they were forged in the effort and the solidarity of sport.

'Everyone knows how it is for children who swim competitively. You get up very early to train, at 5.30am, then you have to go to school, then you eat, you go back to the classroom and then you go to the swimming pool once more before going home to do homework, have your dinner, and sleep. And then it all starts again. It's a routine that hardly leaves time for anything else, but looking back I remember it as one of the best times of my life. It marked most of us who lived through it and it taught us values that will last us our whole lives.'

'I like going back to Llavaneres where my parents Vicenç and Pili live. We are still really close; and I can see my friends and the rest of my family. It is not that far from where Andrés and I live, and going there is like a breath of fresh air with the sea, the calm, the peace and the memories. I get a sort of pleasant melancholy from it. It feels like they are my people; it's the place where I was born. It also gives me a chance to see my sister Marta who also doesn't live there any more. She means so much to me.

And the friends there are the ones that I have had my whole life, that group of seven girls that swam together. They are all there; we are still really close.'

That was, and still is, Anna's world. So what about the world of Andrés? 'He feels most at ease in his own small group of friends. If anyone saw them all together they would think: "That's not Andrés!" but yes, it is. That is where the Andrés that I fell in love with appears,' says Anna. 'Someone who is very interesting, intelligent and enigmatic, and with whom you don't have to talk for too long to realize how fantastic he is.'

Anna's story continues, written in her own hand. 'He is affectionate, respectful, very attentive and always looking out for other people. But the best thing about Andrés is what is hidden; the things which people don't see, the things that only the people close to him know about, and which make us feel fortunate to know him. He appeared in our circle with his jokes (I love the sense of fun that he has) and it surprised everyone because we are accustomed to that serious solemn tone of his. But then when you get to really know him, he has that something special. I don't know what it is, but it hooks you. Until I ended up saying to myself: "I love this guy!" And since that moment, nine years have gone by. It can seem that there are two different versions of Andrés, but it is not that way at all. There is only one and he is unique. I cannot put my finger on why, he just is.

'On this road that we have travelled together we have got to know each other more and more and we have learned a lot from each other. Perhaps that is why often we don't need to speak, I can just look at him and I know that something is bothering him, he doesn't have to say anything. "Are you okay, Andrés?" I ask him. "Don't worry," he says. "I'm just having a bad day." He doesn't explain any more than that and I don't push him any further. If he wants to talk more about it, he knows that he can. Deep down, I know what it is. He is not someone who likes talking about things or for people to be asking him too many questions. If he wants to, then he will go into greater depth. He knows that I am here to help him and give him another point of view.'

That is how Andrés is, or was. Because, according to Anna, something happened to him that changed the way he looked at the world.

'Andrés used to tend to bottle things up, until the moment comes when he is finally ready to talk about things. I suppose it all comes from the relationships you have as a child. Andrés never had it easy. His childhood was different to most other children. It cannot have been easy to be separated from your parents when you are just twelve years old and your personality is being shaped. I think everything he went through then has influenced him a lot and, among other reasons, made him the person he is. We are slightly different in this way. In my close circle we have always shared our experiences and uncertainties. And we were always together. I was lucky enough to live with my parents and my sister; Andrés was not. Now that we are together and we are sharing our lives, we have learned how to tune into each other, something that is not easy for anyone.

'It was not easy for me either to have so many sudden changes when we began our relationship. It was a change of city; I no longer had my family and friends close by, but I did it because I wanted to be with Andrés. He was my great support and he still is. That is why in moments of anxiety, where everything seems up in the air and we are going through so many new things, he showed me that it would all be worth it. And together we have created the most wonderful thing about both our lives – our children.'

Anna uncovers her old world as she dives into a new world. 'Even though my family is just thirty kilometres away, I also had times when I missed them and the times we had spent together. Suddenly my life was different. But bit by bit and with the help of Andrés and his family who supported me and kept me company a lot, and of course of my own family, I adapted to the changes. I suppose if you ask him he will say the same. In the end, both of us overcame the difficulties. We were patient and in the end everything falls into place; everything flows. In the end, we connect more and better every day. If you think about it, life has taken so many turns in these years we have spent together. There have been so many changes and new experiences and we have learned so much about ourselves and grown as a couple and as individuals.

'He has told me time and time again that I have influenced him for the better! That is something that *he* has revealed to me. I have influenced his life and he has influenced mine. We are both better people for being together. That is what love is about, don't you think? Learning together, admiration, respect: I can say with complete faith that that is what we have.'

Suddenly, Anna goes back to the very start. 'What was Andrés like when I first met him? I can only say that I had the feeling that I had known him all my life. At the time he was winning me over, and how he enjoyed it! Just as he is now, he was very good at organizing surprises. He would appear at my front door without any notice and take me off to some unexpected destination. I still have the notes that he would leave me and that he still leaves me; those touches are so important to me. You don't always see it, but he is always there making every moment special. Are we different? Yes, very! Although he doesn't think so. But we share something that has united us since the first day. There is a lot about him that I still have to discover. And I love that. My favourite phrase is that the best is yet to come. That's the way it always is and the way it will always be.

'I didn't like football. I would go as far as to say that it didn't interest me at all. In my family at least, they are all Barça fans. We would watch Barcelona's games, but if I didn't see them then it wouldn't bother me at all, it was all the same to me. Now I don't miss a single game that Andrés plays. I love watching him play. I enjoy it; it makes me feel a lot of pride and admiration and I get excited and suffer too. How things change! When I told my father that I was going out with Andrés, I was a little bit surprised by his reaction. He is a very open-minded man, but one day he approached my mother, who is usually more the worrier of the family, and said to her: "Ah, Pili! What do you think about Anna and this Barcelona player?" That was his moment of being the protective father, but it was just the one comment. From then on, everything went really well.'

● ● ●

'It's true that in that moment I was a little bit apprehensive,' says Vicenç, Anna's father. He and his wife Pili still remember the moment when their daughter came home from Barcelona's midsummer celebration, the festival of San Juan, and told them: 'Yesterday, I met Iniesta.' Naturally they thought:

'Iniesta? Iniesta from Barça?' She had to clarify to her father: 'Yes, that one, Dad.' Everyone in the Oritz household was a bit nervous.

'Pili, can you see our daughter Anna with a Barça footballer?' said Vicenç. 'Don't worry, I think it will all be fine,' said Pili. 'Yes, but . . . you know?' was Vicenç's still concerned response.

'Then we met him and our minds were put completely at peace. That's Andrés for you,' Pili says. 'People still ask me what it is like to have Iniesta as a son-in-law. But I don't think of him as Iniesta, I think of him as Andrés. In fact, when somebody says "Iniesta" to me, it always sounds strange. I get emotional when I speak about him.'

'To us, he is Andrés,' says Marta, Anna's carefree younger sister, the one member of the family who has no interest in football at all. In contrast, how lucky for her best friend Sergi, a big guy almost two metres tall, who is crazy about Barça. But Xavi, Marta's boyfriend, is another who is not passionate about the sport. Marta and Xavi are like aliens in Andrés' world, revolving as it does, around football. 'My boyfriend is also not a football fan. But I believe deep down that is reassuring for Andrés. He is so committed to football and he demands so much of himself. We turn up and we haven't got a clue of what might be going on in the world of football. We talk about so many different things but almost never about football. He has always been very reserved ever since the first day that I met him. I was doing my degree exams when he first came to our house,' reveals Marta. They are complete opposites in terms of their personalities. One is talkative and fun with a contagious sense of humour; the other is quiet, discreet, even secretive. 'Brother-in-law, you know what I have to learn from you? I have learnt how to be quiet.

Sometimes you don't have to talk too much to know what you are feeling. Suddenly, you will just ask one question and with that you will say everything,' she says.

'I will never forget what he did for us during the bad times: when my father had to have an operation, or when Anna lost the baby,' says Marta. 'What Andrés has been through for us is amazing. Every second of every minute of every hour he was there for us; and he was there for me too when I went through bad times. Andrés didn't always need to speak to make his love known. I know that he is a very famous footballer. I know he is very good player and that he is very well loved, but he is also a wonderful person. When he opens up to you, it is wonderful to be with him. He is great. Everything just flows. He is completely devoted to his family.'

●   ●   ●

'Of course, sharing my life with Andrés has changed it completely,' Anna admits. 'It's a completely different lifestyle. But that does not mean that I have changed as a person. Why would I? I am Andrés' wife, but I am the same Anna as before. I still get concerned about the same things and still enjoy the same things. I have the same friendships.'

According to Anna, the more things change, the more they stay the same. 'The fact that both Andrés and I have remained the same helps us, because it means that our world remains ours. Only ours,' she says.

'I have already mentioned that Andrés likes to give surprises. An envelope will appear in the kitchen, or in the bathroom or in the bedroom.

It will have "To Mami" written on it (that's what he calls me now that we are parents, and of course I call him "Papi") and the note will reveal a trip or an outing. I love those notes! At the start, when he used to say to me: "Anna, pack a suitcase, we are going on a trip," I would say: "Andrés, I prefer to know where we are going." Now he says to me: "It's a surprise, Anna, but as I know you like to know where we are going and what we are going to do, then here's the plan." And of course, now we need to plan a little more because of the children. We have so much fun with them and we give them all the time we can. Andrés loves to play with them and they adore him and let him know that every day, as soon as he arrives home.

'The arrival of our little prince and princess has helped him see life differently. Before, if he lost a game he would arrive home under a dark cloud. Now though, he only has to see the children and his face changes completely. Football remains very important but his children are his life. He has changed a lot in that sense. Now if he loses a game it seems as though he sleeps better, or at least he tries to sleep. There are still nights when he will toss and turn but that is Andrés.

'If there is one thing I am sure about, it is that I have found my travelling companion, and with every experience we have shared I am more and more sure about that. He is, and will always be, MY OTHER HALF.'

It's Anna who puts that in capital letters. She had met her other half by chance just before the San Juan celebrations, in a pub in Mataró called El Teatre. Andrés had allowed himself to be taken there by a friend and he could not take his eyes off the girl serving drinks behind the bar. He pursued her that night and never left her in peace until they ended up getting married, celebrating their love with a huge wedding, the best way to share their happiness before returning to their intimacy.

● ● ●

'From the first moment I saw her, I knew that Anna would be my wife,' says Andrés. And he tells exactly how that first moment came about. 'Some days before San Juan in 2007, a classmate of mine from Sant Ignasi College in Sarrià, a lad named Jordi, asked me if I wanted to go to a party he was organizing in Mataró. I told him: "You know I am not a big party-goer. We'll see. I will let you know." In the days before, I tried to convince my friend Jordi Mesalles to come along with me. The problem was that I had not taken down the number of the Jordí who had invited me to the party. I am used to deleting messages from my phone – there is not enough room for all the messages that I receive – apart from the last few. So when Mesalles and I reached the beach zone of Mataró, we had no number to call and couldn't find the party venue, so after spending a while looking for it we decided to head back to Barcelona. Just as we were about to leave my telephone rang and, surprise, surprise, the caller was Jordi. It was a nod from destiny. We went to meet Jordi and a fourth guy named Joel.

'At the party, there was that moment, like at the start of so many parties, when you don't really know what to do, and we started thinking once again about driving back to Barcelona. Then someone mentioned that a new pub called El Teatre had opened in Mataró and we decided to go and have a drink there. It was there that I noticed a girl with long dark hair, who was absolutely stunning, behind the bar. I couldn't take my eyes off of her. It was love at first sight. It was Anna. She didn't even work at the pub, but that evening she was standing in for her friend Silvia – another nod from destiny.

'That is how it happened. I fell madly in love with her, but at first I couldn't find a way of making sure I could see her again. It took Jordi, the guy who had invited me, about a week to pass her number on to me, even though I was asking him for it about two or three times a day. I couldn't understand why Jordí, who said he was a friend of Anna, couldn't get her number for me. So I gave him an ultimatum: "Get me Anna's number or I don't want to hear from you any more!"'

Andrés often sees things that way. He doesn't accept half measures or meanderings: either Jordi had the number and could give it to him, or he didn't have it and that was to be the end of the story. He wants people to be straight with him and in return they have his loyalty. Jordi delivered, eventually giving Anna's number to Andrés.

'I wrote to her,' he says. 'I didn't put anything special in the first message. I just sent her a greeting and not much more. I thought that would do the trick, but it had no effect.' Andrés did not know then that Anna was not interested in football or those who played the game for Barcelona. 'I had to change my tactics. I made friends with her best friend Silvia, the girl that Anna had gone to work in place of that night at El Teatre. I invented some story about needing to do some work for my university course and I never stopped asking Silvia for information about Anna every day. The story lasted for a while and it was months before we were officially a couple. It seemed like an eternity waiting to be able to say that we were. We should remember here that I'm a Taurus, so heavy going, very stubborn and headstrong!

'But once we got together, we clicked very quickly. Everything was very easy. We had so many things in common, in the way we thought and the way we behaved. There were times when I would say: "We are the same personalities in male and female version." Anna gave me back my life. I was going through a difficult time and she helped me find the thrill in living once more. I have no words to describe what she means to me.

'I am someone who believes that in both a person's professional and personal life you have to go through good times and bad to grow and improve, and that is what happened to me with Anna. We have grown a lot as a couple, we understand each other and we respect each other. She appeared at just the right time to keep me on the right road. I am convinced that without Anna I would not have been even half as happy as I am now and I would not have had anywhere near as much fun. It has not been easy, but she has always been there for me.

'I always thought that football and life went together; that they feed each other and that you need both to be working well to feel right. But as time has gone by, I have learned that the most important thing is your personal life. Now it means nothing for everything to be going well on the pitch if I'm not happy at home. And equally, I can be happy with life even if I am going through a bad moment as a player, whether it is because of a defeat or an injury. Valeria, my daughter, has a lot to do with that change in my thinking. Paolo Andrea, my son, as well. I see the proof of it when I get home after a game. As soon as I see them, any lingering anger from the game evaporates and I forget about football. In those moments, you realize what really matters in life. How am I going to beat myself up over a bad game when there are people who are sick or going through a bad time? Why am I going to get angry if I am not playing? Who is going to hold a bad performance against me when I have given everything on the pitch? Anna at first, then Valeria, and now Paolo Andrea too, have put everything in my life into perspective.'

Andrés finishes up: 'Many times I have thought about what would have happened if the call from Jordi had come when we were already on the drive back to Barcelona. Something made sure that Anna and I got together; it was our destiny. She didn't even work in that pub and I didn't live in Mataró, but . . .'

It is not by coincidence that the party before their wedding took place in El Teatre, and neither was it coincidental that Andrés and Anna asked that the pub, now renovated and with a different name, be turned back to look much the same way it had done that night when they first laid eyes on each other. 'We thought about it so many times,' they both say.

Andrés, however, has one more surprise reserved for Anna.

●  ●  ●

*After these eight years, almost nine that we have been together, we have experienced so many things together that I find it very difficult to express in just a few lines all the feelings I have for you, Anna, and everything that you awaken in me as a person. I want you to know that there are many things that I have not mentioned, but I only have words of pride, recognition, respect and affection towards you as a friend, as my partner, my wife and the mother of our children. There are count-*

*less special things that we have lived through together. Meeting for the first time and getting to know each other, trips we have taken, holidays as a couple, the birth of our children, our wedding which was such a magical day. We have enjoyed all of them. But you have also shown me how special you are in the less favourable moments. You are unique, you are brave, you have an enormous heart. You have shown me these things in the life that we have made together. Thank you for the enormous strength you showed when they gave us the news that we had lost our child. After going through all that we went through, we lost it but you were strong. Not everyone manages to get through these delicate moments, Anna. But you did it. I was by your side. We were all by your side. But it was you, Anna, it was you who came through it. It made us stronger and now we will always have an angel that accompanies us. The experience has helped us to grow and improve. And if there is one thing I am sure of, it is that with you . . . the best is always yet to come.*

*Your 'Papi'*

MAMÁ

*'I saw the goal in the World Cup final, but I didn't realize he had
scored it. His father didn't see it. He'd turned the telly off.'*

Mari, Andrés' mother

'It's only recently that people here knew who I was.' Mari is discretion
personified. She goes unnoticed, but once you meet her you don't forget
her: a mother who has recovered a son whose childhood was given up for
football. 'We have been living in this same house in Barcelona for sixteen
years and the neighbours didn't realize until quite recently,' Mari says. 'We
never wanted to stand out. What for? What's the point? I'm no one; I'm
just another mother, one of so many. I'm Andrés' mum and Maribel's mum,
and that's it.'

Mari doesn't talk for the sake of it; she doesn't talk much at all. A bit like Andrés. Everything about Mari has an air of Andrés about it. Sometimes she can seem distant, hard to reach, difficult to work out. Other times she is accessible, close, gentle, engaging.

'I remember one day, when the family had moved in to Barcelona, I went to the doctors,' says Mari. One morning, when the doctor was taking down my name to write me out a prescription, she said: "You know, Mari, I have a very famous patient."

"Oh, right?"

'She said: "Yes, yes, he's very famous, a Barcelona player. Andrés Iniesta. His second surname is Luján just like yours. Do you know him?"

'"A bit, yes," I said, feeling shy.

'"He's not your son, is he?" she said, surprised.

'"Er, yes, he's my son."'

The doctor was a big Barcelona fan and she couldn't get her head around it. 'Why didn't you tell me you were his mum?'

Mari says: 'I thought: "Why would I?" I don't have to go round telling everyone that I'm Andrés Iniesta's mum. I'd much rather no one knows who I am. That's better for me, for him, for everyone. We're just normal people. He's the footballer, not me. Not me, not his father, not his sister, just him.'

Mari prefers to talk about her son, not Andrés Iniesta the footballer, the Barcelona and Spain player who everyone knows, who belongs to all of them now, even though she was the one who gave them Andrés in the first place. 'It's hard enough trying to make up for lost time with my son,' she says. 'Sometimes I feel like I didn't have a son. I know that sounds hard, but it's true.' And that's when she explains how it feels for a mother not to be with her son. 'We were happy in our little town, with our lives, surrounded by our people. And he wanted to go to Barcelona. Lots of people think we forced him to, but that's not how it was. Andrés was the one who decided to follow the ball all the way there. I know that he suffered at first, that he had a bad time of it. We all did. I also know that, now that he is a father himself, Andrés understands a lot of the things we went through when he was away. There were days when he was the one hurting the most; other days when it was his dad; and others when it was me. We all struggled with it, and we all handled it in our own way.

'That's why I resisted it when on that very first night, having made all that effort to get him there, José Antonio wanted to bring him back home again. "I'm bringing the boy back!" I understood that, of course; deep down I felt same way. How could I not understand that? He was so small. And when we left him at La Masía, it wasn't what we expected: we thought he would stay with us that night at the Hotel Rallye and then we would take him to school the next day. But Mr Farrés, the director at La Masía, told us he was staying. José Antonio, me, my dad . . . we left there without him. I don't know how I got through that night. It would have been easy to respond by saying: "Right, get the car, let's take him home." I don't know how we didn't, in fact, but we knew that after all the effort it had taken for him to get there, we had to give it a go; at least let him try. We couldn't just turn round and come back as if nothing had happened. I wanted to, but I didn't. I still don't know why. Maternal intuition, I suppose. I understood José Antonio, because there he was just about to lose his son, this kid he took to every game, who he was with all the time, who he lived for. José Antonio was about to lose everything. *Everything.'*

Mari had hardly seen Andrés play. 'Someone had to stay behind and run the bar, didn't they? José Antonio and my dad were the ones that watched him most. How could I tell his granddad not to go and see him play? I only really saw the Brunete tournament, and I watched that on television. But José Antonio was always there with him.'

José Antonio would tell anyone who would listen how his son was developing as a player. Mari, by contrast, didn't know what to say when the neighbours asked. 'You know what small towns are like,' she says. 'Some people would look at us in a funny way, thinking: "Who do they think they are?" or "How can they do that to their child, sending him away when he's so little?" There were others who supported us, of course. But it was Andrés' decision.'

Mari swallowed it all: the comments, the bad times, the feeling that she had lost her son. She missed him. She knew that he'd never have the kind of life that normal kids in Fuentealbilla had. But it was his decision and she knew that once his mind was made up, that was it. 'I'll never forget something that happened when he was very little,' she says. 'His two grandmothers wanted him to play in the town's band; they even got together to tell me. Every time they saw me it was the same: "Andrés has to join the Fuentealbilla band." So I sent him along. It was only two or three times. At that stage he was already playing football, for Albacete, and I tried to use that: "Look, Andrés, if you don't play in the band, you don't play football either." But he called my bluff: "Okay, I won't play football . . . but I'm not going to join the band either." He was only ten or eleven.'

Once he had gone to La Masia, things happened so fast. That, at least, is how it felt to Mari. 'It's like we still don't fully appreciate what's happened,' she says. 'And even now I don't really enjoy it. Every time Barcelona lose, it's my little boy that loses.'

●　●　●

'Andrés is what you see, there's no pretence,' his sister Maribel says. 'Only there is something that you don't see: the suffering. He carries that on the inside. He swallows it all. All of it. That's the way our family is, especially our maternal grandmother.'

Maribel is two years younger than Andrés and when her brother went to Barcelona she had just celebrated her first communion in Fuentealbilla. 'I was ten years old and very little; it was hard for me not to have my big brother at home. I would see him once a month at most. Sometimes we would go five weeks without visiting him in Barcelona. When I finally went there to live, it was like we were two strangers: one aged seventeen, the other fifteen. I wouldn't let him out of my sight then, I wouldn't let him go, not even for a second. I wanted to do everything with him. It was like I was trying to make up for lost time. I had seen my parents and grandparents suffer and we were only together in the summers and at Christmas. I'll never forget those journeys home to Fuentealbilla after visiting him in Barcelona. The car was silent, no one talked. The journey back felt so long. I was twelve, thirteen, fourteen . . . and we would all sleep in the same hotel room, in the same bed, so that we could go to Barcelona and see him at La Masia.

'Back in Fuentealbilla, our bedrooms were next to each other,' Andrés' sister continues. 'So every time I walked into my room I passed by his and thought of him. All the more so when Dad had a bad day or when there was a family crisis – and there were plenty of those in the five years he was away. It made no difference to me that my friends said: "Your brother is going to play for Barcelona; that's so exciting!" It was no consolation. There were no mobile phones back then. At night, whenever he could, he would call at 10pm. But he couldn't say much because there was a queue building at La Masia, with all these kids waiting to use the phone.

'His dream had always been to play football and he had to give it a try – for himself and for Dad,' Maribel continues. 'All four of us are pretty stubborn. Andrés is just like Dad; they like to have everything under control, to look after everyone. They're always in touch, always there for you.'

So if they're so similar, does Maribel suffer watching Andrés play, too? 'Yes. I really, really suffer,' she says. 'But unlike them I do go to the games, even if I have a bad time of it when I'm there. I don't just watch the game, I try to get inside his head, work out what he is thinking and feeling. And when you're in the stands you hear things sometimes and you think you can't keep quiet any more. You feel like shouting: "Hey, that's my brother you're talking about! My flesh and blood!" But you have to ignore it, just swallow it. My boyfriend, Juanmi, is a lifelong Barcelona fan, all the more so now of course, and he tends to give some back, much more than I do. I only ever responded once and it was because they just kept going on: it felt like someone was drilling in my ear.'

When the moment came, it was Juanmi who broke the news to Maribel. 'Maribel didn't see the goal in the World Cup final,' Juanmi explains, 'and that's despite the fact that we were at least in the stadium in Johannesburg, quite low down just behind the benches, halfway along in Spain's half, some way from where the goal was scored. I was watching the move unfold and it was one of those where somehow you just know that it's going to end up in the net. You're sure of it.

'It was Anna, Andrés' wife; Joel, one of his best friends; Maribel and me; and it was the typical move where you lift off your seat bit by bit, like you can tell that something's about to happen. And it gets closer and closer to the area and you're standing now and when the ball reached Andrés I shouted: "Shoot! Shoot! Shoot, Andrés!" When it went in I went mad. Really mad.

'So mad that Maribel said: "Calm down, you're going to give yourself a heart attack. There's still four minutes left you know."

'And I said: "Darling, you do know who scored, don't you?"

'"No. And I'm delighted that Spain have scored but it's not over yet."

'I couldn't believe it. So I asked again: "Maribel, you do know who scored, don't you?"

'"No."

'"Your brother, Maribel. Your brother scored."

'She went mad then. And I said: "Calm down, it's not over yet. There are still four minutes left."'

They were the four longest minutes of their lives.

●　●　●

Andrés' mum Mari suffers; that's just the way she is. There's something about her that experiences life as a drama. 'We've been through things that are not normal: the titles, the success. But sport is defeat too. Sometimes you feel like you have to win every time and sometimes people treat you as if you have to win every time and whenever you don't it's a disaster. Sometimes you treat yourself like that. Andrés finds it very hard to accept defeat. It's a good job he has Anna and the kids, because if not . . .'

Mari still remembers the look on her son's face the day he missed a penalty in Terrassa. 'He was eighteen and was playing his first final with Barcelona, the Copa Catalunya. He was destroyed, crying, unable to speak or eat . . . he's the same off the field as he is on it. He takes it very seriously; he takes it all in, all of it, carrying that responsibility, that need to win, until it accumulates and becomes intolerable.'

Mari remembers how he suffered before the World Cup in 2010. 'He had all these things going round his head, and then what happened, happened. He's like me. Quiet? Calm? In control? On the outside, sure. But on the inside, we're like a volcano. He thinks things over and over, even things that don't matter; it's like he fills his head with this stuff and it's ready to overflow.

'I never watch his games; I just watch him. As soon as he touches the ball for the first time, I know how he is,' Mari says. She admits that she goes to very few games; just the ones at home and the occasional final, plus a match in Mallorca once because José Antonio was working there with his brother, and one in Almería where his sister lived. 'I don't need to be there; I can tell from the television. I can see it on his face, in his gestures, in the way he moves. I don't know anything about football, not like José Antonio, but I know my son.'

What Mari most likes about the way her son plays is the *pausa*, that moment's pause, the calm he transmits. Because she knows that on the inside, it's different. 'I don't know where he gets that from, because I know that he's like me and his grandmother; I know that he's not as calm as he looks,' she says. 'When he's happy, everything flows. It all seems effortless. If he's right, he never feels overwhelmed; he's in control. The responsibility doesn't weigh down on him, quite the opposite, not even now that he is the captain. You see him confront the referee, and tell him what he has to say, which he never used to do. He used to hardly say a word, but now there are days when I say to him: "Andrés, they're going to send you off." He just laughs; he doesn't say anything.'

There are times when Andrés' mother gets nervous, even when he doesn't. When that moment's pause feels like a lifetime. 'The day he scored a penalty for Spain in the Ukraine in 2012, I was there with Maribel, my daughter. When it went to a penalty shoot-out, we had to leave our seats. We stayed in the stadium, but we left our seats and headed inside. We couldn't take it any more. Penalties are too much,' she says. 'It happens when I am watching on television at home too. I can't watch. And that's despite the fact that Andrés doesn't normally take them. I can't keep watching the telly. I can hear it still, and when it's over I come back in to see it. But that night in the Ukraine, in the semi-final of the Euros, I couldn't stay there. "Maribel, let's get out of here," I said. "Yes, let's do that," she said. "I can't take this either." We didn't know what was going on. Suddenly, one of Maribel's friends sent her a message: "Your brother is going to take one!" She showed it to me and I thought: "Why's he going to take one? That can't be right." And it came back to me: that miss in Terrassa. How could it not? But then the next message arrived: "Scores." I was relieved. "Thank God for that." Still, it was worse for Iker Casillas' mother. She had locked herself in the toilet. That must have been terrible! She's got it even worse than me. Andrés only takes the occasional penalty but Iker is always there, in good times or bad. She was luckier than me with one thing, though: they let her get back to her seat. Me and Maribel couldn't get back in to celebrate.'

Andrés' dad is worse. 'I don't even know where José Antonio was,' Mari says. 'He must have walked off, gone so far that no one could find him. He does that a lot: he takes the car and drives, music up so that he can't hear anything. Maribel gets nervous too. You can't take your mind off him. Above all, you keep thinking about what will happen afterwards if they don't win; what it will be like, everything he will have to go through. It's your flesh and blood that's out there. You suffer with him.'

Mari wasn't there to see the goal her son scored at Stamford Bridge either. That one was even more painful. 'I was here in this very living room, injured. I had hurt my leg at a supporters' club event: Andrés left with a plaque and I left with my knee bandaged up after I tripped on a step. I fell, holding my baby niece in my arms and made a mess of my knee. When I saw Andrés' goal on the television I leapt up in the air, which only made it worse. It was a miracle I didn't break something.'

Neither Mari nor José Antonio went to the World Cup in 2010 and nor did they watch the final together, their son's greatest moment. 'We stayed behind in the town. His wife Anna and his sister Maribel had gone, so had

Juanmi. I was with the members of the Iniesta supporters club in Bar Luján, which used to be ours and had been turned into a mini museum by my dad, with press cuttings and pictures all over the walls. There were lots of people there, the place was packed. I was delighted when Spain scored, but I hadn't realized it was him [Andrés] until people starting hugging me and jumping all over me. "What? What's happened?" "Iniesta scored, Mari!" I ran out of there straight to Andrés' house, which is very near, hardly a hundred metres away. I wanted to reach José Antonio as soon as I could, to tell him. Our son has scored. And there he was, sitting on his own in the living room, the telly turned off. He had no idea what had happened.

"José Antonio, our little boy has scored! He scored! Andrés!"

"What? When? How long is left?"

"I don't know . . . all I know is that Andrés scored!"

'When the game ended, a party broke out in Fuentealbilla. Everyone was there, out in the streets. People came from the neighbouring towns to celebrate with us. And I was still going over and over everything in my head; reliving the game. I had missed Andrés scoring, but I had seen every other detail, including the red card that Van Bommel didn't get, God knows why. That Van Bommel . . .'

That's maternal instinct for you: always protecting, always coming out in defence of her children, always scared that something bad will happen to them. And that instinct, that fear, is sometimes even more powerful than the good stuff. In Mari's mind, the goal had gone but Van Bommel's tackle hadn't.

'When he was young, I didn't know he was going to be a footballer. All I knew was that he wasn't going to be a waiter in the bar. He didn't help out at all, unlike his sister who was making pizzas and serving drinks right from the start. Andrés would turn up with his cousin Manu and just sit there until someone served him. I can still see them now, both of them just sitting there, like two lords, expecting to be waited on . . . waiting to be footballers. I never even dreamed that one day he would score the winning goal in the World Cup final. How could I?

'One day I'm sure it will dawn on us just what he has done, but for now it's like a dream, all these things that have happened to him and to all of us,' Mari says. 'I knew that the playground at school was his life and I knew that he only did things he really, really wanted to do. I knew this was his everything. That feeling is real: he *feels* Barcelona, Spain, football. Everyone knows that. That's why people were so happy when it was him who scored. And yet there I was asking myself why I wasn't even happier and I think others probably wondered too: it was my son, and he had just scored the winner in the World Cup final. My son! I was happy, of course, but I wasn't crying or anything, it was all on the inside. On the outside I can seem as cold as ice, but that's just the outside.

'Look at Andrés: at La Masia he cried all the time and in every little corner, but he would hide away and not tell anyone. And when he went to training no one could tell. They didn't know how hard it was for him. Well, most of them didn't. And the other kids certainly didn't. But later on, some of the staff there, cooks and cleaners, told us that it broke their hearts to see him: they could see he was crying on the inside, however much he hid it. I lost my son for six years. We all did. Things went well, sure. But what if they hadn't? Then what? No one could promise that he would make it; that one day we would see him playing at La Masía and captaining Spain. Now all I want is to make up for lost time. I want to enjoy life with him, to enjoy his talent. Because my son has a talent, something special. And I'm not talking about football. He has something. I'm not sure what, exactly, but something . . . he is a good person.'